References

These Lines marked thus ▬▬ includes the Believers land. Those formed thus ▬▬ are roads. Those formed thus ▬▬ are such as inclose fields, meadows Orchards &c yards. Those buildings that have the letter B affixed to them are brick. Those of F are frame.

Union Village is situated in the State of Ohio in the County of Warren and Turtle Creek Township 30 & ½ degrees with Latitude & 7 miles West South West from Washington and 9 miles East of the State Line That separates this State from Indiana

Shaker Music:
A Manifestation
of American Folk Culture

View of a Camp-Meeting. From The Sweet Singer of Israel *(Pittsburgh: John I. Kay & Co., 1837)*

Shaker Music:

A Manifestation
of American Folk Culture

Harold E. Cook

Lewisburg
BUCKNELL UNIVERSITY PRESS

Associated University Presses, Inc.
Cranbury, New Jersey 08512

Printed in the United States of America

Library of Congress Cataloging in Publication Data
Cook, Harold E.   1904–1968.
    Shaker music.
    Bibliography: p.
    1. Shakers—Music—History and criticism.
    2. Shakers—Hymns—History and criticism.   I.   Title.
    ML3178.S5C6   783'.026'98   71-161507
    ISBN 0-8387-7953-0

*All illustrations Courtesy of the Western Reserve His-
torical Society.*

*Endpaper illustration: Plan of Union Village in 1829.
[Shaker Manuscript Collection.] Courtesy
The Western Reserve Historical Society.*

Contents

Preface

Most of the manuscripts used in the preparation of this study are from the Wallace H. Cathcart Collection of The Western Reserve Historical Society, 10825 East Boulevard, Cleveland, Ohio. This Collection, consisting of over 135 linear feet of account books, diaries, journals, letters, hymnals, and publications by and about the Shakers, is preeminent in this field. Collections of Shaker manuscript material have also been consulted in The Library of Congress, Washington, D.C.; The New York Public Library, New York; The New York State Library, Albany, New York; The Connecticut State Library, Hartford, Connecticut; Berkshire Athenaeum, Pittsfield, Massachusetts; and The New Hampshire State Library, Concord, New Hampshire. Additional manuscript hymnals in the possession of the Shaker Societies have been graciously placed at my disposal for examination.

Only the call number (such as SM15), with pagination when it exists, has been given in identifying references to the various hymnals of the collection of The Western Reserve Historical Society in footnotes and bibliography, since an important part of this work is a collation of these manuscript hymnals in numerical order, presented here for the first time, immediately following chapter 8. All other references are identified by title and by the collection in which they are found. As many manuscript hymnals as possible have been collated, but the collation does not pretend to be exhaustive because of the number of such items in the hands of private collectors.

Manuscript letters referred to in the text may be found in the collection of The Western Reserve Historical Society, filed chronologically by date in the letter boxes marked with the name of the community from which the letter was sent; letters copied into books will be identified by reference to the volume that contains them.

Manuscript material has been quoted extensively, and in most instances consists of the writings of simple, rural folk who were naïve and untutored. Colloquial usage and phonetic spelling found so frequently in these handwritten pages from 1800 on are not peculiar to the Shakers, but, it must be remembered, existed practically everywhere in the rural regions of our country at the time. An expanding and ever-shifting frontier, with few schools and limited book learning, made these unorthodox constructions and spellings the rule rather than the exception, and such quotations fall strangely upon the ear of the reader after the lapse of a century or more. Unfamiliar abbreviations, a great confusion of capital and small letters, a profusion of "&" signs, fantastic and often amusing spellings, and abrupt change of subject matter without any warning, all fill these pages of manuscript, and are far more revealing than the more proper printed pages when information concerning the individuals who made up this communistic venture is sought. These little details reveal the strengths, weaknesses, and personal foibles of a sincere and lovable folk who otherwise are likely to be remembered as the composite group of austere faces under drab hats and bonnets, with regimented gestures of dancing feet and waving arms, portrayed in the clumsy illustrations of nineteenth-century books and periodicals. Details of the manuscripts have been reproduced religiously where they are quoted, but the use of the customary [sic] denoting a departure from standard usage has been omitted unless it was felt that clarity would be lost without it. Not infrequently such departures from standard practice would have constituted half the quotation. All music manuscript material has likewise been copied exactly as it appears in the Shaker handwriting, since this is probably a unique body of folk song, possessing its own notation. The omission of many repeat marks, time signatures, and the like, reveals the "folk" usage, but the omissions rarely obscure the effect intended by the Shakers.

The word *folk* is used in this study in the sense of the definition given in Webster's *New International Dictionary* as referring to "the masses of people of lower culture in any homogeneous social group, as contrasted with the individual or with any selected class; in a people bound together by ties of race, language, religion, etc.," while *folk song* is employed as the same dictionary defines it, as "a song originating and traditional among the common people of a country, and hence embodying characteristic qualities of form and feeling." The argument among musicologists concerning the properties of a folk song is continuous, and definition probably will remain controversial so long as personal opinions continue to be the criteria for classification.

I wish to express my gratitude to the staff of the Western Reserve Historical Society of Cleveland for free use of the fine collection of Shaker manuscripts and artifacts in preparing this work and for their kind permission to print freely from these resources.

Acknowledgments

Grateful acknowledgment is made to the following persons and publishers for permission to quote from published works:

Appleton-Century-Crofts for permission to quote from Donald N. Ferguson, *A History of Musical Thought,* 3rd edition, 1940. Copyright © by Appleton-Century-Crofts, Educational Division, Meredith Corporation.

J. J. Augustin, Inc., for permission to quote from Edward D. Andrews, *The Gift To Be Simple,* 1940.

Hastings House, Publishers, Inc., for permission to quote from William Walker, ed., *The Southern Harmony and Spiritual Companion, 1939.*

Holt, Rinehart and Winston, Inc., for permission to quote from A. Z. Idelsohn, *Jewish Music in Its Historical Development,* 1929.

The family of the late Dr. George P. Jackson for permission to quote from George P. Jackson, *Down-East Spirituals and Others,* 1939; *Spiritual Folk-Songs of Early America,* 1937; and *White and Negro Spirituals,* 1943.

LIFE for permission to quote from Harold F. Dixon, "Three Men on a Raft," LIFE Magazine, April 6, 1942, © 1942 Time Inc.

New York State Museum and Science Service for permission to quote from Edward D. Andrews, *The Community Industries of the Shakers,* New York State Museum Handbook 15, 1933.

W. W. Norton & Company, Inc., for permission to quote from James F. Mursell, *The Psychology of Music,* 1937, and from Curt Sachs, *The Rise of Music in the Ancient World East and West,* 1943.

United States Publishers Association, Inc., for permission to quote from Luther A. Weigle, "American Idealism" (v. 10, *The Pageant of America*). By permission of United States Publishers Association, Inc.

Western Reserve Historical Society for extensive use of the Wallace H. Cathcart Shaker Collection.

Yale University Press for permission to quote from George B.
    Cutten, *Speaking with Tongues, Historically and Psychologi-
    cally Considered*, 1927.

Shaker Music:
A Manifestation
of American Folk Culture

Social and Historical Background

On the 19th of May, 1774, Mother Ann Lee, as she was lovingly called by the Shakers, boarded the ship *Mariah* at Liverpool with eight followers and thus began a voyage which fulfilled the first step of the prophecy that she was to establish the millennial church in America.[1] Her little group of Shaking Quakers, so designated because of the violent shaking that their bodies experienced while they were filled with the spirit, had turned their backs on England, the country that had persecuted them so fiercely, and set "their faces with joy and hope toward the faraway shores of the American colonies, where freedom of religious thought, so they were told, was the acknowledged right of all men and one of the corner-stones upon which the government of the country was to be built."[2]

Overjoyed with this cheerful prospect, the Shakers began to shout and sing exultantly and to shake violently as they marched and danced around the deck, as was their custom when praising God. The ship's captain threatened to put them in chains or throw them overboard for these strange actions which he did not understand, but a violent storm which broke at this time almost destroyed the *Mariah;* Mother Ann's rapt gaze saw two angels standing at the helm giving the ship heavenly guidance, a vision which comforted and encouraged the sailors so that the leaky ship was repaired and all were saved. Without further opposition, the Shakers reached New York on August 6, 1774, to find the colonies on the eve of revolution. Without money, but accustomed

---

1. [Calvin Green and Seth Y. Wells], *A Summary View of the Millennial Church* (Albany, 1823), p. 13.

2. Clara Endicott Sears, *Gleanings from Old Shaker Journals* (Boston and New York, 1916), p. 16.

to hard labor, they found work in their various trades and lived apart for more than a year. John Hocknell, their only member with property, bought a farm at Niskayuna, near Albany, and returned to England for his family, who were to help him prepare the first Shaker home.

During Hocknell's absence Mother Ann was deserted by her husband, Abraham Stanley, because her Shaker belief forbade continuing the marriage relation with him. She had had four children, all of whom died in infancy, and she was convinced that her loss as well as all the world's evils were a result of the lust of the flesh.[3] She never saw her husband again, and the celibacy which she herself practiced became a prominent feature of the Shaker religion.

The century preceding the founding of the Shaker sect in England had been "marked by an affluence in religious sensibility among the common people of Europe,"[4] which took the form of a remarkable psychical development in France, where trance and vision were followed by violent bodily agitation, inspired utterances, prophecies, and denunciations. The recipients of these inspirations suffered much opposition and persecution, and the French Prophets, or Camisards, as they were called, were exiled and spread to all parts of Europe. A group came to England in 1706, and a society led by James and Jane Wardley was formed in Manchester in 1747. Ann Lee affiliated herself with this society eleven years later.[5]

The Camisards and Shaking Quakers had known violence and imprisonment in France and England, and the Shakers were to face it again in America. They were pacifists who denounced all war, and were newly arrived from England; a pretext was not lacking to harass and imprison them while the war for American independence was raging. In their early years they were beset by mobs which included ministers, deacons, and magistrates, along with the lewd and base elements of the countryside,[6] but their sect grew steadily for almost a whole century, seemingly aided by the publicity of the persecutions and by conversions

3. Sears, *Gleanings*, pp. 16ff.

4. Anna White and Leila S. Taylor, *Shakerism Its Meaning and Message* (Columbus, Ohio, 1904), p. 13.

5. White and Taylor, *Shakerism*, p. 14.

6. *Ibid.*, p. 45.

from the ranks of disillusioned members of the very sects that
persecuted them.

A powerful revival, which began in and around New Lebanon,
New York, in 1779, seemed to be at an end within a few months,
and the people "were filled with deep distress and anxiety of
mind"[7] because none of those things of which they had testified
had yet appeared. They turned to the Shakers, believing them
to possess the very things for which they had so earnestly prayed,
and many "from various parts of the country, and of almost every
denomination, embraced the faith of the society."[8]

About 1799 began the remarkable phenomenon known as the
Great Revival, which reached the peak of its intensity in the first
few years of the new century and spread rapidly through the
frontier communities. The frontier church preached a gospel of
salvation for the many rather than merely for the few, and Cal-
vinistic theology with its emphasis on man's unworthiness as a
creature "conceived in sin and born in iniquity" was losing
ground steadily even in New England.[9] The Shakers in the East
had had a prophecy from Mother Ann concerning the opening
of their gospel in the western country and sent John Meacham,
Benjamin S. Youngs, and Isaacher Bates to see if the time was ripe
for such action. These three Shakers set out January 1, 1805, to
walk more than one thousand miles, and arrived in Kentucky
and Ohio in the midst of great religious activities.[10] The Presbyterian New Lights, called Schismatics, having received the
spirit of the revival, separated from that church in 1803. Many
of the subjects of the revival united with them in denouncing
old, established creeds, forms of worship, and church government.[11] John Dunlavy and Richard McNemar were among this
group, and along with many others soon joined the Shakers. It
was estimated that some three hundred people in the West had
joined them by 1807.[12] "These frontier people unaccustomed to

7. [Green and Wells], *A Summary View*, p. 17.

8. *Ibid.*, p. 18.

9. John D. Hicks, *The Federal Union* (Cambridge, Massachusetts, 1937), p. 330.

10. [Green and Wells], *A Summary View*, pp. 70–71.

11. Thomas Brown, *An Account of the People called Shakers* (Troy, 1812), pp.
345–46.

12. *Ibid.*, p. 354.

crowds, had few defences against crowd psychology,"[13] especially in an emotional meeting like the following, where

> there would be an unusual outcry; some bursting forth into loud ejaculations of prayer, or thanksgiving, for the truth; others breaking out in emphatical sentences of exhortation; others flying to their careless friends with tears of compassion, beseeching them to turn to the Lord; some struck with terror, and hastening through the crowd to make their escape, or pulling away their relations; others trembling, weeping, crying out for the Lord Jesus to have mercy upon them, fainting and swooning away, till every appearance of life was gone, and the extremities of the body assumed the coldness of a dead corpse; others surrounding them with melodious songs, or fervent prayers . . . the work would continue for several days and nights together.[14]

Peter Cartwright, the famous backwoods preacher, not too serious about such commotions, gave a vivid description of the "jerks" or the muscular spasms which seized these highly emotional worshipers in the Great Revival:

> They would be taken under a warm song or sermon, and seized with a convulsive jerking all over, which they could not by any possibility avoid, and the more they resisted, the more they jerked. . . . Most usually persons taken with the jerks, to obtain relief, as they said, would rise up and dance. Some would run, but could not get away. . . . To see these proud young gentlemen and young ladies, dressed in their silks, jewelry and prunella, from top to toe, take the jerks, would often excite my risibilities. The first jerk or so, you would see their fine bonnets, caps and combs fly. . . . It was, on all occasions, my practice to recommend fervent prayer as a remedy and it almost universally proved an effectual antidote. To great numbers of frontier folk these involuntary bodily exercises seemed to be manifestations of the spirit of God working in men.[15]

Such was the setting for the early Shaker religion, with its song and dance, its prophetic utterances, and its followers given to a highly emotional type of worship. Such were the types of believers it continued to attract for the next five or six decades: simple people for the most part, devout, honest, and hardworking men and women to whom spiritual direction was given for both work and worship.

Mother Ann's motto, "Hands to work, and hearts to God,"

---

13. From Luther A. Weigle, "American Idealism," *The Pageant of America*, edited by Ralph H. Gabriel (New Haven, 1928), 10:151. By permission of United States Publishers Association, Inc.

14. Richard M'Nemar, *The Kentucky Revival* (Cincinnati: printed, Albany: reprinted, 1808), p. 23

15. Weigle, "American Idealism," *Pageant of America,* 10:151. By permission of United States Publishers Association, Inc.

presents both the religious picture and the temporal economy so closely woven into it, in a few well-chosen words. She said, "You must be prudent and saving of every good thing that God blesses you with, that you may have to give to the needy."[16] Long before labor in the outside world (or "the world," as the Shakers styled all people outside of their own number) had made any general, systematic provision for the working man through unions, insurances, and pensions in America, the Shaker communal life had guaranteed the essential needs to the young, the old, and the infirm, in its plan which shared work and profits equally among members of a family or community. "True some families might differ in their temporal conditions, from fortuitous circumstances, such as location, the business they chose to adopt, the ability to conduct affairs, the number of members" and for other reasons, but "in the case of great loss by one Family the others help bear the burden."[17] They solemnly dedicated themselves in their covenant, "Debtors to God in relation to Each other and all men to improve our time and tallents in that Manner in which we might be most usefull."[18]

Shaker living conditions were of the best; their houses were well built and clean, with good ventilation and plenty of light. Working hours could not have been so long as in many other places, because the average working day in America was from twelve to fifteen hours in length in the first part of the nineteenth century,[19] and the Shakers ate regularly at six A.M. and six P.M. (in summer), had time to meditate, sing, and attend meeting in the evening. An excerpt from the following hymn gives a vivid picture of a Shaker's day:

> I work thirteen hours, in each twenty-four
> Or more if necessity call;
> In point of distinction, I want nothing more
> Than just to be servant of all:
> I peaceably work at whatever I'm set,
> From no other motive but love,
> To honor the gospel and keep out of debt,
> And lay up a treasure above.

---

16. Frederick W. Evans, *Shakers Compendium* (New York, 1859), p. 146.

17. Edward D. Andrews, *The Community Industries of the Shakers* (Albany: *New York State Museum Handbook* 15, 1933), p. 36. By permission of the New York State Museum and Science Service.

18. *Ibid.*, p. 224. By permission of the New York State Museum and Science Service.

19. Richard T. Ely, *The Labor Movement in America* (New York, 1905), p. 49.

I eat for refreshment, my strength to repair,—
Not merely to gratify taste;
Whatever's provided, I thankfully share,
And nothing that's good do I waste;
I still realize that my Elders are nigh,
Their modest example I view,
By which I am furnish'd with power from on high
The beastly old man to subdue.

At half after seven, from work I retire,
And noise and confusion I shun.
And just before meeting I settle the fire,
To see that no mischief be done:
I go into meeting to find some increase,
And never withdraw till it close,
And when we're dismiss'd I retire in peace,
Prepar'd for a pleasant repose.

I sleep seven hours, with little recess,
And O how refreshing they seem:
At four in the morning I get up and dress,
Regardless of vision or dream.
When meeting is over I chuse to give way,
And be at my work very soon,
And more than one half that's laid out for the day,
Must always be done before noon.

I keep in the circle assigned to me,
With which I am fully content,
And nothing beyond it I'm anxious to see,
Unless in a gift I am sent.
In all kinds of company, I am among,
My words I do carefully weigh,
And rather than speak with an unbridled tongue,
I chuse to have nothing to say.

By temperance, prudence, industry and care,
My faith is to lay up in store
A good gospel treasure, enough and to spare,
To give to the needy and poor.
That this is the gospel I have not a doubt,
Nor am I a tittle afraid,
But in true obedience my strength will hold out
Until the foundation is be laid. [sic]

Now this is the manner I fill up my time,
A manner that few will applaud,
Yet I do not see that it is any crime,
To call it the service of God;

> If any have found a more excellent way
> They're welcome to travel therein,
> But from sweet experience, I truly can say,
> My soul is deliver'd from sin.[20]

There were Shakers who were not so convinced of the sanctity of labor as were their leaders, however, and there was the ne'er-do-well who came into the society during the difficult times like the periods of panic in 1819, 1837, and 1857, and who left as soon as times improved; there was another type who likewise spent the cold winter in a warm Shaker house, well fed, and then left when the spring farming and industries demanded his efforts. While the Shaker did not like to mention his worldly goods or the size of Shaker membership, it was estimated at one time by a member that the society had property worth at least twelve millions of dollars,[21] and that it had some six thousand members.

A society which had acquired the property of its members as they entered its ranks, developed its farming and countless industries, and which had generally been frugal and provident, had of necessity developed rules for governing its internal workings, and organized the religious body to direct its spiritual affairs. There were rules for all divisions of church administration, rules for management of farms and industries, rules for travel (in the rare instances when a Shaker was forced to do it and then only for the common good of the group and not for his own personal satisfaction), rules for table behavior, and even strict rules for the least detail of writing their own Shaker music. All these rules applied to their own affairs, however, and they did not vote or participate in any outside government or politics. In *The Testimony of Christ's Second Appearing*, often referred to as the Shaker Bible, the Quakers were condemned by the Shakers because they had "never advanced to a separation between the kingdom of Christ and the kingdom of this world" and because in "taking part in the worldly government under the domination of antichrist, they gained an honorable standing in the world, but lost that degree of the light and power of God, in which they had at first stood for a time."[22] There was complete submission

---

20. Philos Harmoniae [Richard McNemar], *A Selection of Hymns and Poems; For the Use of Believers* (Watetvliet [sic] [Ohio], 1833), pp. 38–39.

21. Ely, *Labor Movement*, p. 12.

22. [David Darrow et al.], *Testimony of Christ's Second Appearing* (Albany, 1856), p. 615.

by all to the authority at the head, as an excerpt from a MS of 1821 shows. A certain Melinda's advice to Shaker youth is that "there must be a lead, and every individual, as well as every rank and order, must yeald Submission to that which is before it. There must be a great deal of conformity or there would be endless confusion."[23]

This yielding to authority by the individual for the common good in practical matters went hand in hand with the "inspired" aspect of Shaker life in the ritual of "gifts," "visions," "speaking in tongues," and prophecy. One recipient of these manifestations who wrote in 1812 after leaving the society, felt "satisfied such things were not caused by the power of God," but that

> those who are subject to these operations have faith in them, and strong belief that they feel the power of God operating to produce them . . . with a passiveness of mind, or willingness to be thus affected. . . .
>
> I had often heard of instances of the Elders taking the power away from individuals while under excessive operations. I inquired, if they were under the power of God, how could the Elders command that power? I was answered—'The Elders have the greater, and the less gives way to it . . . they proceeded from . . . a strong belief and imagination, and oftentimes, a species of insanity; and with others as with myself, when I had those operations (and faith in those gifts and miracles) reason was entirely excluded.[24]

In 1734, Voltaire had written in the third of his English letters concerning the English Quakers:

> This is what contributed most to the growth of the sect. Fox believed himself inspired. He believed, therefore, that he should speak in a manner different from other men. He began to shake, to writhe and make faces, to hold his breath, to let it out violently; the Delphic priestess couldn't have done better. In a short time he acquired quite a habit of inspiration, and soon afterwards he was scarcely able to talk otherwise. That was the first gift that he communicated to his disciples. In good faith, they made the same faces as their master, they shook with all their might at the moment of inspiration. Hence they got the name *quaker,* which means *shaker.* The more humble followers began to imitate them. They shook, they talked through their noses, they had convulsions, and they believed they had the Holy Spirit. They had to have miracles; they made some.[25]

---

23. Copies of Instructions—Letters, Hymns & Anthems—Remarkable Events, &c. (South Union [Kentucky], 1821.) Melinda's Record.

24. Brown, *People Called Shakers,* pp. 296ff.

25. Voltaire, *Oeuvres Complètes* (Paris, 1879), 22:90.

This rather facetious account of the early Shaking Quakers shows what the clear-thinking intellectual's attitude was toward "inspiration," but Voltaire may or may not have had personal observations to rely upon for his comments.

The descriptions of visions which follow are from Shakers actually participating in their faith at the time they wrote:

April 16, 1827. Elder Bro. joined the throng, altho he had but one shoe on. It is impossible for me to describe the operations of this meeting, for everyone went as the spirit moved. . . . Sometimes the Brethren and Sisters were passing & repassing each other—sometimes hugging & kissing the sweetest kisses that ever I tasted, for we felt love enough to eat one another up. Sometimes the Brethren & Sisters would follow each other around & around—sometimes they would have hold of hands, three & four, & sometimes a dozen in a ring, waving up & down.

Anna Matthewson was under a peculiar operation all thro the devotion, which made me think of a pulling mill—especially when she got me into it, for she would have hold of someone, or another of us, both hands at a time, & bow up & down, & back and forth, with almost irresistible power—& for my part I was glad when I got out of the mill, tho it felt to me like a sign that we must bow and humble ourselves, & become more & more like little children. And we really acted as such. It did not appear that any one cared how much like a fool they acted, or what they did, if they could only get their part of the manna while it was dropping down. Each one sung what they felt the most gift in, & every song was full of love.[26]

Jan. 5, 1839. This evening we had meeting in the meeting house. Lemuel Long and Lydiann they all went to hell among the damned Lydiann turned into a Chicken and Lucy turned into a Dog Finaly Lydiann had a vision and come home and then went into vision again and went back to the others.[27]

Sept. 3, 1840. Heard them sing some of their Heavenly Songs, which were cheering in the extreme. Isabella, who was Queen of Spain came and sang a Spanish song to us throu one of the inspired ones. Isabella had not let this sister speak anything but Spanish for a number of days, till today she spoke to us in her own tongue.[28]

The writing in the journals seems to reveal that those most susceptible to the more fantastic phases of Shaker inspiration

---

26. Alonzo G. Hollister, The Book of Moses and of Miscellaneous Writings deemed worth preserving. Copied by A. G. Hollister, chiefly from original manuscripts, pp. 252–53.

27. Entry of Jan. 5, 1839, Common-place Book of P. C. Cramer.

28. Entry of Sept. 3, 1840, Journal of Betty Grove, John O. & Sally L.

were people of limited learning. The realm of inspiration for the leaders, who often had more education than the others, was largely in the field of dogma or ritual, and accounts of their revelations are usually quite factual.

Mother Ann "acquired a habit of industry, but could neither read nor write."[29] She sent a spiritual communication to Father Joseph Meacham, one of her successors, that an evil spirit was loose and had been wandering for many years, and that "His first movement among my children, was to create an undue thirst for nolej [knowledge], after the rudiments, arts & Sciences of this world."[30] This seemed to establish the general policy the Shakers were to have toward "book larnin," as they called it,[31] for a long time. In 1821, the Millennial Laws contained the following regulations:

> 4. No books, or pamphlets, of any kind are allowed to be brot into the family without the knowledge and approbation of Elders. . . .
> 5. Those who teach school should devote their time to teaching their schollars, and not to studying themselves, further than is necessary to enable them to do their duty in teaching, but they should have a good understanding of all the branches they are required to teach.
> 8. In connexion with other school studies the children should be taught to sing.[32]

These rules demonstrate attitudes which were justified as follows two years later:

> to give children literary instructions, without governing them and teaching them to govern the natural propensities and dispositions of their minds, and without instructing them in the principles of moral virtue, would be a ready way to lead them to ruin. Because, in such a case, their literary knowledge would only tend to sharpen their talents, and assist them in their pursuit of evil inventions.

And children were to be given only a common school education because

> it will avail nothing for children to spend their time in acquiring a knowledge of the higher branches of literature, and especially

---

29. [Green and Wells], A *Summary View*, p. 6.

30. [Meacham], Father Joseph's Writings, MS, p. 134.

31. David R. Lamson, *Two Years' Experience Among the Shakers* (West Boylston, 1848) , p. 48.

32. Father Joseph [Meacham] and Mother Lucy [Wright], Millennial Laws, MS, pp. 55ff.

what is called classical learning, unless they can apply their knowledge and learning to some beneficial purpose. Learning without usefulness is, at best, but mere lumber of the brain, and often excludes those things which might have been far more useful in its place.[33]

This common school education lasted three months each year; the girls went to school until they were fifteen years old and the boys one year longer. Teachers were from their own sect and probably could not have been approved by a very exacting committee.[34]

Common schools were the rule rather than the exception in New England in the early part of the nineteenth century, but taught mostly reading, writing, arithmetic, and religion.[35] There was still not a popular interest in education, however, because of "the slowness of the schools to adapt themselves to the needs of a democracy. For the most part they were still operating on the theory that it was their business to educate the leaders of society only, and to ignore the needs of the masses."[36] Shaker schooling had adapted itself to its practical needs from the beginning, had not ignored the needs of its unsophisticated people, and the members learned to keep their accounts and to become frugal in their business dealings with "the world." Father Joseph told his people they were "not called upon to labor to excell to be like others in words according to the letter learning & wisdom of the world. But to excell them in Order, Union, & Peace & in good works that are truly virtuous & useful to man in this life."[37]

The Shakers developed a great many industries and gave a practical training to all of their members. Children were apprenticed to older workmen to learn trades, and women worked in the community shops wrapping and putting labels on packages, weaving, making articles of clothing, spinning, dyeing, drying corn, apples, and pumpkin, and doing many other tasks. Men made shoes, brooms, boxes, mops, the famous Shaker chairs, clay products, and many other commodities; they grew herbs and garden seeds, and produced food for their people and livestock,

---

33. [Green and Wells], *A Summary View*, pp. 64–65.

34. Lamson, *Two Years' Experience*, p. 47.

35. Hicks, *Federal Union*, p. 62.

36. *Ibid.*, p. 331.

37. [Meacham], Father Joseph's Writings, p. 71.

and sold to "the world." The fields and shops were a bustle of activity; the Shakers supplied their own communities' needs, and did a brisk business with a public that was eager to buy their superior merchandise.

All Shaker articles were manufactured with their utilitarian qualities foremost in the mind of the craftsman; they were to be strong, serviceable, and unadorned; but many were also beautiful. The fact that Believers were forbidden "to go into museums, theatres, or to attend carivans or shows," to have any "pictures or paintings," "odd, or fanciful styles of architecture," to use any paint on the dwellings except white (or "a little darker shade" for the shops), to have "fancy articles of any kind, or articles which are superfluously finished, trimmed or ornamented," or "picture books, with large, flourished, & extravigant pictures in them,"[38] undoubtedly caused the making of a beautiful chair or

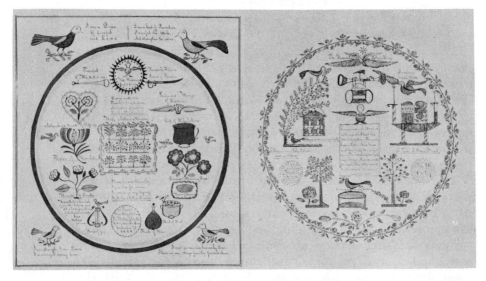

Two Shaker Spirit Drawings. [Scrapbook Broadsides, 3: 60–61].

piece of cloth to be more pleasurable than it might otherwise have been. Even though artistic expression was slowly coming to life in America, regulations forbade its entry into the communities, and lack of travel and communication helped to isolate

---

38. Meacham and Wright, Millennial Laws, pp. 53ff.

the Shakers further from its influences. The type of humble person who united with the communities probably would not have been greatly interested in such matters outside of group life in this period, but there did seem to be a real longing for self-expression among some Shakers, and a desire for the things which "the world" could offer and had given in some measure to many of them, which kept coming to the surface in the life of constant denial they were leading. The repeated allusions to "a golden leaf," "golden trumpet," "shining gems," "golden seals," "plum cake," "manna," "wine," "gold chain," "gold cross," "shining cross," and a great many "Reward" songs might be mentioned, as well as processions and ceremonies in visions where the "instrument" who received it saw himself and other Shakers wearing "beautifully colored sashes," and elaborately embroidered garments and articles of clothing forbidden to the uniformly dressed Shaker. A sister who worked in the herb industry wrote:

> The rose bushes were planted along the sides of the road which ran through our village and were greatly admired by the passersby, but it was strongly impressed upon us that a rose was useful, not ornamental. It was not intended to please us with its color or its odor, its mission was to be made into rose-water, and if we thought of it in any other way we were making an idol of it and thereby imperiling our souls. In order that we might not be tempted to fasten a rose upon our dress or to put it into water to keep, the rule was that the flower should be plucked with no stem at all.[39]

With most of the outlets for self-expression and pleasure eliminated, the Shaker turned to the ritual of song and dance with great intensity. "The original Shaker dance was not an organized form of worship. Shaking or trembling, whirling, reeling, dancing, marching, running, stamping, shouting, gesticulating, falling to the ground—such exercises were in large part involuntary operations, precedents for which may be found in the history of many cults."[40] In the earliest period in Manchester, England, a meeting was described as "singing, shouting, or walking the floor, under the influence of spiritual signs, swiftly passing and repassing each other, like clouds agitated by a mighty wind."[41] After Mother

39. Andrews, *Community Industries*, p. 102. By permission of the New York State Museum and Science Service.

40. Edward D. Andrews, *The Gift to be Simple* (New York, 1940), p. 143. By permission of T. T. Augustin Incorporated *Publisher*.

41. [Darrow et al.], *Testimony of Christ's Second Appearing*, p. 617.

Ann became the spiritual leader, the manner of worship was "singing and dancing, shaking and shouting, speaking with new tongues and prophesying,"[42] and on the voyage to America "they went forth, in obedience to their inward feelings, to praise God in songs and in dances."[43] It was said that American-born Father Joseph saw the hosts of Heaven "laboring," as the Shakers called these movements and exercises, and gave the vision to his people that they might use it in their worship. He was entirely lacking in natural ability for such dancing, but had such a keen desire to attain perfection that the "floor boards of a vacant room over a shop on the premises were said to be worn smooth by his constant practice in these exercises."[44] Some of the Shakers were thrown into prison in England for breaking the Sabbath with this manner of worship,[45] and in their newly chosen country they were accused of witchcraft, sorcery, and having the evil eye because of their "shouting and whirling, and the rhythmic dancing."[46] By the time they had arrived in America, "dancing was a well-established amusement not only among the socially privileged of Boston—largely Anglican in their religious connections—but also among some of the more democratic social elements."[47] It was not because they danced that the Shakers were persecuted so cruelly, but because they used the dance in their religious worship, and it was easy for those who objected to go one step further and accuse them of dancing naked, and all other possible forms of licentiousness. Believers undertook to justify the dance in their worship by many quotations from Scripture such as "Thou hast turned my mourning into dancing," "Praise His Name in the dance," and "Praise Him with the timbrel and dance" after they had met with so much criticism. "Typical Dancing," a hymn from the first printed hymnal (1813), contains this same Biblical defense:

> At Shiloh was a yearly feast,
> Where virgins met from west to east;

---

42. *Ibid.,* p. 620.

43. *Ibid.,* p. 621.

44. White and Taylor, *Shakerism,* p. 101.

45. [Green and Wells], *A Summary View,* p. 12.

46. Sears, *Gleanings from Journals, p. 33.*

47. Arthur C. Cole, "The Puritan and Fair Terpsichore," in *Mississippi Valley Historical Review* 29 (1942) : 17.

These virgins were a type at least,
Of those that follow Jesus;
If they went forth in dances then,
Why should our dances now offend,
Since from the filthy lusts of men,
Our blessed Saviour frees us?[48]

In 1823, members wrote that they were "aware that a strong prejudice prevails against the exercise of dancing, as an act of divine worship, in consequence of its having been for many ages, perverted to the service of the wicked."[49] but in spite of the prejudice, people flocked to the Shaker meeting houses to see this strange worship and some found it beautiful and inspiring, others grotesque and ridiculous. Dances varied at different periods; the revival of 1827 and the manifestations of the decade 1837 to 1847 brought on many lively changes in the simple patterns, but "all stemmed from the fundamental operations." During the awakening, or revivals, "conscious control of ritual would often be lost in the cumulative excitement of worship,"[50] and then would settle back again into what Shakers admitted was "originally an involuntary motion" and "now repeated as a voluntary duty."[51] One member who was gifted in turning, said that the skill in turning was acquired by practice and that the dancers fell prostrate on the floor, not because of the gift, but because they were too dizzy to stand alone.[52]

The earliest meetings in England had mentioned "singing" in connection with the bodily exercise, and music appears closely interwoven with the dance in the Shaker ritual throughout its development except for a brief time near the end of Father Joseph's life when the exercise "was suspended altogether [1793] and the meeting consisted of a solemn song without words, followed by instruction and reproof."[53] The early Shaker communities were anxious to keep away from worldly influences and were told

---

48. *Millennial Praises* (Hancock [Massachusetts], 1813), pp. 24–25.

49. [Green and Wells], *A Summary View,* p. 88.

50. Andrews, *Gift to be Simple,* p. 150 *passim.* By permission of J. J. Augustin Incorporated *Publisher.*

51. Charles Lane, "A Day with the Shakers," in *The Dial* 4:168.

52. Lamson, *Two Years',* p. 88.

53. White and Taylor, *Shakerism,* pp. 330–31.

to rely on the inspiration of God rather than on the knowledge of any science which the mind of man had developed. Hence, the study of musical science with other branches was at first wholly neglected and for a time rather depreciated. Lengthy anthems and hymns, thousands in number, were learned by hearing. Those musically inclined by nature were employed to communicate the music to others; and in the exchange of social visits among the societies attention was particularly given to an interchange of music. This proved very satisfactory, and for a number of years between 1792 and 1821, no change was deemed necessary.[54]

From 1823, musical instruction was given to both Brethren and Sisters and it was recommended that twenty or thirty minutes be devoted to singing every day. A system of "letteral notation"—the use of the letters of the alphabet instead of notes—was developed to make the learning and writing of Shaker songs easy, and books of music theory appeared explaining their new system.[55]

Isaac N. Youngs, a Shaker historian, wrote that the songs and tunes used for several years after the New Lebanon meeting house was constructed (1795) were often "such as originated in the world."[56] This statement is supported by the researches of George P. Jackson, who has made a study of the origins of our early American folksong and revival literature. He writes:

> The disciples of Mother Ann had sung from the start. But possessing no body of song suited to their own purposes, they borrowed at first largely from the ubiquitous sober psalm-tune stock, the songs which the later Shakers still used to some extent and called "solemn songs." Paul Petrovich Svenin tells how he heard the Shaker colony in Alfred, Maine, between 1811 and 1813, singing "the Psalms of David . . . in an abominable drawl."
>
> It was in the western branch of Shakerism that a great new wave of song arose. The wave was at first organic with that of the Kentucky Revival as a whole. The Shakers quickly altered the texts or made new ones to suit their "Mother Ann" (Ann Lee) worship, and in this guise the song swell swept eastward into the older settlements.
>
> The new songs out of the west were of two general sorts, Shaker-historical ballads and "exercise" songs, the latter so-called because they accompanied their dancing and other "exercises."[57]

---

54. *Ibid.,* p. 336.

55. White and Taylor, *Shakerism,* pp. 337–38.

56. Andrews, *Gift to be Simple,* p. 83. By permission of J. J. Augustin Incorporated *Publisher.*

57. George P. Jackson, *White and Negro Spirituals* (New York, 1943), p. 111. By permission of the family of the late Dr. George Jackson.

A paper, probably of a late date, pasted on the inside cover of a hymnal dated 1812–1824 (without music) contains the following unsigned note: "Brought from Union Village [Ohio]. I have understood that our first hyms were composed in the West—I think this a rare collection of some of the earliest—perhaps written in the West & brought home by one of the missionaries. . . . Last hym assures that it was composed in the West."[58]

It is also revealed in Jackson's comparisons that at least ten of the 140 compositions in the *Millennial Praises,* the first published hymnal (1813), were found widely in the books of contemporary separatist sects, or are textual adaptations of their songs.[59] Many songs came from the "New Light" orders and Baptist "Merry Dancers" in the East in the early revival period around 1780, and others two decades later came from the "New Lights," "Schismatics," and "Christians" who had rebelled against the orthodoxies of Baptist, Methodist, and Presbyterian faiths. The number from the latter revivals far exceeded those from the earlier one.[60]

Church music in colonial America had fallen to a very low level, partly as a result of the antipathy of Puritan congregations toward music in the worship, and partly because pressing matters of frontier existence had not given people time to learn to sing by note. Congregational singing became so restricted that only five Psalms were said to be in general use, as a result of the limited number of books and of the inability of the singers to read music. The propriety of "Skilfulness in singing," or singing by note, nagged at the Puritan conscience and brought forth such objections as "the names given to the notes are *bawdy,* yea *blasphemous,*" and "it is a *needless way,* since their good Fathers that were strangers to it, are got to heaven without it."[61] About 1720, eminent clergymen like Mather, Edwards, Symmes, Dwight, and Eliot, began an ardent campaign for improvement in the musical part of the service,[62] which led to the establishment of singing-

---

58. Papers of Shakers, No. 189, Ohio, Union Village (1812–1824), Hymns, MS (in Library of Congress), inside cover of hymnal.

59. Andrews, *Gift to be Simple,* p. 14. By permission of J. J. Augustin Incorporated *Publisher.*

60. *Ibid.,* pp. 10–11. By permission of J. J. Augustin Incorporated *Publisher.*

61. Frédéric Louis Ritter, *Music in America* (New York, 1890), pp. 9ff.

62. *Ibid.,* p. 11.

schools and the appearance of the itinerant singing-teacher on the American scene. "The reform in singing was set on foot by two books": John Tuft's *Introduction to the Art of Singing* (1721), and Thomas Walter's *Grounds and Rules of Music* (1721).[63] At least 375 tune books, which usually contained a few pages on the rudiments of music, appeared before the Civil War period in this country. Until about 1830, the "original instinctive efforts toward popular training in the rudiments of singing, toward what is now called 'community music,' and toward the discipline and enrichment of church services—these all remained in force."[64] With the emphasis upon choral singing, and the skill finally attained in both singing and choral directing, a separation of interest came about between the democratic congregational singing and the skilled choir about 1850. Soon after 1830 these same trends began to affect the American hymn book, and it developed in two general directions: one became the dignified and artistic hymnal of the present day; the other "veered off into the music of the choirless assembly—the Sunday-school, the camp-meeting and the revivalist's campaign."[65] Of the latter sort, at least in spiritual and emotional content, were the Shaker hymns and tunes. The most distinctively Shaker music is contained in the hundreds of MS copybooks left by the Believers in the period roughly covering the years 1820–1860. These copy-books include the hymns and tunes of the fertile revival periods of 1827 and 1837, the intensely productive years, when the sect in its ascendancy was most independent and exacting in its dogma, and those of the Civil War era, which saw the rapid decline of the societies.

The Shakers were the first real communal group in America, and a few members still exist. Mother Ann Lee's doctrine of celibacy forbade a normal increase within their own ranks and they are now practically extinct. Some seventy-five years after the first family order of Shakers was formed, communal groups like those at Zoar, Oneida, Economy, Amana, Brook Farm, and many others, were organized, but have for the most part now been abandoned. All were either a direct result of that mysterious wave of religious enthusiasm which swept the country in the middle of the nineteenth century, or of the desire for Utopian schemes of life for the common man. Brook Farm, Fruitlands, and Oneida

---

63. *Grove's Dictionary of Music and Musicians* (New York, 1928), 6:385–86.
64. *Ibid.*, p. 391.
65. *Ibid.*, p. 392.

were founded by people with more general cultural advantages than those of the other societies, but the common man was becoming conscious of his class and of his rights and was striving to get his "part of the manna while it was dropping down," as the Shaker Sister said.

Mother Ann was one of the first advocates of equal rights for women in America, and all of the Shaker Sisters shared work and profits equally with the men of the sect; temperance rules and anti-tobacco regulations were adopted in the Shaker communities, and many of the movements in the societies anticipated similar movements in American life by years. However, these many Shaker communities represented a similar number of social islands in nineteenth-century American life. Shakers were not interested in war, voting, or temporal government, nor did they hasten to adopt the cultural offerings of a fast-growing country. In spite of his shrewdness in business dealings, the Shaker never worried about the prices that his competitors demanded for commodities which he had to sell. The general lack of concern for the world of antichrist, and the Shaker's own self-sufficiency, isolated him from outside activity as the limitations of a special geography isolated other folk groups. As a result of this cultural independence, insisted upon from within, the Shaker fund of religious folk tunes continued to grow over a period of several decades. The needs of the dance and song ritual were the incentive for many hundreds of new songs "inspired" and composed by Shaker musicians who more often than not remained anonymous.

Each song was a renewed expression of Shaker faith or a testimony to inspiration, hence the practice was not discouraged by the "lead"; it expressed eagerness for conformity and a pride in the characteristics which were believed to be distinctly Shaker. The society soon made ironclad rules for tonality and tempo in an attempt to make the songs as uniform as the Shaker bonnets in these matters. Analysis shows that the rules could not be followed by the folk instinct; rules summarize practice but fare less well when they precede it. The music of the hundreds of hymnbooks so beautifully copied by loving Shaker hands bears testimony to the fact that the natural expression of the Shakers often won in the struggle between folk ideals and the man-made rules of the Shaker music theorists.

2

The Development of
Shaker Hymnody: Text and Tune

An account of the state of music among the earliest Shakers in Manchester, England, in the years following 1747 is to be found in *A Summary View of the Millennial Church,* published in 1823, which states that "This infant society practiced no forms, and adopted no creeds as rules of faith or worship; at . . . times they were exercised with singing, shouting and leaping for joy at the near prospect of salvation."[1] From the same source we know that they sang and danced on the voyage to America in 1774,[2] but there is no mention of the songs that they sang.

When the gospel first opened in America, those who embraced the Shaker faith came to the society with nothing but their natural faculties of singing and usually could not do more than sing the melody. Establishing the community took so much effort that little time was devoted to music, and Shakers had no hymns or anthems adapted to their faith, nor were they able for many years to create any that expressed their doctrines or belief.[3]

By 1793, Shaker singing had become so slow and monotonous that the dancing was suspended altogether and only a solemn song without words, probably from the early Psalm-tune stock, was used in the worship.[4]

---

1. [Calvin Green and Seth Y. Wells], *A Summary View of the Millennial Church* (Albany, 1823), pp. 4–5.

2. *Ibid.,* p. 1 3.

3. Calvin Green, Remarks on Music, Instrumental and Vocal, MS, pp. 1–2.

4. Anna White and Leila S. Taylor, *Shakerism its Meaning and Message* (Columbus, Ohio, 1904), pp. 330–31.

Five years later the same manner of singing was described in an account by a Shaker to a prospective convert:

> As to singing, though we sing vocally, we seldom sing hymns, or a composition of words . . . our singing is that which St. John heard (Rev. xiv. 3, 4.) that no man could learn, (or understand) but those who were redeemed from the earth, and not defiled with woman, or rather (according to our travail) the song of redemption and complete salvation. Vocal prayer, and singing a composition of words, are accepted when done in the gift of God; and at some future time we may be so led to pray and praise.[5]

On the same trip to Niskayuna (August 1798), this visitor attended a meeting where the Shakers "sat silent for a few minutes, then arose and stood in their order, and sung a tune without words; after which, four or five sung a more lively tune, to which the others *danced*."[6]

Concerning these years just before 1800 when dancing had been reinstated in the Shaker ritual and was causing much opposition from a hostile public, a former member wrote: "the principal objection that people far and near made against us was, dancing, and singing jig tunes, and hornpipes, particularly on the Sabbath, under pretence of worshipping God."[7]

A hornpipe, probably by one of the most prominent early Shaker hymn-writers, was found in a Shaker MS hymnal, and is given just as it was found:

MC NEMAR'S HORN PIPE[8]

[Richard McNemar?]

---

5. Thomas Brown, *An Account of the People called Shakers* (Troy, 1812), pp. 19–20.

6. *Ibid.*, p. 15.

7. *Ibid.*, p. 84.

8. Papers of Shakers, 208, Ohio, Union Village (in Library of Congress), p. 70.

In 1808, Samuel [Hooser] wrote from Union Village, Ohio, to Calvin [Green] of the central society at New Lebanon, sending him the words of Richard McNemar's hymn, which was later printed as "The Seasons" in *Millennial Praises,* the first printed Shaker hymnal. The letter shows how a secular English Morris Dance tune was adapted to a Shaker religious text:

> I have a feeling to make the a little present of a hymn; Compos'd by Richard McNemar to the Tune that was formerly cauld Black Joke We begin upon the low part of the tune to Sing and not repeat that part and in the last Virce you will find one line more than what is in the Other Virces, repeat that part of the tune giving the Seventh line much the Same Sound of that above it—[9]

THE BLACK JOKE[10]

(English Morris Dance)

George P. Jackson notes a similar usage in his *Spiritual Folk-Songs of Early America,*[11] where he shows that the "Cross of Christ" is a close variant of "James Harris" (or "Daemon Lover" or "House Carpenter") "turned around; that is with the second

9. Letter from Samuel [Hooser], Union Village, Ohio, Feb. 28, 1808, to Calvin [Green], New Lebanon, N. Y., p. 1.

10. Cecil Sharp and Herbert C. MacIlwaine, eds., *Morris Dance Tunes,* Set II: new ed. (London, Novelle & Co. Ltd., 1912), pp. 12–13.

11. (New York, 1937), pp. 117–18. By permission of the family of the late Dr. George Jackson.

THE SEASONS

(Words: *Millennial Praises,* pp. 217–20; tune reconstructed from "The Black Joke" and the letter p. 34.)

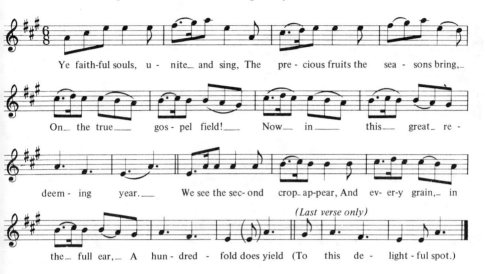

Ye faith-ful souls, u - nite_ and sing, The pre - cious fruits the sea - sons bring,_

On_ the true____ gos - pel field!___ Now__ in ____ this__ great_ re -

deem - ing year. ___ We see the sec- ond crop_ ap-pear, And ev- er-y grain,_ in

(Last verse only)

the_ full ear,_ A hun - dred - fold does yield (To this de - light - ful spot.)

part of the . . . tune coming first in the secular ballad tune."

Mary Dyer, an apostate who withdrew from the Shakers and then proceeded to "expose" Shakerism, wrote that their

> family and church worship is to sing songs of their own composition (no form or appearance of prayer) in adoration to *Ann Lee,* in the most merry tunes, such as "Yankee Doodle," and "Over the river to Charley," &c. with·the most ridiculous gestures, and motions and dance.[12]

Other secular tunes which are said to have accompanied Shaker songs and dances in the early stages of their development were "Scots wha' ha'e wi' Wallace bled," "Chevy Chase," "Nancy Dawson," "The D———l among the Tailors," and "Moll in the Wad."[13]

The following secular tune called "Wood Cutter" appears frequently in Shaker manuscript hymnals as a shuffling tune:

---

12. Mary Dyer, *A Portraiture of Shakerism* [New Hampshire?], 1822, p. 279.

13. Edward D. Andrews, *The Gift to be Simple* (New York, 1940), p. 85. By permission of J. J. Augustin Incorporated *Publisher.*

WOOD CUTTER[14]

Also SM197, p. 100; SM314, p. 217; SM359, last page

Joel Turner's "Stack Song" of 1809 (SM314, p. 20) probably has a secular origin; a tune called "Duke of York" appears in SM309, p. 50, but is not the popular march by the same name found in other early collections of dance music.

A shuffling dance called "Drawer tune" is found in SM314, p. 107, and in SM313 [n.p.]; *Webster's Dictionary* defines "drawer" as "one who draws liquor for guests; a waiter in a taproom." This may have been a tavern tune or drinking song of the period:

_____

14. Samuel Holyoke, ed., *The Instrumental Assistant* (Exeter, Newhampshire [sic.] [n.d.]) , 1:38.

DRAWER TUNE (1834)

Another evidence of continued Shaker interest in the secular dance tune is the "Fiddle Tune" in SM103 [n.p.], copied in the years between 1853–1864:

FIDDLE TUNE

The justice of the accusation that the Shakers sang "jig-tunes and hornpipes" may be seen in these illustrations. Both by literary account, which is practically all that can be relied upon for the tunes used before the Shakers began to record their music, and by the nature of the written music, it is evident that there is a close relationship between the body of British and early American dance tunes and those of the Shakers.

"Solemn songs" of the Psalm-tune type, and the adapted secular dances, appear to have constituted a large part of the Shaker music literature until 1807. Both solemn songs and dances were word-less; words came into use only after the Ohio and Kentucky so-

cieties were established. The frontier converts were accustomed
to using words, and the Shakers found that hymns provided a
fine manner of teaching their strange doctrines to their new
followers.

The Shaker missionaries who left the central ministry at Niskayuna on New Year's day, 1805, for Ohio and Kentucky, found
the communities they were sent out to visit in the midst of a
stirring religious revival. Converts from the Methodists, Baptists,
and Presbyterians, and the "Schismatics," "Merry Dancers,"
"New Lights," and "Christians" who had become dissatisfied
with the more firmly established sects, all were among those who
came into the Shaker fold. Unlike the believers in the East, who
had neglected music in their worship for several years until it
had lost its vitality,

> the subjects [the believers] of the great opening at the West, were
> accustomed to sing hymns & Anthems, hence when they embraced
> The Gospel They were not required to abandon that manner, but
> new compositions were formed adopted to their faith & state . . . &
> for years it greatly increased the life and power of our worship; it
> brot forth talents which had lain dorment for it was found that there
> were many able faculties among the people, capable of producing
> beautiful & appropriate compositions adapted to music which were
> very instructive & edifying.[15]

"Appropriate compositions *adapted* to music" suggests the
early practice of the Western Shakers in much of their musical
output. Most of this adapting at the beginning was done by
Richard McNemar, Isaacher Bates, and Samuel Hooser. McNemar
was by far the most prolific member of the group, and John P.
MacLean says in his Shaker bibliography that

> while it may not be fully susceptible of proof that he was the father
> of Shaker songs, yet in the infancy of music he did more to promote
> hymnology than any other person. Indeed he wrote most of the early
> songs.[16]

The great number of Shaker religious poems in the early manuscript hymnals signed by these three men make it seem reasonably

---

15. Green, Remarks on Music, p. 2.

16. John P. MacLean, *A Bibliography of Shaker Literature* (Columbus, Ohio,
1905), pp. 5–6.

sure that the "hymnology" and "songs" refer, at least for the most part, to the *texts* and not the music.

The interval between 1807, when hymns were first introduced into Shaker worship, and the 1820 period when definitely dated notation of Shaker hymns begins, leaves some doubt as to what the practice with regard to the tune may have been. The first hymns with notes were sent between communities in 1815 and hymn singing had begun eight years earlier in the societies. Letters are filled with the literary portion of the hymns which were exchanged during those years, suggesting that the tunes must have been well known to all, and that they must have come from the general stock of the Baptist, Methodist, and Presbyterian churches, and from revival melodies which would have been familiar to the new members.

Early Hymns (1809) antedating Shaker music notation. [SM391, pp. 6–7.]

By 1811 they had "near an hundred [hymns] composed on the different subjects of their faith,"[17] and in 1812 appeared the first printed hymns (words only), which were bound together in 1813 as *Millennial Praises*.

Shaker policy was proclaimed openly in one of these newly printed hymns:

> Lift up your heads, ye righteous few!
> A joyful theme belongs to you;
> Let justice sieze old Adam's crew,
> And all the whore's production:
> We'll take the choicest of their songs,
> Which to the Church of God belongs,
> And recompense them for their wrongs,
> In singing their destruction.[18]

The tune of "The Hallelujah Hymn" (SM255 [n.p.]) is a variant of "Shout Old Satan's Kingdom Down,"[19] but the words, which appear in Shaker hymnals without music as early as 1809, are different:[20]

Another set of words in the same hymnal of 1809 was probably sung to the same tune:

> Children of the latter Day Halla
> As you march the living way Halla
> Raise your Voice with Solemn Sound
> Tell the world what you have found Glory[21]

Words of "The Voyage to Canaan" are also in this same hymnal without the music, and were included in *Millennial Praises* (pp. 26–27) in 1813: these words and the tune that the Shakers used for them are the same as "The Spiritual Sailor" used by other sects of the period.

---

17. Brown. *An Account of Shakers*. p. 359.

18. *Millennial Praises* (Hancock, 1813), p. 169.

19. George P. Jackson. *Down-East Spirituals and Others* (New York, 1939). p. 265. By permission of the family of the late Dr. George Jackson.

20. SM391, pp. 9–10.

21. SM391, pp. 48–50.

SHOUT OLD SATAN'S KINGDOM DOWN
compared with
THE HALLELUJAH HYMN

(Non-Shaker)

(Shaker)

This day my soul has caught new fire, Hal-le, hal-le-lu-jah! I

What could mean the— sol-emn sound? Hal-le, hal-le-lu-jah!

feel that heav'n is com-ing nigh'n, O glo-ry hal-le-lu-jah!

On the old en-camp-ing ground, Hal-le, hal-le-lu-jah!

Chorus:

Shout, shout we're gain-ing ground, Hal-le hal-le-lu-jah! We'll

Fields and for-ests— all a-broad Hal-le hal-le-lu-jah!

shout old Sa-tan's king-dom down,O glo-ry hal-le-lu-jah!

Vo-cal with the— praise of God, Glo-ry hal-le-lu-jah!

THE SPIRITUAL SAILOR[22]

compared with
THE VOYAGE TO CANAAN[23]

The peo-ple call-ed Christ-ians Have man-y things to

A peo-ple call-ed Christ-ians How— man-y things— they—

tell A-bout the land of Ca-naan, Where saints and An-gels

tell A-bout a land of Ca-naan, Where— saints and An-gels

dwell; But here a dis-mal o-cean, En-clos-ing them a

dwell; But sin that dread-ful O-cean— En-clos-es them a

round,With its tides, still di-vides Them from Ca-naan's hap-py ground.

round,With its— tides, still di-vides Them from Ca-naan's hap-py ground.

22. William Walker, ed., *The Southern Harmony and Musical Companion* (New York, 1939 [orig. ed., 1835]), p. 41. By permission of Hastings House, Publishers, Inc.

23. Tune: SM412, p. 6; words: *Millennial Praises,* 26–27.

The practice of adapting a tune to any one of a large number of hymns having the same meter was common in Puritan Psalm singing and is prevalent in our own day. The Shakers used the same tune for "The Reapers" as for "The Shakers,"[24] and this practice may account for the fact that Isaac N. Youngs, the prominent Shaker musician, in writing out the tunes for *Millennial Praises* (in MSS, SM412), at a later date, omitted certain melodies.

A letter of 1808, in which a hymn was sent between communities, states that: "This Hymn we Sung in the Song [to the tune] that was sung to welcome Mother home to New-Lebanon."[25]

Funeral hymns were written at the death of many Shakers and were sung at the funeral. Burial was most often the day after the death, and it is reasonable to believe that a familiar tune was chosen for most of the poems written upon such short notice, or they could not have been learned by the singers. In the hymnal SM335 a funeral poem written upon a loose leaf and entitled "Farewell to Sister Abigail Cook" is marked "Tune of How fleeting and Transient."

A Shaker copyist gives the Adventist sect credit for five hymns in the Shaker song literature in SM314, p. 246: all of the tunes are dated 1846. Titles are "The Glory of Zion," "Christ is Coming," "Hail Happy Day" "Lots Yfe [Wife]," and "To the Mariner." The tunes are without words. The Shaker–Adventist version of "To the Mariner" is almost identical with "Mariner's Hymn" in Jackson's *Down-East Spirituals*, p. 253:

"Missionary Hymn," "Hoe out your Row," and "New England" are found in a collection dated 1867,[26] suggesting outside origins, and "Swede March," "Sweet By and By," "Beautiful River [Shall We Gather at the River]," and "Sweet Hour of Prayer" from outside sources penetrated Shaker Hymnology (1873) in its less picturesque days.[27] *The Musical Messenger*,[28] a short collection of

24. Tune: SM314, p. 228; words: *Millennial Praises*. pp. 239–41.

25. Letter from Caleb, Daniel, Ruth, Betty, to the Elders of the first Family [?]. Harvard, July 10, 1808.

26. Andrew D. Barrett. "A Collection of interesting matter written for the Edification & perusal of writer Commenced October 12" 1867 [n.p.].

27. SM102, p. 91, *passim*.

28. *The Musical Messenger*, (Union Village and Lebanon, Ohio [n.d.]), pp. 62–63.

TO THE MARINER
Compared with
MARINER'S HYMN

(Non-Shaker)

Male voice:

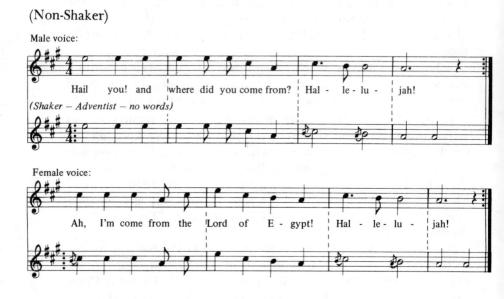

Hail   you!   and   where did you come from?   Hal - le - lu - jah!

(Shaker — Adventist — no words)

Female voice:

Ah,   I'm come from the Lord   of   E - gypt!   Hal - le - lu - jah!

melodies published by the Shakers, included "Rescue the Perish-
ing," a revival number popular among other religious sects, but
there is no evidence that these non-Shaker hymns were ever used,
even though they appear scattered through the hymnals.

A rare, if not unique, case of an American tune book taking
over a Shaker hymn and giving credit for it is to be found in
The American Vocalist, which printed "The Gospel is Lovely"[29]
with the words "[A Shaker tune.]" above it. (See page 48)

Shaker hymnology adapted not only tunes from the outside
world but many texts as well. Since, for the most part, the early
Shaker hymnals and letters up to the 1825 period contain words
only, it would seem reasonable to suppose that in many instances
the tunes were those commonly sung by other denominations
when the words are found in other sources, and when Shaker
membership consisted of substantial numbers recruited from the
ranks of other prevailing religious denominations. The Youngs

29. *The American Vocalist* (Boston [n.d.]; title page partly torn off), p. 338.

manuscript[30] already quoted, however, does not always give the tune found in other tune books, and in one case it gives six alternative tunes for one set of words. SM255 (1846) and SM314 (1838–1857 period) give alternative tunes for many of the hymns in the *Millennial Praises* of 1813; these two hymnals, as well as the six alternative tunes in the Youngs manuscript mentioned above, seem much later in date than the single tunes Youngs gives for accompanying the printed hymnal, suggesting that the early use of outside tunes to some of these hymns may have given way to original Shaker tunes once Believers started composing.

Evidence that Shaker words may have been adopted by other religious sects is found in "Babylon is Fallen" from *Millennial Praises*, pp. 50–51. Jackson says, "The earliest appearance of the text—six stanzas and the refrain . . . is in the New Hampshire Shaker *Millennial Praises* of 1813.[31] The tune is not the same as that given in the Youngs manuscript. The following comparison shows the manner of adaptation:

A PRAYER MEETING AND REVIVAL HYMN BOOK, HARRISBURG, 1825. p. 18, Appendix. Hymn 17.

1. Hail the day so long expected,
   Hail the year of full release;
   Zion's walls are now erected,
   And her watchman publish peace.
   Through the Shiloh's wide dominion,
   Hear the trumpet loudly roar—
   Babylon is fallen, is fallen, is fallen,
   Babylon is fallen, to rise no more.

MILLENNIAL PRAISES, HYMN XXIII, Babylon is fallen, pp. 50–51.

1. Hail the day so long expected!
   Hail the year of full release!
   Zion's walls are now erected,
   And her watchmen publish peace:
   From the distant coasts of Shinar,
   The shrill trumpet loudly roars,
   Babylon is fallen! is fallen! is fallen!
   Babylon is fallen to rise no more!

2. Hark, and hear her people crying,
   "See the city disappear!
   Trade and traffic all are dying!
   Lo, we sink and perish here!"

30. SM412.

31. George P. Jackson, *White and Negro Spirituals* (New York, 1943), p. 172. By permission of the family of the late Dr. George Jackson.

2. All her merchants stand with
  wonder,
  What is this that comes to pass;
  Murmuring like the distant
  thunder,
  Crying, Oh! alas, alas!
  Swell the sound ye kings and
  nobles,
  Priests and people, rich and
  poor,
  Babylon, &c.

3. Sing aloud ye heaven'ly choir,
  Shout ye followers of the Lamb;
  See the city all on fire,
  Now it sinks beneath the flame.
  Now the day of compensation,
  On the mystic church with gore.
  Babylon, &c.

4. Blow the trumpet in mount
  Zion,
  Christ will come the second
  time;
  Ruling with a rod of iron,
  All who now as foes combine.
  Babel's garments we've rejected;
  And our fellowship is o'er.
  Babylon, &c.

Sailors who have bought her
  traffic,
  Crying from her distant shore,
  "Babylon is fallen, . . . etc."

3. All her marchants cry with
  wonder,
  "What is this that's come to
  pass?"
  Murm'ring like the distant
  thunder
  Crying out, *Alas! Alas!*
  Swell the sound, ye kings and
  nobles!
  Priests and people, rich and
  poor!
  Babylon is fallen, . . . etc."

4. Lo, the captives are returning!
  Up to Zion see them fly!
  While the smoke of Babel's
  burning
  Rolls across the darkened sky!
  Days of mourning now are
  ended,
  Years of bondage now are o'er,
  Babylon is fallen, . . . etc."

5. Zion's children raise your voices,
  And the joyful news proclaim!
  How the heavenly host rejoices!
  Shout and echo back the same!
  See the ancients of the city,
  Terrify'd at the uproar!
  Babylon is fallen, . . . etc."

6. Tune your harps, ye heavenly
  choir!
  Shout, ye foll'wers of the Lamb!
  See the city all on fire!
  Clap your hands and blow the
  flame!
  Now's the day of compensation
  on the scarlet colour'd whore;
  Babylon is fallen, . . . etc."

The following parallel columns will show some other cases in which words from the *Millennial Praises* hymnal of 1813 existed in non-Shaker tune books:

MILLENNIAL PRAISES	NON-SHAKER SOURCES
"The Journey to Canaan," pp. 247–50.	"The Old Israelites," *Christian Songster*, pp. 98–101,[32] and *The American Vocalist*, p. 339.[33]
"My Feelings," pp. 65–66.	"Desires after Holiness," *Christian Songster*, pp. 84–87.
"Voyage to Canaan," pp. 26–27.	"The Spiritual Sailor," *The Southern Harmony, and Musical Companion*, p. 41;[34] *A Prayer Meeting and Revival Hymn Book*, pp. 376–77.[35]

Other manuscript hymnals also reveal similar adaptations of text, but it is not possible to produce conclusive proof that the Shakers had the words first, or vice versa, because the manuscripts were recopied many times and are impossible to date accurately:

SHAKER MANUSCRIPTS	NON-SHAKER SOURCES
"Midnight Cry," SM255, pp. 9–10.	"The Midnight Cry," *The Southern Harmony*, p. 32.
"The Patriarchs, SM288, pp. 287–89.	"Safe, in the Promised Land," *Christian Songster*, pp. 248–50.

A free version of the words to "Sweet Home," written by Robert Smith in 1829, probably used the well-known tune:[36]

---

32. *Christian Songster* (title page missing; no data), pp. 98–101.

33. *The American Vocalist*, p. 339.

34. Walker, *The Southern Harmony*, p. 41. By permission of Hastings House, Publishers, Inc.

35. *A Prayer Meeting and Revival Hymn Book* (Harrisburg, 1825). pp. 376–77.

36. SM397, 1823, pp. 70–71.

A Shaker tune in a non-Shaker tune book. [**The American Vocalist,** p. 338.]

SWEET HOME Philadelphia, 1829.
A Hymn Written by Robert Smith

Midst a world fill'd with sorrow vice folly & crime
And with mis'ry replete in each nation & clime
How sweet to the soul that in sorrow did roam
To find with believers a sweet tranquil home
    Home, Home, sweet, Sweet home
The heart broken wand'rer may here find a home.

Here the bond of friendship & kindness most sweet
Holds this firm little band in a union complete
And the tempest & billows around them may foam
Sweet peace spreads her wings, o're their thrice happy home
    Home, home, Sweet, Sweet home
There's no place on earth like a true Shaker home.
    [six more verses follow]

From the time of the arrival of the Shakers in America in 1774 until the decade following 1820, there were many adaptations in Shaker hymnody. The frontier musician read little by note, if at all; hymnbooks were scarce almost to the point of nonexistence, and many tunes were learned from the mouths of other singers

who likewise had probably never seen the tunes written down
and would not have understood them if they had. Old tunes and
hymns formed a common fund from which all denominations
drew freely, and from which they cut and pieced to suit their
special needs of religious dogma and peculiar poetic meter. (Jackson shows this interdenominational relationship in *White and
Negro Spirituals*.) The folk composer often accomplished this re-
creation of music "by altering the time, the rate of movement, the
relative length of the notes, or the mode (major to minor or vice
versa) or by differently combining the several phrases; and not
unfrequently all these changes were made in one melody."[37]

Abraham Whitney, a music teacher and musician in the War
of 1812, joined the Shirley Shakers in 1816 and soon began teaching Believers to write notes. As a result of this training, they
became less and less dependent upon the outside world for their
music, and adaptations gave way to original Shaker songs. Shaker
music had had its beginnings in the Kentucky Revival, and
flourished in such highly emotional surroundings. Another wave
of spiritual manifestation swept over the communities in 1827,
which gave fresh impetus to Shaker song writing and new songs
abounded; however, this revival was of comparatively short duration and was entirely eclipsed by the revivals of the decade 1837–
1847 in which it was estimated that between one and two thousand Shaker songs and hymns were brought forth and learned.[38]

Elder Henry C. Blinn wrote: ". . . on the 16th of August, 1837,
a new era commenced in the society at this place [Watervliet,
New York]. At first some of the little children, who were learning
to sing and to read, were suddenly entranced. . . . At 7:30 p.m.
they were taken to their chambers for the night, but they soon
began to sing and to talk about the angels."[39] This phenomenon
spread through the communities, especially among the children
at first, and the following year children at North Union, near
Cleveland, "heard some beautiful singing which seemed to be
in the air above their heads."[40] Shaker sisters soon began hearing
songs and before long the "gift," as the Shakers called this strange

---

37. Phillips Barry, "Polish Ballad. Trzy Siostry (The Three Sisters)" *Bulletin of
the Folk-Song Society of the Northeast* 11 (1936) :2.

38. White and Taylor, *Shakerism,* p. 337.

39. Henry C. Blinn, *The Manifestations of Spiritualism Among the Shakers
1837–47* (Canterbury, New Hampshire, 1899), p. 15.

40. Blinn, *Manifestations of Spiritualism,* p. 88.

manifestation, had spread to the brethren and through all of the communities. The recipients of these gifts of song were known as "instruments," who went into trances, had "visions," and frequently also were able to "speak with tongues," as did the Biblical characters, and who were also able to interpret these same strange messages and to prophesy. An early Shaker hymn writer described these favored few

> Moving in their ranks before us,
> Things immortal they discern;
> These can join the heav'nly chorus,
> None but such the song can learn.[41]

Shaker accounts of these gifts of song show that they were often accompanied by such bodily exercise as jerking, whirling, falling stiff and cold on the floor, prophesying in unknown tongues, moaning, bowing, barking, shaking, etc.; they are usually described with great reverence and amazement by the devout Believer who held the manifestation to be of divine origin. Because the record of these visions kept by Isaac Youngs is most revealing, a few of the entries concerning Shaker songs will be given:[42]

[February 1838?] . . . at Sodus—Mathilda Southwick is said to have had 50 songs in a week!

April 4th 1838: . . . their songs were wonderful; one of them (Emily) sung an anthem ½ hour long! & other songs, very beautiful.

May 21, 1838: [concerning children in vision jerking], I dont know what our hired workmen think to see so much going on, as they must see in our door yards!

May 29, 1838: Giles . . . heard Emily Babcock sing a song in english that Mother gave her, because she had not talked much of late—She also sung one they had heard before, this she could sing in english too, but what was remarkable was that she could not speak a word in english, only while singing these songs—this Giles witnessed himself

It is evident that some individuals held power over others who

---

41. *Millennial Praises*, p. 101.

42. Isaac N. Youngs, Sketches of Visions And various spiritual Gifts of which I obtain Information in various ways (1838) , p. 9, *passim.*

were zealous for a divine gift of song, speaking with tongues, or prophesy, and it is also clear that Youngs saw nothing but the working of divine power in the following entries from the same manuscript:

[No date; p. 10] The boys have songs, from Saml Southwick jr— one woman by the name of——? has the gift to communicate power to individuals & to take it away as she chooses!

July 17, 1838: . . . a peculiar case occurred with Nancy Wicks on Sab-evening the 15th in union time. In singing a certain song with the rest she was taken with jerk' and shak'—Brother Rufus.B. came came [*sic*] in about that time, & asked her to sing a song, but she jerked so she could hardly speak; She tried to sing, but could not, then she told br. Rufus if he would release her from jerking she would sing, he then said he was willing she should stop long enough for that; if she would then continue her shaking. Whereupon she immediately ceased shaking & sung her song, and when that was done she went right to shaking again. She wanted br. Ru. should release her forever, but he was not willing she should be wholly released. Mary kept on shaking after union meeting, & was much mortified about it and begged of Eliza Sharp to go & ask elder sister if she might not be released. E. was backwards about it, but Mary being urgent she went. E[lder] sister told her she might—& when Eliza bro't word to Mary, she immediately stopped!

There has been a number of instances I understand, with Mary, simillar to this, being released from jerking by applying to some of the elders which must have been effected by supernatural agency to show the order of the gospel in the dependence of souls on their lead or elders.

August 4th, 1838: This evening after meeting, there were 4 of them [four sisters operating *"very evidently against their wills"*], I understand that went to see the elder sisters to get released, & what is no less true & equally remarkable with the rest, the elder sisters have the power to release them, for it has been very frequently the case of late, that when these young sisters have applied to them to be released, & the elder sisters, one or both of them have expressed their consent that they should be released, they have uniformly been released, as was the case this evening with Miranda B. Mary W. Harriet S and Abigail H. if I understood their names.

[No date; pp. 63–64] I have watched these gifts and operations among believers of late closely to see if any pretence went undetected. There have been, I learn, some cases of pretence, or overstepping of the real gift, but as far as *I* know anything, it has been severely reproved and exposed by a true gift.

In a letter exchanged between ministries in 1838 the writer tells of "visionists" who are not "susceptible of any feeling from the prick of a needle," and adds that "our counsel has been to all . . . to yield submission to their elders."[43] George B. Cutten described this same submissive attitude which characterized all relations between Shaker Elders and members when he said, "In the modern Pentecostal meetings there is another element which is also ncessary to successful sleep or hypnotism, and that is the emphasis laid upon 'yielding oneself.' When this is accomplished, suggestion has full sway."[44]

A member who withdrew from the society described the Shaker "gift" of song with some skepticism and less religious awe than Isaac Youngs:

> The ministry inform the brethren, and sisters, generally through the elders, that there is a certain gift for them, and then *they must all labor for this gift, that is, mentally to be inspired with this gift.* [My italics.] For example, the elders inform the brethren and sisters, assembled in meeting, that 'the ministry tell us there is a gift of songs, for us brethren and sisters, now let us every one labor for a song. We must go forth in the *gift*, brethren, and sisters, if we would receive a blessing.' So then, for *days, or weeks, the brethren and sisters dwell upon the subject.* [My italics.] Until some Holy Spirits come and inspire them with a song; communicating to their minds by impression, or otherwise, the *language,* and the *tune.* And the songs that are brought forth on such occasions are a curiosity.[45]

It was with the suggestion that there were songs for them and that to receive one was a special blessing that these willing Shakers labored to attune their minds to an outside force that would put "language" and "tune" on their lips. Persons who could not sing were sometimes said to be able to do so under such conditions, and some who could not write verses found that they rhymed easily while under this force.[46] Zealous Believers went into trance, which in one case lasted as long as "6 days & 6 nights or 139

43. Letter from the Ministry at Shaker Village, Merrimack Co., New Hampshire, Jan. 29, 1838, to the ministry at Watervliet, pp. 3–4.

44. George B. Cutten, *Speaking with Tongues. Historically and Psychologically Considered* (New Haven, 1927), p. 167. By permission of the publisher, Yale University Press.

45. David R. Lamson, *Two Years' Experience Among the Shakers* (West Boylston, 1848), p. 80.

46. Cutten, *Speaking with Tongues,* pp. 83–84. By permission of the publisher, Yale University Press.

hours!"[47] in an effort to receive some special favor from the spiritual world, and at the same time to do something that could in no way detract from their prestige with the elders.

Frequently "speaking with tongues," whirling, shaking, prophesying and other strange acts, like barking and imitating those seen in the spirit world, accompanied the gift song. Sometimes descriptions of the methods of reception accompany the song and give a picture of how it was received, such as the one following the long anthem "Paradise of Rest":

> Mother Lucy says "this Anthem was sent to us from our Heavenly Father, by a holy Angel when the Chh was first established [sic] in gospel order upon earth;" she says we received the *spirit of it but not the letter.* [My italics.][48]

Other statements suggest that often the idea was given by inspiration in a trance or dream, but that the working out had to be accomplished later. The following dedication follows the song, "Love for the Faithful":

> This song was sung, as far as rejoice; by four little Angels that were sent from Jesus Christ to stay with the Elders. Mother Ann [her spirit] wanted Semanthia to have this song if the elders were willing. Mother Ann sung the remainder of the song for Semanthia F.[49]

A similar piecemeal method of giving the song is related in the same hymnal, which states that Mother Ann "then joined in praises and finished out the song."[50]

A long anthem was learned from a roll that

> Father James & Saint John brought into the meeting house Dec. 1st 1839; Father read apart of the roll then said that brother Daniel B. & Philliman might take the roll, & dance around the singers & they must labour for a gift to read the rest."[51]

Again this seems to have suggested the idea of tune and words for the singers to take up and complete.

---

47. Letter from the Ministry at Shaker Village, Merrimack Co., New Hampshire, Jan. 29, 1838, to the Ministry at Watervliet, p. 2.

48. SM105, p. 60.

49. SM106, p. 61.

50. *Ibid.*, p. 81.

51. SM105 [n.p.].

The "instrument" usually received the song from a Shaker in the spirit world such as Mother Ann, a prominent elder, or a recently departed member who had been well known to the favored recipient: sometimes a personage such as Queen Isabella, the Prophet Jeremiah, Christopher Columbus, Lafayette, or George Washington, who had become Shakers in the realm beyond, sent a song to the inspired one.

Rough scrapbooks were kept in which the songs were "scratched" down as they came along, and from which they were "drawn" or recopied, and probably revised, as the Shakers found time.[52] The dedication "Sung to Tabitha Lapsley by Elder Sister Olive in our Sab. morning meeting Oct. 5th 1839. Learned by Anna Dodgson," shows the method frequently used. Elder Sister Olive [Spencer] who had died five years previously in this community sent the song from the spirit world to Tabitha Lapsley, and it was notated by Anna Dodgson, a New Lebanon Shaker musician, and contemporary of Tabitha Lapsley as she "learned" it from the actual singing.[53]

Some of the mediums fasted while they were engaged in spiritual labors, and often would exist for six or eight days on a fare of bread and water.[54] The strange effect upon the mind produced by fasting is illustrated in the following description of an Omaha Indian rite. It was customary for the tribe to send a youth out to fast in a lonely place, and to sing a prayer for four nights and days in a trial of endurance.

> When at last he fell into a sleep or trance, and the vision came, of bird, or beast, or cloud, bringing with it a cadence, this song became ever after the medium of communication between the man and the mysterious power typified in his vision. . . . In this manner all mystery songs [for his rites] originated.[55]

Another more modern example illustrates the same effect of fasting. Fliers whose plane had been forced down in the Pacific and who had floated on a rubber raft for thirty-three days without food wrote that

---

52. Letter from Isaac Youngs, New Lebanon, New York, to Beloved Brethren (?), Aug. 11, 1837, p. 1.

53. SM106, p. 63.

54. Blinn, *Manifestations of Spiritualism*, pp. 19, 39.

55. Alice C. Fletcher, *Indian Story and Song* (Boston, 1900), p. 26.

By now our minds were growing weak with hunger. Sometimes they strayed away and imagined queer things. Tony imagined he heard choral voices singing. The voices were low and sweet and beautiful. They sang sentimental songs of home. Once he asked, "Don't you hear those voices singing?" I heard nothing but the winds and the waves.[56]

Songs sent to individuals in dreams and visions are not uncommon in history. About A.D. 720 a school of Chinese actors, known as "The Garden of Pear Trees," was founded by one Yuên-tsoūng, who wrote for the first play to be interpreted by his artists "music which a spirit had dictated to him in a dream."[57]

St. Godric, who died A.D. 1170, wrote what are thought to be the earliest extant lyrics in England after the Norman Conquest. All of these songs were said to have been dictated to him through angelic vision "by the son of his dead sister, attended by angels, in answer to his persistent entreaties of God to know how she had fared in the spirit world."[58]

After Thomas à Becket had been dead three years, his life inspired an English antiphon, which a group of angels allegedly dictated to a sleeping Norfolk priest. The account of the inspiration states that it was sung three times to the sleeping priest.[59]

Precedent was not lacking for the inspirational methods of song reception which the Shakers practiced, but the exact processes involved are not revealed to us by the meager bits of information that these devout and astounded minds left. Even if they had considered these inspirational songs other than a divine gift, they probably would have been incapable of examining and analyzing the functioning of their own minds. A hundred years later we are still struggling to follow the creative mind as it discovers and develops an idea and gives it to the world, and like the Shaker who could create thirteen songs in one vision without any scientific explanation of that feat, we still have only the result, and not the process involved in obtaining it.

In conscious composition, as in the case of Beethoven's crea-

---

56. Harold F. Dixon, "Three Men on a Raft," *Life Magazine* 12 (April 6, 1942) : 76. © 1942 Time Inc.

57. Louis Laloy, *La Musique Chinoise* (Paris [n.d.]) , p. 111.

58. Gustave Reese, *Music in the Middle Ages* (New York, 1940) , p. 241.

59. *Ibid.*, p. 242.

tions, for example, an idea may have come suddenly and have been the original starting point for hard work for ten years to come; a well-trained and disciplined mind sorted, weighed, revised, and calculated the details which evolved from the original inspired idea until at last a beautiful and finely balanced work of art appeared. In such a case there are two major divisions in the process: original inspiration and development of that inspiration through deliberation. Shaker inspirational composition differed from this in both categories: suggestion from outside sources played a large and important part in the original idea involved in this type of music, and the Shaker mind was not usually the well-trained and disciplined sort that could develop the original idea, but left an emotional expression in which religious fervor outweighed intellectual development.

In the fragmentary vision song which follows, the nice balance of the four two-measure phrases may be the result either of the rhythmic dancing which accompanied much Shaker singing, or of careful revision and organization by a copyist after it was given. The single idea is "Love," and the word is an emotional shout each time it appears. It is not improbable that an elder had said "There is a gift of love for the brethren and sisters," as was often done, which would have sufficed to inspire the singer with his song. Notice that the idea occurred to the instrument to mention that it was "heavenly" love, and not "carnal" love, but words failed at the end and it became a wordless tune:

SM190 [n.p.] "Vision song Elliett's"

Organization is practically absent in the next fragment. The singer's flow of words failed in English and he continued in "the gift of tongues." Cutten says of this common practice in inspired singing and speaking:

Those who speak in tongues are generally the most illiterate among the Saints, such as cannot command words as quick as they would wish, and instead of waiting for a suitable word to come to their memories, they break forth in the first sound their tongues can articulate no matter what it is.[60]

Pictures of Shaker musicians. [Shaker Photograph Collection.] Courtesy The Western Reserve Historical Society

---

60. Cutten, *Speaking with Tongues,* pp. 73–74. By permission of the publisher, Yale University Press.

SM45, p. 1 "Dec. 4th 1839 Sent by a little spirit to L.T."

This is Moth-er's pret-ty   path Se - ne   vo   Se - ne   ve

All the shorter gift songs show that the melodic and textual ideas are terse and very simple in nature. The repeats may have been the idea of the copyist:

SM45 [n.p.] 2nd order 1840

Press____ on,   press____ on,   press_____   ye   on.

Lamson remarked that the "gift" partook of the character of the visionist. "If the instrument be a shallow weak minded person, this quality will also characterize the gift. If an ignorant person, ignorance will be manifested in the gift. If of a strong imagination, the gift will be proportionately brilliant."[61] The next example is almost like a primitive tribal tune, dwelling chiefly on four tones, G, A, C, and D (if we discount the sliding of the voice), and with exact repetition of one simple literary phrase:

SM272, p. 105

Lo lo   lo lo   here   is___ Christ Lo   lo   lo   lo here   is___ Christ
Lo   lo   lo   lo   here   is Christ Lo   lo   lo   lo here   is Christ

61. Lamson, *Two Years' Experience,* p. 80.

An intermediate stage between the fragmentary examples just quoted and the cases mentioned in which one visionist "sang the song as far as" a certain point and another finished it is the song entitled:

I AM MOTHER'S

SM3 [n.p.], No. 35

"The 1st line was sung by Joanna K. in meeting. The next by Sʳ Lucy in answer. 1839–"

Many of the songs given by inspiration must have been lost for lack of musicians adequately equipped to notate them with but one hearing. There was an instance in which a Shaker wrote that

> Mother stood on a little knowl close by the village of South Union, and sung a song which sounded in the air, and some of the believers heard it, & learned it or she thought that they would gather it. It was a worded song, and the sisters repeated the words; but Hannah could only remember a line or two, & I have not retained them.[62]

Quotations like this, and the fact that many skilled musicians cannot take down a long musical phrase from dictation, without repetition, make it evident that in the case of the longer anthems, the Shakers probably "received the spirit of it but not the letter," and that there must have been many alterations later to render the music at all singable. The explanation of this step in the song creation must be left largely to conjecture because the books in which they "scratched down" songs and from which they copied them later as they found time have not been available, if they still exist.

Songs given in a dream do not differ noticeably from those

---

62. Copies of various letters from different societies written 1817–1841, letter No. 15; Hancock, June 20, 1838 to the Ministry by Olive Spencer, pp. 111–12.

given in trance or vision. The following song, which is entirely in the "gift of tongues," was "Rhoda Blake's sung to her in a dream 1838." The jingle quality of its rhythm suggests a parallel to a school cheering song:

SM68 [n.p.]

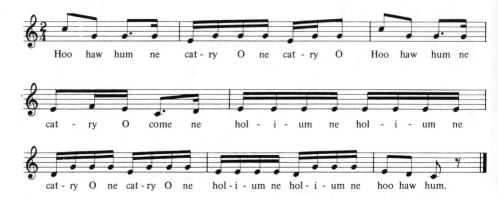

"Speaking with tongues" is a common phenomenon: it existed in Biblical times; among the Jansenists in France in 1731 and among the Quakers in the time of Cromwell; and the Welsh, Primitive Methodists, and Mormons all practiced it.[63] The foundation of this peculiar gift

> is the abnormal state of trance or ecstasy in which certain mental powers are exalted, chief among which are the memory and the power of expression. At the same time the higher judicial and regulative mental functions are almost entirely inhibited. While in this state, the suggestion of being another person has all the effect of such a suggestion during the hypnotic state. The glossolalics endeavor to carry out the part and that without the confusion of bashfulness which would come were the person in a normal state.[64]

Cutten says the whole phenomenon of speaking with tongues is "a childish reaction, showing itself not only by its appearance among the most primitive and untrained in a community, but by its similarity to the reactions of children."[65] The person so gifted

---

63. Cutten, *Speaking with Tongues,* p. 67, *passim.* By permission of the publisher, Yale University Press.

64. *Ibid.,* p. 86. By permission of the publisher, Yale University Press.

65. *Ibid.,* p. 162. By permission of the publisher, Yale University Press.

seldom has the power to interpret his own words, and interpretation is usually performed through another "instrument" who has the meaning revealed by the spirit world in the same manner that the original message in "tongues" is revealed. Many examples appear without interpretation. In some instances the meaning is given in a general sort of way, suggesting the spirit of the message but not the actual words; a few interpretations pretend to be literal, and the meaning is given for such revelations line by line. Alliteration is a prominent feature of speaking with tongues, and, as the following parallel columns will show, one syllable or one group of syllables does not necessarily have a fixed meaning each time it appears.

MOTHER ANN'S PRAYER[66]

SM267, pp. 38–39.
Vi vo vive vum vum vi vive vum
    ve
  o vum
vi vo vive vum vi vo vum

vi vo vive vum vi vive vum vi vo
  vive vum
ve o vum vum vi vive vum ve o
  vum vi vi vive
vum vum.

O Lord give me Wisdom, O give
  me strength to
direct my poor needy children on
  earth!
O Lord do protect them from the
  judgement
O Lord in thy mercy do bless
  them,
  O Heavenly
Father! don't leave my poor needy
  children.

THE LILLY

SM3 [n.p.], Song No. 2.
O ne nin ve vi vum, ne nin ve
  vi vum
O ne nin ve vi vum Ne Vane O
O ne ninve Vi vum O ne nin ve
  vi vum
ne vane O.

O the lilley does bloom, The lilley
  does bloom,
O the lilly does bloom in the lowly
  Vale

SM3 [n.p.], Song No. 15.
  "Examination"
Wene wane woo, We ne wane
  woo,
  wif waf-
We vo vane voo.
  2nd order 1839.

    "Enterperetation"
Faithful faithful souls, faithful
  souls shall dwell
with my faithful children here.—

---

66. It is interesting to note that most of the gift songs in "tongues" which have "vive vo vum ve" syllables similar to this one are attributed to Mother Ann Lee.

SM272, pp. 21–22. ANTHEM "A SURE PROMISE"

(by sure and liv ing streams that never more will fail)
so con di re ne va so ka kan le ne vi

(A safe and sure protector a safe and sure protector)
ve vi vo viv e vum va va van ve vi vo viv e vum va van
lin se len vo len, se leen len vo
(appointed chosen) (annointed few.)
March 24, 1839

SM45 [n.p.].
O come si hil e ka ne, O re an
den cany
A le anson, a le v, a in you de
fancy
There E van te, & sel e te vest,
O how hack any
te van, far e vas een, & tinse
I veen I nos in te le ve.

SM225, p. 113 (in WISDOM'S
PLEASURE).
O ka den, des pre den van

SM225, p. 123
Co la es ka wa wah co la es ka
wa wah
Co la es ka wa wah wa wah wa
wah
Co la es ka wa wah wa wah wa
("Turn to next page for the en-
terpretation.")

O come my children dear, here in
heavenly treasures
Here's a mansion far above, all
earthly fleeting pleasures
The weary soul can here find rest,
O how happy & peaceful—
Here the Lord doth freely bless,
his holy chosen people.

deep sorrows of time.
Pure love and union is a flowing
freely
Pure love and union O come to
me
Co la es ka wa wah wa wah wa
wah
Co la es ka wa wah wa wah wa.

MODA'S DOM NE TE

SM247, p. 58.
Ah lah, ah lah le Mo da An es
Dom ne
te oo ve lan co dex a lon

. . . . .

Ah co din vun se vin se
Ah co tan dal vil lo dal vil lo
di vin se,
Le des dom ni te
Dom ne te of Mo des Dom ne to of
Moda's
Dom ne te ov Moda An's
I an de ka le va len.
Ah Mo des ka le tan dom ne te.
"Learned at Queen Isabella's
Society, in the world of Spirits,
January 10th, 1840."

(Interpretation to the foregoing,"
SM247, p. 59.)
Oh lo O ho In Mother Anna's
pretty way of freedom
Come march along

. . . .

O come be lively lively
O come and dance around, dance
around be lively
in this pretty way.
Pretty way of Mother's, Pretty
way of Mothers
Pretty way of Mother Ann's
And the holy Saviour
O Mother's holy and pretty way.
"Sent to Elder br. & br. Daniel
B. January 31st 1840."

SM272, p. 16.
Lone ve ureve See Cak a dak a ne
Uron dollevon Sara ak a ne ne.
I o ok a se Let e ve let e ve
Urosok a see Sara ak a ne ne
Jan. 1839.

Interpretation
Here flows Mother's love. It is
  a pretty treasure;
Pure love, precious love. Partake
  and live forever.
I have a little store. I'll strive
  to gain more.
All must be increasing; Partake,
  and live forever.

SM25 (page numbers are
  confused).
O Praise the Lord Praise ye the
  Lord,
Give honor & glory to His name
  thro his chosen Annointed

Vas keen vi Lero, vas keen ve
  Lero
Le a O len pre za ven to sen he
  fe holen Lensen volen.
("Note. The last part of the tune
has the meaning of the forepart—")

Augustus Blase, to whom the following German Song was sent, was born in Germany and wrote his Shaker diary and journals in German. The sounds written down by the recorder, who probably knew no German, present quite an accurate and literal German version of the English translation when pronounced phonetically, in spite of their formidable appearance in writing.

GERMAN SONG

SM45 [n.p.].
O himmel, himmel, himmel, O
him ma lis hu le bah, le bah, le
  bah,
O diece ist, Mutus himma lis ha le
  bah;
O mutus le bah, de ist
hi le, hi le, hi le, O mutus
le bah, de ist hile ut rine.

Interpretation
O heaven, heaven, heaven, O
heavenly love, love, love,
O this is Mother's heavenly love.
O Mother's love, it is
holy, holy, holy—O Mother's
love, it is holy & pure!
"Sent to Augustus Blase, from
his Sister Algebrine a german-
family. from Watervliet 1840."

A song attributed to Queen Elizabeth likewise gives a liberal version in Latin, if read phonetically, of the English interpretation which accompanies it. Abraham Whitney was a singer and music teacher before he became a Shaker, and may have known and sung some Latin before joining the Shirley community. The caption with this hymn suggests that the ungarbled version of the words came from a printed Latin text:

SM3 [n.p.]. "The following was copied from the public print & inter-preted by Br Abraham Perkins of Canterbury n.h. It is said to be from Queen Elizabeth, sung by her while imprisoned in the 16th Century".

O Dom I ne Deus, spera vi en te,	O God my Creator I've trusted in thee
O Carry me Jesu munce libera me.	O Jesus my Saviour now liberate me
In dura ca te ne, mass er a po e na	In fetters I languish in sorrow & anguish
dis idder O te. Lan qwen do, gem en do	I still look to thee. In the depths of affliction
a do ro im-plore ut liber us me.	I worship & pray that I yet may be free.

Mother Ann herself was reputed to have spoken by inspiration in many foreign languages. In the early days of Shakerism there must have been few in the society who could have questioned her ability to speak some thirty or forty languages when they wrote their own English so poorly and had had so little schooling and travel. Cutten states that it was not uncommon in groups other than the Shakers to find "speaking of some words in a foreign tongue; but the language is always one with which the subject has come in contact, even if he can consciously speak no words in that language,"[67] and the "psychological explanation is that of exalted memory, due to the abnormal condition of the individual."[68] Since a great amount of this phase of Shaker tradition was unrecorded in the early years, it will probably never be a certainty where the line can be drawn that divides fabulous legend and trickery from true psychological phenomena. That part of the process which was willful and conscious on the part of the individual and that which can be attributed to hypnosis, post-hypnotic suggestion, mob psychology, and all of the other circumstances or conditions in which one mind can influence another, are difficult to disentangle. Consideration of this kind of Shaker song creation must be approached with the knowledge that Shaker accounts in diaries and journals show Believers to have been devout and sincere about their inspirational gifts, but just as unaware of the possibilities of its psychology as they were eager to accept blindly all that appeared to be of divine origin. It is probable that most elders with the power to make individuals shake or sing and the ability to "release" them when they so chose did consider such a strange gift divine rather than in any sense an

---

67. Cutten, *Speaking with Tongues*, p. 170. By permission of the publisher, Yale University Press.

68. *Ibid.*, p. 176. By permission of the publisher, Yale University Press.

act of cunning, for little was known about such matters at the height of its use among the Shakers. The number of people who created songs seems high in proportion to Shaker membership when compared with a non-Shaker community, but music early assumed an important role in the Shaker societies and was the one diversion which replaced all of the pleasures enjoyed by members of a general American community—family, travel, personal possessions, and other forms of self-expression. A study of style may reveal at some future time whether there are as many distinct musical personalities in Shaker music as there are names, or whether the few who were more richly endowed were sources for supplying suggestions to the minds of the many who were less gifted. The difficulties in the way of such a study are first of all the self-effacing anonymity of many of the writers to avoid any false pride or prestige, and second, the practice of keeping "gift" songs in notebooks which were later copied and revised in their final form by a few copyists. When revision is practiced, the song is no longer a pure "gift" or vision song and conscious composition begins. The "scratch" books are not available, and data are often lacking concerning the personalities involved in the reception of a "gift" song, namely, the spiritual donor of the song (usually in the spirit world) ; the "instrument" who received it in vision, trance, or dream; the person or persons who wrote it down when the "inspired" person sang it; the copyist who transferred it from the rough copy to a neat manuscript hymnal; the multitude of Shakers who recopied it into their own hymnbooks if it was well liked, making it impossible to tell which copy was the earliest to come from the scratch books; and finally, the person who heard it sung and wrote it in his hymnal from memory without ever having seen it written out, perpetuating variations which take place in any folk singing and at any one of the numerous stages in the development of the song.

Conscious composition seems to have existed hand in hand with adaptation and inspiration at all stages of the growth of Shaker music. It is not uncommon to find such a phrase as "Words from Union Village Ohio and tuned at New Lebanon" written after a song, showing that a Shaker musician *composed* a melody for a hymn which had been sent from one society to another.

There is no infallible way of telling whether a song which is not marked is a "vision" song or one that was consciously composed; hymnals often state explicitly that a song was "given in vision," and many tell where and by whom the words were "tuned"; the third category is without any identification, but Shakers considered their music, regardless of the manner of acquisition—adaptation, inspiration, or conscious composition—as a spiritual gift. Phillips Barry said:

> If out of a ceremonial dance, as was the Shaker Dance, executed by the members of a homogeneous community, as the Shakers were, folk song has grown, we should expect to find at least a reversion to the primitive way of communal song-composition. Yet we do not find it. The Shakers regarded song-composition as a spiritual gift; following Biblical precedent, they believed that the spirit inspired not communities, but individuals.[69]

This is true only in a sense. Individuals were "inspired," but it often took several members of the community to notate, to copy, and, in some cases, to revise a song before it reached its final form.

In one period of less than eleven months, Isaac Youngs wrote 360 new songs,[70] and Eunice Wythe, who died at the age of 36, had written about 600 poems.[71] Composers and hymn writers and their songs were legion among the Shakers for almost a century. Sometimes the poet and musician were the same person, and sometimes an entire hymnal was "A Collection of verses written & Pricked [the tune written]" by the same Shaker;[72] often only the author or the composer is designated, and it may not be clear whether one or both are intended: initials, a date, or the name of the community are frequently the only identification. Other songs give absolutely no clues.

The following list of names of people who participated in Shaker music is by no means complete: the above explanation shows the impossibility of arriving at such a goal. Included are musicians, poets, copyists, and visionists, all active throughout the hundred-year period and all found in varying degrees from one to hundreds of times in Shaker journals. Since Shakers frequently changed communities, the society where they spent most of their

---

69. Phillips Barry, "Heavenly Display," *Bulletin of the Folk-Song Society of the Northeast* 1 (1930) :6.

70. Letter from Isaac N. Youngs [New Lebanon, N.Y.], Aug. 11, 1837, to Beloved Brethren[?].

71. Letter from Harvard Ministry, Jan. 21, 1830, to "Beloved and much esteemed Ministry" [?], p. 2.

72. SM386.

years is usually given. Dates represent birth and death; if the Shaker withdrew from the society, such information is given if known; a blank is left when no data are available.

ALFRED, MAINE
Holmes, Oliver, there 1827
Pote, Elisha, 1764–1845

CANAAN, NEW YORK
Green, Ellen, 1843–?
Hollister, Rhoda R., 1819–1890
Offord, Miriam, 1846–1914
Sizer, Daniel, 1804–1880

CANTERBURY, NEW HAMPSHIRE
Blinn, Henry C., 1824–1905
Brown, Elijah, 1772–1851
Durgin, Dorothy, 1825–1898
Fletcher, Sarah, 1780–1829
Sanborn, Joseph, 1780–1841
Stickney, Asenath C., 1826–
    1916
Williams, Tabitha, 1779–1853
Wright, Thomas, 1794–?

ENFIELD, CONNECTICUT
Blanchard, Zilpha, 1829–1874
Haskell, Russell, 1801–1884
Lyman, Amelia, 1831–1892
Lyman, Marie, 1833–?

ENFIELD, NEW HAMPSHIRE
Curtis, Miriam, 1803–1844
Dickey, Reuben, 1795–1851
Perkins, Abraham, 1807–1900
Randlett, Timothy, 1815–1892
Russell, Isabella, 1833–?
Russell, James G., 1843–1888

GROVELAND, NEW YORK
Lockwood, John, 1791–1879
Love, Anna Maria, 1835–left
    1860

HANCOCK, MASSACHUSETTS
Augur, Mary Ann, 1830–1861
Cogswell, Anna, 1761–1829
Goodrich, Joshua, 1781–1854
Williams, William, 1781–1867

HARVARD, MASSACHUSETTS
Bathrick, Eunice, 1793–1883
Blanchard, Louise B., 1810–?
Bridge, Hanna, 1781–1875
Hammond, Thomas, 1791–
    1880
Hildreth, Amos, 1794–?
Parker, Joseph, 1805–1854
Warner, John, 1758–1834
Wood, Mariah, 1820–1914
Wyeth, Eunice, 1756–1830

NEW GLOUCESTER, MAINE
Cummings, Ada S., 1862–?
Frank, Eva, 1870–?
Hill, Mary Ann, 1799–1890
Littlefield, Lydia, 1793–1877
Sawyer, Otis, 1815–1884
Stickney, Prudie, 1862–?
Whitney, Nellie O., 1857–?

NEW LEBANON, NEW YORK
Agnew, Hannah Ann, 1820–
    1905
Allen, Catherine, ?–?
Anderson, Martha J., 1844–
    1897
Annas, Angelina, 1807–1847
Avery, Eliza, 1814–1886
Barber, Miranda, 1819–1871
Barrett, Andrew D., 1837–1917
Bates, Isaacher, Sr., 1758–1837
Bates, Sarah, 1792–1881
Bennet, Derobigne, 1818–left
    1846
Bennet, Molly, 1782–1870

Bennet, Roby, 1798–1880
Bennet, Willie, 1866–left?
Bishop, Amos, 1780–1857
Bishop, James B., 1778–?
Blake, Hannah, 1811–1893
Blanchard, Electa, 1801–1837
Brown, Angelina, 1856–?
Bruce, John, 1771–1829
Buckingham, David A., 1803–
    1885
Bushnell, Richard, 1791–1873
Clark, Stephen, 1776–1819
Clough, Jacob, 1754–1834
Copley, Luther, 1800–1851
Crocker, Fanny, 1827–?
Crossman, Abigail, 1807–1889
Crossman, Daniel, 1810–1885
Curtis, George, 1806–1873
Dean, John H., 1797–1873
DeWitt, Henry, 1805–1855
Dibble, Chauncey, 1821–1889
Dodgson, Anna, 1818–1897
Doolittle, Antoinette, 1810–
    1886
Evans, Frederick W., 1808–
    1893
Fairbanks, Olive, 1812–1834
Fairbanks, Semantha, 1804–
    1852
Fortier, Andrew, 1823–1890
Fowler, Edward, 1800–1878
Gates, Benjamin, 1817–1909
Gates, Lucy, 1816–1848
Gates, Oliver, 1785–1847
Ginnings, David, 1771–?
Greaves, William H., 1835–?
Green, Calvin, 1780–1869
Harwood, Jesse, 1800–1874
Haskins, Horace, 1812–1885
Haskins, Orin, 1815–1892
Hazard, Mary, 1811–1899
Hollister, James, 1832–?

Jacobs, Adonijah, 1764–1846
Jacobs, Clarissa, 1833–1905
Johnson, Samuel, 1775–1856
Ketchel, Joanna, ?–?
Lannuier, Augusta, 1823–1862
Lannuier, Elizabeth T., 1822–
    1852
Lapsley, Mariah, 1821–1901
Lapsley, Tabitha, 1819–1900
Lawrence, Garret K., 1794–
    1837
Lewis, Sarah Ann, 1813–1877
Lockwood, Hortency, 1815–
    1852
Long, George, 1825–left 1860
Long, Peter K., 1816–1885
Loomis, Sally, 1751–1827
Lovegrove, Elizabeth, 1791–
    1844
Lyon, Benjamin, 1780–1870
McLean, Myra, 1842–?
Mantle, Mary Ann, 1808–1886
Matthewson, Lydia, 1777–1850
Meacham, John, 1770–1854
Parker, David, 1807–?
Potter, Eleanor, 1812–1895
Reed, Mathilda, 1817–1902
Reynolds, Minerva, 1819–1904
Robe, John, 1818–left 1872
Sampson, Rachel, 1803–1886
Sears, Florinda, 1825–1901
Sears, Louise, 1826–left 1853
Sharp, Eliza, 1797–1881
Simons, Sarah, 1820–left 1849
Sizer, Charles, 1810–1881
Smith, Emily, 1824–left 1871?
Smith, James H., 1806–1888
Smith, Phebe, 1810–1881
Smith, Ransom, 1795–1876
Smith, Sarah, 1819–1856
Spencer, Olive, 1778–1834
Spier, Nathan, 1775–1827

Spires, Samuel, 1760–1826
Standish, Sarah Ann, 1809–
    1895
Stephens, Rosetta, ?–?
Stewart, Philemon, 1804–1875
Stone, Betsy, 1813–?
Strever, Marietta, 1847–1890
Sutton, Elizaette, 1820–1903
Thompson, Gabriel, 1835–left
    1861
Tiffany, Daniel, 1767–1793
Travers, Mortimer, 1825–1846
Turner, Jethro, 1764–1853
Turner, Joel, 1772–1855
Turner, Samuel, 1775–1842
Vail, James, 1819–1865
Valentine, Robert L., 1822–
    1910
Van Houten, Phebe, 1817–1895
Vedder, Angelica, 1796–1882
Vedder, Catherine, 1799–1891
Vining, Joanna, 1802–1888
Weed, Charles, 1831–left 1862
Wells, Seth Y., 1767–1847
Wheeler, Olive, 1802–1882
White, Anna, 1831–1910
Wicks, Mary, 1819–left 1846
Williams, Nathan, 1781–1869
Wood, John, 1791–1861
Woodrow, Richard B., 1828–
    left 1853
Youngs, Elizabeth, 1782–1865
Youngs, Isaac N., 1793–1865

NORTH UNION, OHIO
Ingalls, Jeremiah, 1797–1858
Thayer, Moses, 1823–?

PLEASANT HILL, KENTUCKY
Cooney, James, 1799–1854
Dunlavy, Banjamin B., 1805–
    1886

Hooser, Samuel, 1778–1854
Pearson, Fanny, 1803–?
Pool, Sarah, 1797–?
Redmon, Susannah, 1786–1877
Runyon, Vincent, 1790–1846
Rupe, Polly M., 1826–1875
Shields, Joel, 1780–?

POLAND, MAINE
Bangs, Anne, 1797–1827

SHIRLEY, MASSACHUSETTS
Barret, Susannah, 1762–1847
Crispe, M. J., came 1855–left
    1889
Elston, Mary O., 1833–1904
Morse, Mary R., 1849–1879
Orsemont, Nancy, 1803–1874
Prouty, Lorenzo D., 1824–1891
Randall, Joanna, 1820–1902
Wheeler, Huldah, 1806–1881
Whitney, Abraham, 1785–1882

SODUS, NEW YORK
Blakeman, Elisha, 1819–1872

SOUTH UNION, KENTUCKY
Eades, Sally, 1782–1859
Freehart, Hannah, 1803–1893
Gill, Harriet, 1803–1882
Houston, Prudence F., 1804–
    1873
McComb, Mary, 1795–1874
Moore, Nancy E., 1807–1889
Price, Maria, 1807–1879
Rice, William, 1784–1863
Whyte, Molly, there 1830

TYRINGHAM, MASSACHUSETTS
Allen, William, 1751–1828
Stanley, Eleazer, 1777–1852
Storer, Harriet, 1817–1890

UNION VILLAGE, OHIO

Belcher, Eunice, 1802–1836
DeWitt, Lucy, 1803–1877
Eades, Hervey L., 1807–1892
Houston, Isaac N., 1795–1859
King, Solomon, 1775–1858
McNemar, James, 1796–1875
McNemar, Richard, 1770–1839
Morrell, Prudence, 1794–1855
Risley, Lucinda, 1820–left
    185–?
Russell, Sanford, 1818–1900

WATERVLIET, NEW YORK

Avery, Giles B., 1815–1890
Ayres, Mary Ann, 1819–1912
Bates, Isaacher, Jr., 1790–1875
Bates, Pauline, 1806–1884
Blase, Augustus, 1813–1884
Boler, Daniel, 1804–1892
Bowie, Semantha, 1839–1892
Brackett, William C., 1807–
    1887
Bragg, Ambrose, 1785–left 1820
Buckingham, Ann, 1804–1892
Budine, Justin, 1829–1905
Butler, Samuel S., joined 1880
Clark, Emeline, 1793–1873
Dole, Laura, 1820–1899
Johnson, Eunice, 1780–1861
Laurence, Polly, there 1866
Lowe, Jeremiah, 1798–1878
Reed, Polly, 1818–1881
Seeley, William, 1790–1863
Williamson, Emily S., there
    1862
Wood, Joel, ?–1820

WATERVLIET, OHIO

Hampton, Oliver C., 1817–
    1901

NO DATA:

Bartlett, George C.
Bottom, Eleanor
Bowers, Lucy
Browser, Richard
Burnam, Eunice
Collins, Elash
Coyman, Carrie
Doolittle, Julia
Foy, Flora
Gelispie, Mary A.
Paterson, M.
Richard, Isaacher J.
Robert, Anthony
Shutley, Maria
Sidle, Mathilde
Staples, Florence
Stout, Mercy
Whitney, Harriet
Woodford, Oliver
Woodworth, Emma

3

Shaker Notation

Dating Shaker notation by means of hymnbooks is a dangerous procedure. Hymns were copied and recopied and sent between communities so frequently that many hymns actually composed at an early date were copied later, possibly decades later, in the style of notation most familiar to the scribe. If no accurate record was kept, one can only trust the memory of the copyist for the date of composition. Some hymnbooks started at a given date were abandoned and finished many years later, and often by another hand. It was not uncommon for a friend or visiting Shaker to write one or more hymns in a manuscript book as a gesture of friendship, much as verses were once exchanged in autograph albums. The notation used would probably be the one that the writer knew best or the one used in his community.

Letters are more accurate than hymnals as sources for fixing dates, but Shakers frequently made several copies of important letters, sometimes long after the original had been written, thus increasing the possibility of inaccuracies. Some letters were carried by Shakers traveling between communities. The dates on such letters might be accurate enough, but only letters with official postmarks on the paper can be regarded as trustworthy evidence in fixing the probable dates for the composition of the hymns specified.

There was also the difficulty caused by the variety of systems or styles of notation. The existence of communities removed from each other by hundreds of miles, with members recruited from those several localities and possessing widely varied musical experiences, gives the Shaker systems of notation a highly complex and sometimes confusing appearance. Styles and periods overlap in spite of the Shaker desire for conformity in all things, even in music notation, and the overlapping was caused partly by strong-willed individuals who wanted to keep a system they already knew, and partly from inadequate communication in the remote rural communities.

A whole hymnbook with the complete contents of several hundred tunes all dated the same year, or dated consecutively by months and years, has usually been considered as reasonably accurate evidence of notation date. It is possible, however, that any one of these may have been recopied, so that final judgment concerning dates has been based on both the hymnals and collateral information contained in letters, and upon the evidence in the manuscripts and general Shaker writings.

Shaker music literature before 1807 consisted chiefly of wordless solemn songs and was so limited in quantity that it could easily be remembered and required no notation. The Shaker missionary work carried on in Ohio and Kentucky in the wake of the Great Revival resulted almost immediately in the writing of many original hymns and adaptations describing the doctrines and experiences of a struggling but determined little sect, trying to gain a foothold among the numerous and long-established frontier religions. The members of the established denominations were highly wrought emotionally by the revival years, and did not take kindly to the Shakers. The persecutions which resulted brought to light many latent talents among Believers. A worship ritual that had become lifeless about 1793, in which even the "exercise," or dancing had been suspended for a period by command of Father Joseph, suddenly sprang into new prominence after 1807 and demanded the best efforts of Shaker poets and composers.

Hymns (words only) sent from the western communities to the leading society at Mount Lebanon were warmly received and "by the summer of 1807, the singing of hymns had become a custom."[1] Soon after 1810, the Shakers who were musically inclined began to teach the others the great body of song that had come into existence, and "lengthy anthems and hymns, thousands in number, were learned by hearing."[2] Isaac N. Youngs, who later was to become one of the leading Shaker musicians, wrote in his journal May 9, 1815: "Daniel Wood's Song entitled the Lambs War—The Anthem entitled Mother's Children is sent to

---

1. Anna White and Leila S. Taylor, *Shakerism Its Meaning and Message* (Columbus, Ohio, 1904), p. 331.
2. *Ibid.*, p. 336.

Ohio, with the Songs pricked [written] down:—the first thing of the like among us. It was pricked by William Seeley."[3] Thus is recorded the first instance of the exchange of music between Shaker communities, a practice which was to serve as a potent factor in unifying the many remotely located societies, and which even then was a valuable means of spreading religious propaganda among Shakers and nonbelievers. The following year an exchange of several pieces was made between the Society at Mount Lebanon, near Albany, and the Community at Union Village, in Ohio.[4] These were probably in round-note notation on a five-line staff, unbarred, and without rhythm or key signatures, since they emanated from New Lebanon as did the other earliest examples of round-note writing in this form. Youngs copied the tunes for the first 129 pages of the *Millennial Praises* hymnal (1812–1813) in this style of notation, but it is undated.[5]

A system of notation was becoming a necessity with the great numbers of tunes to be learned and retained, and with the growing practice of exchanging songs with other communities. The Harvard society of Shakers began experimenting with the use of letters for notes about 1816 and the unidentified author claimed that the system was imparted by inspiration from Mother Ann as an easier method than the one in common use by Believers.[6] That it was slow in being adopted is revealed in a letter from D. A. Buckingham of Watervliet to Russell Haskell of Enfield, Connecticut, in which he states that the Patent System was introduced and adopted at Watervliet about the year 1818, the *"letteral System* not then existing as a form."[7]

The Shakers were trying to find a notation to suit their needs in these early years, and had at least three systems, round notes, letter notes, and patent or shaped notes, all being practiced simultaneously. They were also permitting the more musical to learn notation, as Youngs' diary entry for March, 1819, relates:

3. Isaac N. Youngs, Journal. Narrative of Events. Beginning Apr. 1815. Papers of Shakers, No. 42 (in the Library of Congress), Shakers, New York, Canaan 1815–1823; entry, May 9, 1815.

4. White and Taylor *Shakerism*, p. 336.

5. SM412.

6. White and Taylor, *Shakerism*, pp. 336–37.

7. Letter from D. A. Buckingham, Watervliet, Nov. 12th, 1834, to Russell Haskell, Enfield, Connecticut, p. 1.

About these times there are several getting hold of singing by notes. Joel began upwards of a year ago—I began to get some knowledge last summer—some of the sisters are labouring in that line, particularly Sarah B. & Joanna K. We have had several songs from elsewhere and we hope, ere long, to be independent on others for pricking down songs.[8]

The entry for April 8, 1819 says that the Elder

then spoke in relation to one branch of learning which was getting in among us, viz. singing by note; he signified there was freedom felt for some to get the knowledge of that art, so that when we had songs sent to us from other places, we might be able to understand it, without being dependent on others out of our order. . . . As to the five that were spoken of, they were not named but were known to be Joel T [urner,] I. Y [oungs], G. Lawrence, Sarah B [ates], and Joanna K [etchel]. But in the course of two or three days Garret resigned . . . so Richard B [ushnell ?] was nominated.[9]

New Lebanon was definitely using the round-note notation in dated hymnals and letters sent to other societies between 1821 and 1839, even though New Lebanon was the seat of the central Shaker governing body which later insisted upon a uniform "letteral" notation in all communities. A five-line staff was employed and note values were those generally accepted in ordinary printed music. Rhythm signatures and bar lines, except at main divisions and at the end, were generally omitted. This practice was common in printing early American psalm tunes; according to Frédéric Ritter the first bars were printed in American music in 1721.[10] Key signatures likewise rarely appeared in this early Shaker music. Comparisons with later versions of the tunes in "letteral" notation show that the bottom line and top spaces of the staff frequently represent *do,* or the keynote of the tonal scheme. Occasionally a sharp or flat, or diamond-shaped note marking the leading tone, as in the patent-note system, appears at the beginning to show the line or space that is to serve as *do* for that tune. In other cases, no clue appears, either from neglect on the part of these unskilled early Shaker copyists or from the fact that the tunes were so well known to them that it was an unnecessary precaution for those who understood music, and use-

8. Isaac N. Youngs, Diary, Papers of Shakers, No. 42 (in the Library of Congress) [n.d.]; entry before Mar. 19, 1819, 152.

9. Youngs, Diary, pp. 153–54.

10. Frédéric Louis Ritter, *Music in America* (New York, 1890) , p. 39.

less for those who had not learned to read notes. In this early form, round-note notation extends from 1821–1839, definitely dated, with the greatest concentration of literature in 1824 and 1825. It appears sporadically down to the beginning of the twentieth century but usually not with these special features, but as it is used in "the world" by non-Shakers.

MOTHER'S MANTLE

Letter to the Ministry at Buors, Indiana, from the New Lebanon Ministry. Feb. 18th, 1821

Our Mother has finish'd her work here on Earth,
And gone to the Mansions of heavenly mirth:
From all mortal sorrow her soul is releas'd,
To reap the reward of her labours in peacè.
(7 more stanzas)

In 1802 the non-Shaker, Andrew Law invented a patent-note system for printing music without the use of a staff, employing four different shapes of notes.[11] Patent-note tune books were very common in America during the first half of the nineteenth century and even later, and Buckingham, in the letter already

11. *Dictionary of American Biography* (New York, 1933) , 11:38.

mentioned, states that this system was adopted by the Watervliet Shakers in 1818. An undated letter from Union Village, Ohio, containing an example of it has "1820?" written upon it in pencil. The first patent-note usage definitely dated is the manuscript copy of "The Patent Gamut or Scale of Music, 1823," by the non-Shakers Wm. Little and Wm. Smith. Their *Easy Instructor* appeared in Albany in 1798 and was frequently reprinted until 1831.[12] This instruction book was followed by two hymnals, partly in patent notes, in 1824 and 1825, but this style of noting songs seems to have been most popular in the 1831–1839 period, with the greatest concentration in the three years 1837–1839. The style extends feebly to 1853 and appears in 1873 in one of the manuscripts.

The idea of the shaped notes, character notes, or patent notes, as they were variously called, was to present four notes of varied shape to the singer, which would suggest by association and with a minimum of effort the characteristics of the various pitches within the octave in relation to the keynotes. The following example will show the general plan of the octave which could be transposed the same as our "movable *do*" to begin on any pitch:[13]

The first three shapes, triangle, circle and square repeat, since the interval relationships of C–D–E are identical with those of F–G–A, or whole steps apart. The leading tone possesses peculiar properties normally demanding resolution upwards to the keynote, a quality which is vital in establishing tonality. To show this characteristic and to give the clue to the location of the keynote, it has the diamond shape, typical of no other pitch. Likewise, it is given the syllable name *me,* which for the same reason belongs to no other pitch.

---

12. "Tune-Books," *Grove's Dictionary of Music and Musicians* (New York, 1928), p. 387.

13. William Walker, ed., *The Southern Harmony and Musical Companion* (New York, 1939 [orig. ed., 1835]), p. xiii. By permission of Hastings House, Publishers, Inc.

Lebanon January 10th 1840.

Beloved Ministry.

According to brother Trefurer's request and my promise I will now write a few lines to you, respecting Elder brother's health, we think he is getting along as well as could be reasonably expected; for three or four days after you left here, he was very much distressed: but for two days past he seems to be gaining slowly, and we think it will be a considerable length of time before he can recover. Mother and the good Spirits told us, through the inspired ones, that they were not willing that Elder brother should leave us quite yet. Mother Lucy said she desired that we, with her, would pray to God for his recovery, and told us we must pray earnestly, we all united with Mother with all our hearts, and prayed according to the best of our ~~understanding~~ understanding, and from that time he seemes to be more released from his distress, so we have gathered some hopes. Mother Ann, sent a little Dove into Elder brother's room, and it flew about and finally lit upon Elder brother's head, he sensibly felt the pain leave his head at the time, the Dove sung a beautiful little song and Elder brother desired me to send the song to you, with his kind love, As to my health, I am thankfull to say it is much better than it has been for some weeks past. the rest of the family are well We heard from the first order yesterday, Brother Jonathan is quite confined with the Rheumatise, Desire Sanford fails quite fast, is not expected to continue long. Brother Chancey, Marilla and I send our kind love to all the Ministry, and do be so kind as to remember us in your prayers to God, for we feel very needy.

the little dove's song

I am Mother's little Dove
She has sent me from above
She has fill'd me with her love
For her true Solinda

Truly I have come to bring
True comfort unto you
And loud praises I will sing
Coo coo coo coo coo coo

Shaker letter illustrating manner of exchanging songs between communities. [Shaker Letter Box, New Lebanon, Jan. 10, 1840.]

Note values appear in this system exactly as in regular round-note writing. The Watervliet Shakers[14] had a system that was similar but much quicker to copy with a pen, which was also widely used in their societies. This system did not use the black notes which had to be inked in, and did not close all of the geometric figures. The stems and flags on the notes called for the same scale of values represented as when the notes were black. The following styles, with and without bars, but usually barred, appear in manuscripts:

SM248, p. 143 from "Grateful Thanks" Watervliet, 1829

which in regular notation would be written as follows:

A curious variant of the patent-note style with words written on the staff between the notes appears but once in the known manuscripts:

SM117, p. 164

---

14. Letter from Isaac N. Youngs to Beloved Brethren (?), Aug. 11, 1837.

Hucbald, 10th Cent.

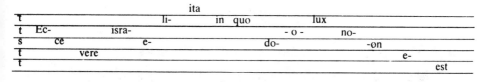

Hucbald of St. Amand placed the words on a six-line staff in the
tenth century, but the six lines represented the strings of the
cithara and not actual pitches. Only the spaces indicated pitches,
and tones (t) and semi-tones (s) were marked on them to show
interval relationships.[15]

If the Shakers did begin to experiment with letteral writing
in 1816, information is scarce concerning its origin and development between that date and 1824. A note written on a blank
check and attached to "Elder Giles Tune Book"[16] states that
"Letter notes were introduced by Abram Whitney, of Shirley,
who informed me the plan originated with Mother Ann. He
received it from her. But few among Believers could read music.
The letter notes enabled many to learn both to read & write it."
A letter from Russel Haskell to Isaac Youngs in 1834 says, "I am
aware that the treatise on music which I wrote and sent to the
second order at New Lebanon about 10 years ago, is quite im-
perfect; as I was not then sufficiently qualified for such an under-
taking. My principal object however was to bring the *letteral
notes* into use."[17] Almost simultaneously in 1824 and 1825, examples of both capital-letteral and small-letteral writing appear
in the manuscripts. The dates of composition marked on the
music are usually earlier when it is capital-letteral than when it
is small, and the following statements affirm the priority of the

---

15. Donald N. Ferguson, *A History of Musical Thought* (New York, 1940), p. 82.
By permission of the publisher, Appleton-Century-Crofts.

16. Papers of Shakers, No. 190 (Library of Congress, Box 33).

17. Letter from Russel Haskell, Enfield, Connecticut, Feb. 10, 1834, to Isaac N.
Youngs, p. 24.

Shaker manuscript song of 1821. [New York Public Library.]

capital letters: "The first seven letters of the alphabet in capitals were employed," when the Harvard Society began to make use of letters for notes,[18] and a letter from Thomas Hammond of Harvard to Isaac Youngs of New Lebanon, June 7, 1830, says,

---

18. White and Taylor, *Shakerism*, pp. 336–37.

"we have adopted the small letters in room of capitals, and like them very well, for they are quicker made, and answer every purpose."[19] The capitals gave way to the small letters because they were "quicker made," and Harvard, where the system had originated, was now taking orders from Youngs of the central ministry at New Lebanon. Youngs had learned to note music in 1818, two years after the system was said to have been instituted at Harvard.

The capital-letteral system employed the first seven letters of the alphabet. Roman letters designated quarter notes; italics, eighth notes; and half notes were notated with an additional line beside the letter. The following example is from a Shaker letter of 1830:[20]

(Travelling tune)

19. Letter from Thomas Hammond, Harvard, June 7, 1830, to Isaac Youngs, New Lebanon.

20. Letter from the Enfield, New Hampshire, ministry, Feb. 11, 1830, to the Harvard Ministry, p. 3.

(Regular notation)

This style of notation also appears without the staff.

SM261 [n.p.]   Sally Lomas'

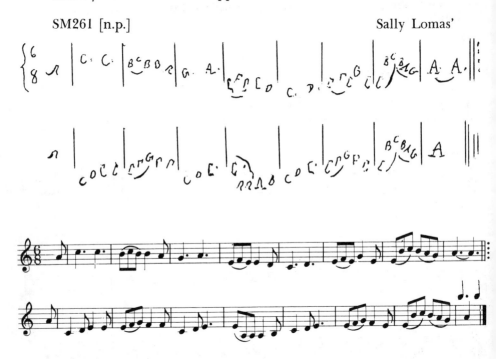

Capital-letteral writing was paralleled by round-note, patent-note, and small-letter styles in its date range, and was used between 1825 and 1839. A similar type of notation using the first seven letters of the alphabet "about the year 1100," and "somewhat resembling the tablature for the lute; but without lines," appears in Burney's *A General History of Music*, as follows:[21]

---

21. Charles Burney, *A General History of Music* (New York, 1935), 1:485–86.

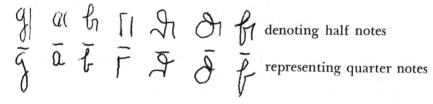

denoting half notes

representing quarter notes

Capital letteral gradually was replaced by small letters. Youngs, the untiring worker for uniformity in Shaker music, wrote in 1830:

It is very desirable to us that believers should all have one uniform manner of writing music; on this account we have conformed to the manners of others in a great measure. The use of letters we consider a great improvement, & that of small letters to claim the preferance, as they are so simple and compact. As to timing and barring of tunes, we have heretofore been backward about it, but are now conforming more to it, for the satisfaction of others, especially in the east. I have always felt shy of this, as I considered it required great exactness, & would increase the labor, & the songs be no better. it is also a matter in which even good writers of music would greatly vary in many cases.[22]

Russel Haskell's contribution to this problem of unifying a notation that would be understood by all the communities was another (or rather his rewritten) treatise on music, the title page of which reads: "A Musical Expositor: Being an index or key to the reading & writing of music according to the letter method Enfield, Hartford county, Conn. 1831." This was written in an effort to make the Watervliet community adopt the small-letteral system. D. A. Buckingham seems to have been the spokesman for the Watervliet nonconformists, and to him Haskell wrote:

My principal object in composing the musical expositor, and sending it to you, was to aid in introducing the letter method at Watervliet. But I am somewhat surprised on finding that you still continue to make the patent notes, apparently almost to the total exclusion of the letters, notwithstanding the letteral notes are used and approved by the Society at New Lebanon, Harvard, Shirley, New Enfield &

---

22. Letter from Isaac N. Youngs to Beloved brother Andrew [Houston?] New Lebanon, Aug. 6, 1830, p. 3.

at the eastward; and of late they have been brought into common use by the music writers among the Believers in Ohio and Kentucky.[23]

Buckingham's strength as a good Shaker was in not "yielding" to the musical "lead" and he replied: "I am perfectly willing that others should make use of any form, manner or System they choose, unmolested; and it is my desire to be allowed the same privilege."[24] In this same letter, he also states that "the letteral notes were introduced long after the Patent ones were established [1818] at Watervliet," and that New Lebanon learned the letteral system before it became acquainted with patent notes "consequently, were more in favor of the former; because, in them, they possessed the greatest knowledge."

The small letters seem to have been used at first on the five-line staff. The manuscripts and references to notation indicate that from 1824 to 1830 there was little if any such noting without lines. Note values were represented as follows:

Rests were represented by our standard symbols, but seldom were used. Any line or space might serve as *do* or the keynote, and was usually chosen, as in the case of our movable C clef, to accommodate the range of the tune without the necessity of going above or below the staff.

---

23. Letter from Russell Haskell, Enfield, Hartford county, Conn. to D. A. Buckingham, Sept. 25, 1834, pp. 1–2.

24. Letter from D. A. Buckingham to Russell Haskell, Watervliet, Nov. 12th, 1834, p. 2.

SM359 [n.p.]
Betsey Smith

There was much experimenting with this style, as there was with the others. Concentrated in the 1833–1834 period is found small-letteral notations on one level, sometimes with one line, and sometimes without any.

SM242, p. 33   Sally Eads' book dated 1833

The copyist of one of the hymnals wrote:

As it is the more speedy manner of noting, or writing tunes in a straight line, and takes up less room, at present, [1834], we prefer

Then rise thou inhabitant, rise and rejoice;
For God is thy Maker in him is thy trust;
With saints & with angels uniting thy voice,
His goodness proclaim who is holy & just:

"The Beauty of Zion"; words "heighted" on staff with open shaped notes. [SM117, p. 164.]

this manner, & we believe tunes may be as correctly written, & as correctly learned, when so written, as on the staff. The horizontal "breviture" "—" will show the rise and falling of the notes. . . .

As long as we rise from one note to another, we set the mark above, & when & as long as we fall from one note to another, we set the mark underneath, and when we rise or fall to a second note or letter, of the same kind, or over [an octave or over], use two marks . . . and when the sounds are the same we make no further marks.[25]

DANCE TUNE (1834)

SM197, p. 12

Appearing sporadically from 1835 to 1870, the small letters appear with one line, which serves to guide their approximate height, suggesting pitch to the eye by their relative position as well as by letter.

A NEW YEAR

SM245, p. 107

In 1837 Youngs wrote in regard to this manner of noting songs: "We have grown into the practice of lessening the labor of writing our new songs by not using the staff, but using common ruled

---

25. SM197, pp. 4–5.

paper; it answers well & I think it will be generally practiced here."[26] The writing paper lines often served as a guide in the very latest music manuscripts found.

The "Micrologus" of Guido d'Arezzo written about A.D. 1025 presents an interesting parallel to these last two types, with one line and letters "placed at different elevations with respect to that line, according to their different degree of acuteness or gravity."

Burney, 1:460

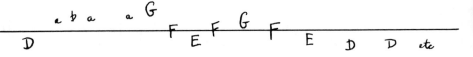

"In most of the examples, however, the letters were placed of an equal height, and without a line; but perhaps this was the transcriber's fault, and to save time."[27]

Here for the sake of chronological order must be mentioned the figure or numeral notation which had a limited vogue and seems to have been used by the individualists at Watervliet. It appeared once in 1839 and once again in 1873 in two hymnals. Buckingham was in favor of its use in 1834 and evidently had been using it. Quarter notes are designated by 4, and eighth notes by 8 placed upon the line or space. Thomas Harrison patented a system of numeral notation in 1839,[28] and numerals were in limited use in

SM140, p. 47   S. O. Watervliet, 1839

---

26. Letter from Isaac N. Youngs, New Lebanon, to the Beloved Brethren [?] Aug. 11, 1837, p. 1.
27. Burney, *A General History of Music* 1: 458–60.
28. Thomas Harrison, *Juvenile Numeral Singer*, 1852, Preface.

Top: Capital-letteral notation. [SM270, p. 1.] Middle: Isaac Youngs'
MS of tunes for the 1813 Millennial Praises in early round-note nota-
tion. [SM412, p. 10.] Bottom: printed Shaker song leaflet, "Happy
Land." [Mounted broadside in Scrapbook Broadsides, 5: 6.]

printed American song books, six others having been located, ranging from 1842 to 1867.[29]

Youngs wrote Buckingham in 1842 that "Believers are now approximating so near uniformity in writing music, that it seems encouraging."[30] The small-letteral system without lines, except where they existed on the writing paper used, became the accepted notation, and this style appears in more than seventy-five percent of the known manuscript hymnals. The earliest instance found appears in 1830, and for almost a decade five-line letteral and staffless letteral were both prominent. Both exist down to the very late stages, although the five-line staff is used much more rarely after the 1840–1845 period.

Shaker rhythm will be taken up separately in chapter 6, but the rhythmic signatures, when they do not appear the same as in our regular printed music, are as follows:[31]

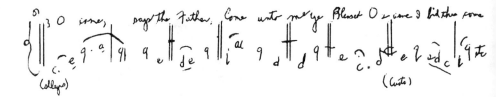

Various speeds within each group were designated by numerals placed above these symbols. There does not seem to have been any consistency in their use in the Shaker manuscript hymnals. Some hymns use them while others in the same book have no markings.

MOTHER ANN'S WELLCOME IN HEAVEN
SM326, p. 30 Watervliet   (1841)

29. *Davids Harp,* 1842, *Numeral Harmony,* 1846, and *One-Line Psalmist,* 1849, all by H. W. Day (from *Grove's Dictionary of Music and Musicians,* p. 390) ; *The Temperance Musician* (Cincinnati, 1853) , *Fillmore's New Nightingale; and Sunday School Singer* (Cincinnati, 1862) , and *The Violet* (Cincinnati, 1867) , all by A. D. Fillmore.

30. Letter from Isaac N. Youngs, New Lebanon, Nov. 16, 1842, to A. D. Buckingham.

31. Russell Haskell, *A Musical Expositor* (New York, 1847) , pp. 23–25.

In 1839–1840 this staffless small-letteral notation was used on "song leaves" given by inspiration, but its use constitutes nothing new in notation. They may be found in SM169, p. 120; SM218, p. 50; SM316, p. 63, and SM318, p. 2. "A [nonShaker] Canon of Four in One" written in circular form with patent notes on five-line staff presents an appearance much like this "song leaf" and antedates it by three or four years (1836).[32]

Shaker music, as far as has been discovered, had been mono-phonic in style until 1844. There must have been converts from other denominations accustomed to part singing before this late date who had experimented with such a practice in Shaker hymns; Shakers continued to use the monophonic style they had used of necessity in the early days when their members had little or no instruction, until a message came by inspiration from the spirit world in 1844 to sing music written in parts. On December 30 of that year D. A. Buckingham as the inspired instrument wrote "The Harmony of Angels," an anthem which added one, two, or three parts in brief passages. The parts were notated in colors,[33] to keep the various voices from being confused on the same staff. The top voice constitutes the principal part, and the other voices are added below. Buckingham wrote a letter to the Societies the month after receiving this anthem, giving directions for its per-formance, in which he says: ". . . be it understood that when there are no notes leading from the main or principal part all are to sing together on one part the same as any other tune."[34]

32. Samuel Wakefield, Esq., *The Christian Harp* (Pittsburgh, 1836), opposite p. 60.

33. For examples of coloration in medieval music notation, see Willi Apel, *The Notation of Polyphonic Music 900–1600*, The Mediaeval Academy of America (Cambridge, Massachusetts, 1945), pp. 126ff.

34. Letter from D. A. Buckingham, Watervliet, Jan. 24, 1844, to the Societies, p. 1.

HARMONY OF ANGELS

SM9, p. 10 (D. A. Buckingham, Dec. 30th, 1843)

Join the chor - us bright Arch An - gels, Join ye Ser - aphs swell_ the

sound, Join in the har-mon-ious con - cert,This the heav - ens all_ a round.

This new style produced many imitations for one or two years, and a variety of colored inks were used to notate the different voices in the letteral manner. However, at almost the same time, Professor B. B. Davis, of Concord, New Hampshire, "was engaged to give a course of lessons to the singers at Canterbury. This new departure was more or less subject to criticism, but the round notes soon led to a deprecation of the other styles,"[35] and as if determined to maintain the letteral writing intact against the inroads of the round notes, Haskell published *A Musical Expositor* in 1847, explaining the letteral system used by Believers.

Part writing appeared frequently for two, three, or four voices in the years that followed, and the notation used seemed to be entirely a matter of whim or training of the copyist. The following excerpts will give an idea of some of the styles; different versions are not necessarily identical in barring, notation, or rhythmic signatures.

SM9, pp. 4–5   D. A. Buckingham, Dec. 30th, 1844

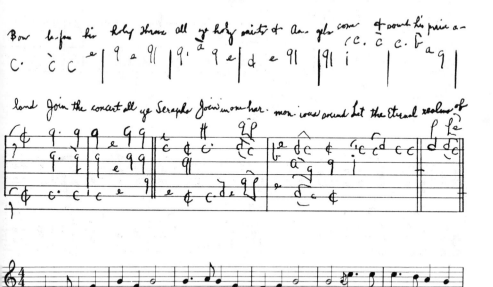

Bow be-fore his   ho - ly Throne all   ye ho - ly   saints & An - gels come & sound his praise a-

---

35. White and Taylor, *Shakerism*, p. 338.

loud Join the con-cert all ye Ser-aphs Join in one har-mon-ious sound Let the E - ter - nal realms of

SM370, p. 77 (1871–1878)

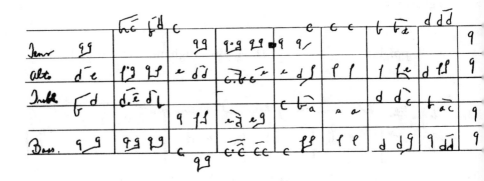

56

qeecdleeedlldedeldedleccdleaaeeldedeldeellegqqlabealqaqeldeqlqaaqlqaeelodeeledeellu

Come arise let us be going
Let us join the holy throng
Who are marching on before us
Praising God with a new tongue
Enfield Mass 1835.

We may gain a lasting treasure
That will never fade away
O my soul be up & doing
View the realms of endless day

Jeelqqqagledqeldeedeflqqeflqqqagledqeldeaqleelldleeegqlededleqqeflqqqelqaedllefqedleeedleel

Dear friends we're bound for the land of praise
How precious is our calling
Come let unite in a song of praise
Let every harp be sounding
Col 11th 1835 N.L.

O praise the Lord for that heavenly rest
Which unto those are given
Who bid farewell to the joys of earth
To gain a prize in heaven
Abagail Crofman

eledeqalaqqdleeedelqqqleeebelddelecfedlledleedelddleedeljqeldedllbqqfljqqqleelebedlddel eeelbdddleddeflqqqqlaffqaljqqqllefedleeqlefedlee

O freedom lovely in my eyes
To thee I'm bound in duty
In thee is an eternal prize
Thy ways are ways beauty
Enfield N.H.

As fawns upon the Mountains heigh
Or as the Eagles in their flight
To be in perfect liberty
My dove long to be as free
Abraham Perkins

eqqelqeqeleqeqldeeqlaqqll
eellaqqqlaqqelfedlqedeleleIll

My Mothers love is flowing!
My Mothers love is flowing
Flowing flowing flowing!
To all hl faithful Children!
N.L. N.Y.   Joel Turner
May 1835.

edleelqqqlaeeleelbbalallaqalqqlaedlelqqqaleeleaqlan

I will be free I'll not be bound
Haughty self it shall come down
A wicked nature I will fight
I have a sword that sheen & bright

Five tunes in letteral notation on one level. [SM198, p. 56.]

SM250, p. 183

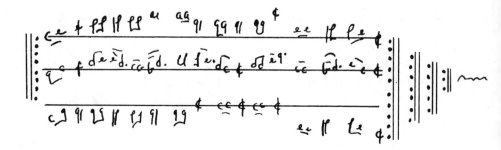

SM235 [n.p.] (last page)

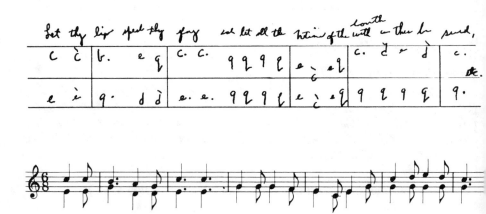

The above example, having the parts written out like the madri-
gal and motet part books of the Elizabethan period, and apparently unique in Shaker writing, appears in SM250, p. 184.

The first printed Shaker hymnal that contained tunes was *A
Sacred Repository of Anthems and Hymns,* printed at Canterbury,

New Hampshire, in 1852. The preface (p. iii) says that in this work they are able "to furnish the tunes, printed in musical form, which is the first of the kind ever issued among Believers. It will be observed that the music is placed on three lines—viz., the intermediate or medium note occupies exclusively the middle line while those above, are placed in a line above, and those below in a line below." The style is similar to the small-letteral and is the first case of its use in print:

THE PRECIOUS FAITH[36]

Between November 21, 1846, and January 30, 1847, six songs in the letteral style were printed in the *Day Star* magazine,[37] but because of difficulties in setting the type at the various levels the practice was of short duration. This following example is from the issue of November 21, 1846, 11:40: there are only three levels, the keynote level and one above and one below it; eighth notes have no spaces between them; the comma gives the quarter note twice its value, and a star represents an octave higher than written:

---

36. *A Sacred Repository of Anthems and Hymns* (Canterbury, New Hampshire, 1852), p. 61.

37. *The Day Star* (Cincinnati), Vols. 1–13, No. 3, 1841–July 1, 1847 (?).

HEAVENLY CITY

The Musical Messenger, published by the Union Village Shakers in Ohio [n.d.], is printed in letters resembling the written characters, all on one level. Large letters represent the pitches in the octave above the keynote, and small letters the notes below it; a wavy line above a note denotes a pitch found in the second octave above the keynote; a line at the side of a letter or under it has the same significance as in the written letteral style.

THE SAVIOUR'S CARE[38]

---

38. *The Musical Messenger* (Union Village, Ohio [n.d.]), p. 55.

The difficulties of printing the letteral notation to which the Shakers had become accustomed, and the introduction of round notes by singing teachers from the outside world, gradually led to the decline of letteral notation in the Shaker communities. Another important factor in this change was the acceptance of part singing, which had been introduced largely by teachers from "the world" who had learned and used round notes. Shaker practice had been largely determined by the efficiency and usefulness of the style; letteral notation served the great numbers of Shakers who had a limited amount of musical knowledge, and was a quick way of noting the monophonic tunes in the earlier years. With four voices instead of one, both noting and printing were facilitated by the round notes; so they were permitted and adopted.

As has been pointed out, some of these styles of notation were a part of the general American scene, and Shakers took over what they had known before they came into the society or what they learned from tune books then on the market in this country. A few of these manners of writing music echo the styles of the tenth and eleventh centuries, the period when our present manner of standard music notation was in its infancy. It is not probable that the Shakers had access to this knowledge concerning medieval notation, and since they were facing problems similar to those faced by men like Hucbald and Guido d'Arezzo centuries ago, and the later organ and lute players, it may be that these notations were just rediscovered by the Shaker musicians in their efforts to solve anew the same problems the medieval musicians faced. Regardless of the real sources of most of these styles, which will be difficult to prove conclusively, Shaker music notation was an original, often fantastic, means of preserving one of their most voluminous and important expressions, and remains as testimony to the Shaker love of the utilitarian and to Yankee ingenuity.

Three Shaker tunes; dark and open patent notes; numeral notation.
[SM140, pp. 40, 41, 47.]

"De Muder's Song": Indian song in "tongues" and spirit writing in a letter. [Shaker Letter Box, New Lebanon, Feb. 2, 1845.]

Table I. Shaker Notations Used at Different Periods

Date	Round note	Capital letteral	Patent notes	Small letteral	Numeral notation	Part writing in letteral	Part writing round notes
1815	▨		▨	▨			
1825	▨	▨	▨	▨			
1835	▨	▨	▨	▨	▨		
1845	▨		▨	▨	▨	▨	
1855				▨		▨	▨
1865			▨	▨	▨	▨	▨
1875				▨		▨	▨
1885				▨			▨
1895				▨			▨
1905							▨

4

Shaker Theory and
American Tune-Book Theory

There was an impromptu air about many things in Shaker communal living in the earliest stages. With a small group, the early leaders relied upon the inspiration of the moment for decisions concerning ritual and matters of daily living. As their membership and the number of Shaker communities, increased, rules had to be formulated to run the societies; once formulated, the power these rules placed at the disposal of the "lead" or head bishopric at Mount Lebanon encouraged the ministry to make regulations for every least detail of Shaker life. Music, which played such an important part in all of the communities, did not escape, and a rigid set of rules was formulated for the musical practice. Many of them were based upon the American tune-book theory then in use in singing schools all over the country, but some ideas appear to have been the personal opinions of those Shakers who were in a position to demand attention. There were strong-willed musicians in the different communities who did not agree with much of this theorizing and who followed the dictates of their own musical feelings, but the pecularities of their *practice* will be ignored entirely here, and a résumé of purely theoretical concepts will be given.

In 1818 Isaac N. Youngs wrote from the central bishopric at New Lebanon, New York, to the community at Union Village, Ohio, and "sent a couple of moddles of songs, one to a little anthem from Harvard, composed by a youngish believer, and the other to a quick dancing verse."[1] It was this same Isaac Youngs,

1. Letter from Isaac N. Youngs, New Lebanon, New York, June 18th, 1818, to Eldress Molly (?), Union Village, Ohio, p. 1.

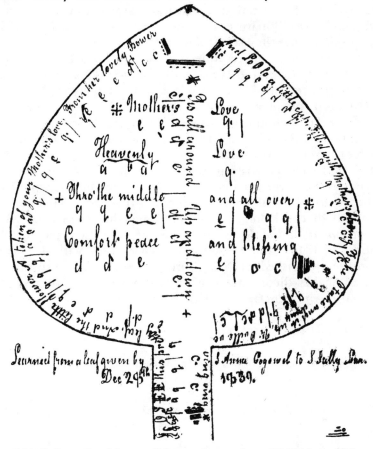

"Gift" Song Leaf in small-letteral notation. [SM316, p. 63.]

who had only recently learned to read notes, who continued to send "models" to Shaker musicians for nearly fifty years, and who, in attempting to set up standards of uniformity among the various communities, became their outstanding theorist.

Hervey L. Eads, one of the leading musicians of South Union, Kentucky, wrote to Youngs on April 22, 1833, belatedly thanking him for "the little *Gamut* you sent us, thro the medium of our good Ministry in 1827."[2] Youngs early acquired a prestige which caused the prominent musicians of all communities to consult

---

2. Letter from Hervey L. Eads, South Union, Kentucky, Apr. 22, 1833, to Isaac N. Youngs, p. 1.

him by letter for direction in musical matters, and his generous, and usually kindly nature, responded with advice and examples. It is possible, that the Gamut Eads referred to was the MS Gamut in the Cleveland Shaker collection (SM503), dated 1823, and marked "Wm. Little and Wm. Smith," non-Shakers who compiled a gamut printed in 1811 from which it was largely copied.

The need for some treatise to satisfy the many inquiries from the different communities concerning musical practice became apparent, and Russell Haskell of the community at Enfield, Connecticut, wrote *A Musical Expositor*, the manuscript of which is dated 1831,[3] to demonstrate the letteral method of reading and writing music. Two years later (1833) Youngs' manuscript called "Rudiments of Music"[4] was written. Setting his own type and doing all of the labor, Youngs published his ideas as *A Short Abridgement of the Rules of Music*, at New Lebanon in 1843 (reprinted 1846), and Haskell followed in 1847 with *A Musical Expositor*, published in New York. These books constitute the printed Shaker theory. Many of the same ideas have been copied into various manuscript hymnals.

Characters Used in Shaker Theory

(1)   *The Staff*—the five lines and four spaces on which music is written.

(2) — *Ledger line*—for notes above or below the staff.

(3)   *Initial*—the sign of the beginning of a tune.

(4) *Notes*—represented by various forms of the first seven letters of the alphabet, and the corresponding *rests:*

Whole	Half	Quarter
ABCDEFG		
Eighths	Sixteenths	Thirty-seconds

---

3. SM504.

4. Papers of Shakers, MT .Y56 case 149 and 150 (two copies) (in the Library of Congress.)   7

(5) | *Single bar*—divides the music into measures.

(6) || *Double bar*—indicates the mode (rhythmic signature) and usually appears with a figure above it or with crossbar attached, to show meter and tempo. (Discussed fully under rhythm.)

(7) |||| *The close*—shows the end of the tune.

(8)   ⌒   *A Slur*—shows that all notes under it are to be sung to one syllable.

(9)   \   *Brevitures*—are affixed to notes to shorten them. (𝄐)

(10)   .   *Dot*—placed at the right of a note adds one half of the original value to it.

(11)   :S: *Sign of repetition*—marks portions of music to be repeated.

(12)   ❢   *Staccato, or mark of distinction*—shows that the note under it is to be sung very distinctly.

(13)   e / c   *Choosing notes*—show that either pitch may be sung.

(14)   ⌢•   *Pause, or hold*—shows that the note under it is to be held longer than usual.

(15)   ᴗ   *The curved breviture*—"shortens a note at least one fifth, and at most one fourth, when placed over or under it." (Haskell only, p. 11).

(16)   ⁓   *The horizontal brace*—(like the tie), "is put over or under two notes that are on a level, when they are sung as one." (Haskell only, p. 12).

(17)   ∿⌐   *Direct*—at the end of the staff, shows the place of the first note on the following staff.

(18)   ♯   A *sharp*—before a note raises it half a step.

his chosen people on the earth. Yea let your voices chord in sweet harmonious

sounds, in holy Alleluiahs, alleluiahs, alleluiahs, alleluiahs, alleluiahs to

his holy name, for great and wonderful are all his works & of his glory and increase

of his Kingdom there is no end. Ho! Ho! Ho! Praise & glorify his holy name

forever & ever, forever & ever. O rejoice, rejoice in holy praises, new, in sweet

harmonious sounds of holy praise & true thanksgiving, Ul ye chosen of the Lord

"Harmony of Praise & Adoration"; part writing in small-letteral notation. [SM243, n.p.]

(19)   ♭   A *flat*—before a note lowers it half a step.

(20)   ♮   A *natural*—"restores a note to its former air." (Youngs only, p. 7.)

(21)   ♪   *Appoggiatures, transition, or diminutive notes*— indicate "a short graceful slide of the voice, from one note to another" (both treatises).

(22)   tr   A *trill*—"a kind of shake in the voice" (both treatises).

(23)   ∪   *The enclosure*—"is used in case of changing theme [the leading-tone; therefore, the tonality or key], to show what letter or note, the last of the former changes into." (Youngs, 7 and also Haskell in substance).

(24)   ◁   *Crescendo*—denotes an increase of sound.

(25)   ▷   *Diminuendo*—denotes a decrease of sound.

(26)   1.2   First and second endings; the note or notes under 1. to be omitted the second time through the tune.

(27)   2.   —"Over or under any three notes . . . shows that they are to be sung in the time of two." (Youngs only, p. 6).

(28)   3.   —"shows that three notes . . . are to be sung in the time of two." (Haskell only, p. 13). (Neither Haskell nor Youngs mentions an existing duple or triple scheme in using a 2 or 3.)

(29)   :||:   *Prisa*—a repetition of words and not of the music. (Youngs only, p. 6.)

(30)   ⌣⌣   A *double slur*—a phrase which may include both articulate sounds and slurred groups.

(31)   • • •   —"signifies so many repetitions of the preceding syllable." (3 repetitions in this case; Haskell only, p. 10.)

(32) P e a c e—"indicate that the word is to be spelled in singing." (Haskell only; p. 15.)

Nearly all of the symbols are common to the great number of
early American tune books published at this period. Youngs
wrote in the introduction to the second edition of his treatise
(1846) : "The substance of this little work is compiled from various authors of former times," and Haskell's Preface (1847) says:
"some part of several sections has been taken from the writings
of others." Many definitions in these two treatises are found to be
almost identical with definitions in other such sections at the
beginnings of early American tune books, showing that all were
freely plagiarized by compilers who probably learned what they
knew about theory from these common sources. Numbers 3, 4,
6, 15, 16, 23, 31, and 32, seem to be rather specifically Shaker
symbols; if they appear in other contemporary tune books, such
cases are rare.

Shaker Theory of Tonalities

The manuscript (1831) of Haskell's *A Musical Expositor* presents two systems of tonality as follows:

Soft-sharp air or tone of melody	*Shrill-mild air*
C D E F G A B C	D E F G A B C D

Modal names are not mentioned in the writings, but these two
systems will be seen to be the major scale (Ionian mode) and
Dorian mode.

Youngs presented what he termed "Major and Minor Keys" in
A Short Abridgement of the Rules of Music (1843) pp. 17–18:

Major tonic scale

C D E F G A B C   C B A G F E D C

Minor tonic scale

A B C D E F♯ G♯ A   A G F E D C B A

While the C major scales are identical in both treatises, the Dorian
mode is not Youngs' choice for the tunes which do not fit the
major feeling, and he presents the melodic form of the minor.

Equivocally enough, a note at the bottom of p. 19 of Youngs' *Abridgement* says: "The places for the semitones, and the flats and sharps in the minor key, are purposely omitted after the first lesson," and in the ten pages of lessons which follow, no accidentals ever appear. In describing the formation of his melodic minor scale, he says that "this scale commences on A. . . . But it is not always the case that G is raised in the minor key; in tunes when A does not immediately succeed G . . . it is not likely to be raised. The tones of this key are more uncertain than those of the major" (p. 17). The "Minor" on p. 19 is the Aeolian Mode:

A B C D E F G A   A G F E D C B A

Youngs' 1846 edition of the treatise has not changed his first concepts of these tonalities.

If the point of view Haskell took in adopting the Dorian form of minor instead of the customary Aeolian is not unique, it must at least be very rare in American tune-book theory. No other case of it has been discovered in the great number of such tune books examined. He still was as determined as ever that Dorian was correct and that the Aeolian was wrong after sixteen years, and it is presented the same way in his published treatise of 1847. If the A should be employed as tonic, he insists upon removing the half-step between E and F by sharping the F, which again gives Dorian tonality (transposed),

A B C D E F♯ G A

or *re* to *re* in our G major scale, instead of *re* to *re* in our C major scale; he justifies his stand by saying, on p. iv of the preface: "for so it is proved by our common singing."

In reply to Haskell's rather haughty letter containing the statement: "I insert d sol and not a law for the first governing sound in the minor key, I always do so . . . for I certainly know it to be the only right method, whatever may be said to the contrary,"[5] Buckingham does not make it sound as if theory had merely classified existing practise, as Haskell had suggested in his arbitrary choice of the Dorian mode as something "proved" by their common singing.

You advance an Idea, relating to the governing note in the Minor Key, which is different from any thing, heretofore exhibited to

---

5. Letter from Russell Haskell, Enfield, Conn., Sept. 25, 1834, to D. A. Buckingham, Watervliet, New York, p. 2.

the Public. Here again is an intended improvement, which seems to be delaying this *desired uniformity,* which we are all so strongly advocating. I cannot unite with you on this subject, without going in direct opposition to my own understanding,[6] and the universal opinion of Music writers, both ancient and modern, with which I am acquainted. Admitting that, by making D the governing note or sound in the minor Key, the semitones are brought between B, C, and E, F;—Yet it gives the notes or sounds an unnatural air, and thereby destroying the beauty & melody of the tune, I am satisfied that by making D occupy the place of A, in the minor Key, the air of the tune is very much varied from its natural style."[7]

It was the opinion of Abraham Whitney of Shirley, Massachusetts, in 1835 that scholars should be "taught the 7 sounds called the Gamut which should be commited to memory, both in the Major & in the Minor mode, without the least variation by flats or sharps . . . whether the sound or Key note be C, or A,"[8] a statement which shows that he sanctioned the Aeolian mode for the minor.

All four treatises point out the location of whole and half steps in these tonalities in the standard manner, which needs no further discussion here since it presents no deviation from regular tune-book practice.

The Haskell manuscript of 1831 and his printed treatise both show the "first governing tone" (tonic) and "second governing tone" (dominant) in both the Ionian and Dorian systems of tonality mentioned above. In the Ionian, Haskell calls B, F, and D "interflowing" tones or dissonances, while C, E, G, A, and C he terms consonances; similarly in Dorian, B. G. and E are dissonances and D, F, A, C, and D are consonances [n.p.]. Youngs does not venture into this domain in either of his editions.

The following condensed table shows Haskell's version of intervals and the unorthodox names he gave them in the 1831 manuscript. Notice that each interval as Haskell designates it is actually one count smaller numerically than in our standard usage:

---

6. Buckingham's chart (1848) on p. 110 shows the melodic form of beginning on a minor with f and g sharped ascending and natural in the descending scale.

7. Letter from D. A. Buckingham, Watervliet, New York, Nov. 12, 1834, to Russell Haskell, Enfield, Connecticut, p. 3.

8. Letter from Abraham Whitney, Shirley, Massachusetts, May 25, 1835, to Isaac N. Youngs, p. 1.

Table II. Interval Classification in Haskell's Manuscript of 1831 [n.p.]

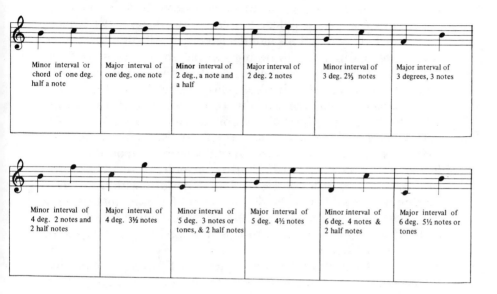

Minor interval or chord of one deg. half a note	Major interval of one deg. one note	Minor interval of 2 deg., a note and a half	Major interval of 2 deg. 2 notes	Minor interval of 3 deg. 2½ notes	Major interval of 3 degrees, 3 notes
Minor interval of 4 deg. 2 notes and 2 half notes	Major interval of 4 deg. 3½ notes	Minor interval of 5 deg. 3 notes or tones, & 2 half notes	Major interval of 5 deg. 4½ notes	Minor interval of 6 deg. 4 notes & 2 half notes	Major interval of 6 deg. 5½ notes or tones

In this effort to simplify the system of interval classification, Haskell has reduced all intervals to major and minor. Fourths and fifths are classed as *perfect intervals* in standard nomenclature; since Shaker tunes rarely called for alterations, there is no category for diminished or augmented intervals except in the cases of the augmented fourth, F to B, and the diminished fifth, B to F.

Youngs clings to standard usage and says both extremes are reckoned in interval naming "as A and B, being two degrees, or notes, is called a second; from A to C is called a third," and so on (p. 16), but recognizes only major and minor intervals. In the printed version of Haskell's treatise, his system has not changed except that he adds that the interval of one degree may be called a "second" and so on (pp. 51–55). Both Youngs and Haskell differentiate between the words "chromatic" and "diatonic" according to our standard usage, but do not illustrate these differences or pursue the subject further, since Shakers did not use chromatics.

Shaker Theory of Rhythm

Thomas Hammond, a leading musician of the Shaker com-

munity at Harvard, Massachusetts, wrote Youngs June 7, 1830:
"I received the letter you sent by Br. Abraham last fall, respecting
the use of small letters in putting down tunes, and of timing, &
. . . we feel it a great privilege to unite with whatever is felt most
proper at Lebanon."[9] Two months later Youngs wrote to another
Shaker community: "As to timing and barring of tunes, we have
heretofore been backward about it, but are now conforming more
to it."[10] These are the first references found in Shaker letters
which denote a concern for the rhythmic element in writing
down Shaker tunes. Many of the worded tunes until this 1825–30
period were without bars, and appear to have been sung very
freely; such songs were probably quite dependent upon the words
for their rhythmic properties. Other melodies were well known
to all and needed little conscious effort to perform with the correct
rhythm or tempo. It was the development of Shaker notation and
the exchange of songs between the several communities that demanded a definite and uniform plan for specifying the rhythmic
element in the music.

One of the Kentucky singers questioned Youngs "respecting
the *Moods* of time" in a letter in 1833 and enclosed a tune which
he said had been "sung about to the second according to our
printed book."[11] Since the first Shaker theory printed was Youngs'
1843 treatise, it would seem reasonable to believe that standard
American tune books were furnishing the Shaker musicians with
their theoretical information at this time. Corroborating this
assumption, are both Abraham Whitney's letter of 1835, containing counsel to Youngs for teaching music, in which he says: "The
next lessons are the characters & modes of time simply expressed
(according to the old movement) very much as it is in your
M.S,"[12] and the already quoted preface of Youngs' 1846 treatise
saying that the substance of his work was "compiled from various
authors of former times."

Since it is apparent that Shakers used the standard tune book

9. Letter from Thomas Hammond, Harvard [Massachusetts], June 7th, 1830, to
Isaac N. Youngs, New Lebanon, New York, p. 1.

10. Letter from Isaac N. Youngs, New Lebanon, New York, Aug. 6, 1830, to
Beloved Brother Andrew [?], p. 3.

11. Letter from Hervey L. Eads, South Union, Kentucky, Apr. 22, 1833, to
Isaac N. Youngs, New Lebanon, New York, p. 1.

12. Letter from Abraham Whitney, Shirley [Massachusetts], May 25, 1835, to
Isaac N. Youngs, New Lebanon, New York, p. 1.

"Moods (or Modes) of Time" and also based their own system upon it, a table will be quoted here from *The Missouri Harmony of 1835*,[13] showing the plan in general use at that time in smaller American communities. Modern metronome markings not found

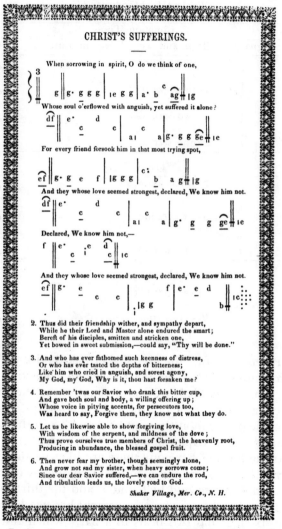

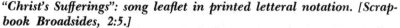

"Christ's Sufferings": song leaflet in printed letteral notation. [Scrapbook Broadsides, 2:5.]

13. Allen D. Carden, *The Missouri Harmony* (Cincinnati, 1835), pp. 15–16.

in the tune books have been added in the last column since they are more familiar to the average reader than "sung in the time of two seconds," or "a third quicker."

Table III. Moods of Time

Mode	Signature		Beats and seconds per measure	(Metronome)
Common Time				
First	C	$[{}^4_4]$	4—four seconds	♩ = 60
Second	¢	$[{}^4_4]$	4—three seconds	♩ = 80
Third	Ɔ	$[{}^2_2]$	2—two seconds	♩ = 60
Fourth	$\frac{2}{4}$	$[{}^2_4]$	2—one second	♩ =120
Triple Time				
First	$\frac{3}{2}$		3—three seconds	♩ = 60
Second	$\frac{3}{4}$		3—two seconds	♩ = 90
Third	$\frac{3}{8}$		3—one second	♩ =180
Compound Time				
First	$\frac{6}{4}$		2—two seconds	♩. = 60
Second	$\frac{6}{8}$		2—one second	♩. =120

"The Patent Gamut," the non-Shaker manuscript of Wm. Little and Wm. Smith (1823) in the Cleveland collection of Shaker hymnals, which has Shaker letteral notation at the end, follows the above plan. In Section I of the 1831 manuscript, Haskell omits the first mode of common time, and 3-2 and 3-8 in the triple mode, but groups as three triple moods, 3-4, 6-4, and 6-8. He states that "In the triple form of harmony there are likewise three degrees of movement. The first in our manner of singing is marked by the figures 3 and 4, the second by 6 and 4, and the third by 6 and 8," but says later that "the six-four movement has two beats to a bar," and "the six-eight has two beats to a bar," which restores it to a duple conception. He states that the characters are not always "intended to represent" a precise time, but that each classification can be varied to "include the whole time between the quickest and the slowest movement, so as to leave no room for any more intervening ones" [n.p.]. This explanation represents an attempt at simplification, but Haskell confuses an easy plan in general use at the time by his unorthodox phraseology, according to tune-book standards, at least.

A letter copied in SM162 (pp. 131–38) shows that by 1840 Youngs had a new and highly individual system of modes worked out which took the eighth note as the basis for calculating all measures; 4-4 had eight eighth notes, 2-4 four eighths, 3-4 six eighths, but the 6-8 which also had six eighths was to be designated in the signature by a 7 to avoid confusion with the 3-4. In all other signatures except compound mode, "the upper figure denotes the speed & the lower fig. the number of quavers or their quantity—" (p. 132).

A late variant of small-letteral notation invented too late (1871) to be used elsewhere. [SM345, pp. 116–17.]

Table IV. Improved Modes (1840)

Even Mode

Mode	Symbol	Seconds to sing	Beats per measure	Beats per minute	Length of string in inches (See p. 127)
Adagio	1st/8	3	4	80	22
Largo	2nd/8	2⅛	4	91	17
Allegro	3rd/8	2¼	4	106	12½
Presto	4th/8	1⅞ to 1½	4	128 to 160	8¾ to 5½

Sub-measures

Sub-Adagio	1st/4			
Sub-Largo	2d/4	sung in half the time of the above	Two beats to a measure	"The number of beats per minute & length of string the same as in full measure."
Sub-Allegro	3d/4			
Sub-Presto	4th/4			

Triple Mode

Adagio-triple	1st/6	sung in 2¼ seconds		
Largo-triple	2d/6	1⅞	Three beats to a measure	The number of beats per minute and length of string the same as the preceding
Allegro-triple	3d/6	1⅝		
Presto-triple	4th/6	1⅜ to 1⅛		

Compound Mode

Symbol	Seconds to sing	Beats per measure	Beats per minute	Length of string in inches
1st/7	2¼	4	106	12½
2nd/7	1⅞	4	122	9½
3rd/7	1⅝	4	142	7
4th/7	1⅜	4	170 to 213	4¾ to 3⅛ or less

However, these signatures never appear to have been popularized by the Shaker musicians, and in Youngs' published treatise of 1843 (pp. 30–32) he adopts another set of symbols to denote the various rhythmic signatures which appear to be unique in American tune-book theory. He mentions that they still call "them by their names, or by saying first 8, second 8 &c." (p. 30), but the symbols have changed as follows:

Table V. Table of Modes

[Common Time] [4–4]

Mode	Symbol	Seconds to sing	Beats per measure	Beats per minute	Length of string in inches
Adagio	$\Vert^{1}$	3	4	80	22
Largo	$\Vert^{2}$	2⅝	4	91	17
Allegro	$\Vert^{3}$	2¼	4	106	12½
Presto	$\Vert^{4}$	1⅞ to 1½	4	128–160	8¾ to 5½

Sub-measures [2–4]

Sub adagio $\nparallel^{1}$	Sub-largo $\nparallel^{2}$	Sub-allegro $\nparallel^{3}$	Sub-presto $\nparallel^{4}$

"The quantity, time and beats, in these measures, are of course just half as much as their corresponding full measures require; but the number of beats per minute, and length of string are the same."

Triple Mode [3–4]

First, Adagio triple $\nparallel^{1}$	Second, Largo triple $\nparallel^{2}$	Third, Allegro triple $\nparallel^{3}$	Fourth, Presto triple $\nparallel^{4}$

"There are three beats to this mode; two down and one up; the quantity and time to a measure is 3-4 that of a full measure; but the number of beats per minute is the same as in even mode."

Compound Mode [6–8]

Symbol	Seconds to sing	Beats per measure	Beats per minute	Length of string in inches
¢ $\Vert^{1}$	2¼	4	106	12½
¢ $\Vert^{2}$	1⅞	4	122	9½
¢ $\Vert^{3}$	1⅝	4	142	7
¢ $\Vert^{4}$	1⅜ to 1⅛	4	170 to 213	4¾ to 3⅛

Sub-measures [6–16]

First $\sharp^{1}$	Second $\sharp^{2}$	Third $\sharp^{3}$	Fourth $\sharp^{4}$

Youngs says that the above sub-measures of compound modes are new, but because "the fourth speed was not quick enough for exercise songs, there were two speeds added as a supplement" (p. 32).

Supplement

Mode	Symbol	Seconds to sing	Beats per measure	Beats per minute	Length of string in inches
[Fifth]	¢⁵	1⅛	4	213	3⅛
[Sixth]	∦⁶	⅞ to ¾	4	250 to 300	2¼ to 1½

He expresses his dissatisfaction with this system because it is "a violation of true system, in singing a tune faster than the written form of the notes indicate; second, because these speeds are not quick enough for the quickest compound tunes; third, because the notes in a triplet, in compound exercise tunes, are sung as quick as semiquavers" (p. 32), and in the 1846 edition the "supplement" is omitted.

Haskell's *A Musical Expositor* (1847) owes much to the Youngs treatise, but is not without the mark of Haskell's strong personality. He has changed the scale of values for the timing and has seven newly classified divisions in compound modes. His system of modes (pp. 23–25) is as follows:

Table VI. Haskell's Modes

Even Mode

Mode	Degrees	Time of a beat	Length of thread	Beats per measure
Adagio	∦¹	¾ second	22 inches	4
Largo	∦²	⅝ second	15¼ inches	4
Allegro	∦³	53/100 of a second	11 inches	4
Presto	∦⁴	44/100 of a second	7½ inches	e e e e |

Sub-measures

Mode	Degrees	
Sub-adagio	♯¹	
Sub-largo	♯²	"These are the same as half measures in
Sub-allegro	♯³	the corresponding degrees above and have
Sub-presto	♯⁴	the same time to a beat." e e |

Triple Mode

Mode	Symbol	
Adagio triple	♯¹	"Time of a beat, the same as in Even Mode.
Largo triple	∦²	Three beats to a measure—two down, and
Allegro triple	∦³	then one up.
Presto triple	∦⁴	e e e |

Compound Mode

¢¹	Allegro	Four beats;	¢⁵	Sub-allegro	Two beats
¢²	Presto	eee eee|	¢⁶	Sub-presto	per
¢³	Sub-adagio	Two beats for	¢⁷	1-5 quicker than sub-Presto, length of thread,	measure
¢⁴	Sub-largo	a measure		4¾ inches	eee eee|

Both Youngs and Haskell give four beats for the slower 6/8 except in the 1831 Haskell manuscript which gives two beats for all 6-8 movement. No explanation is given about the location of up-beat, and the practice of using four beats in 6-8 measure does not seem to occur as common practice in early American tune book theory. The eeeee's show the number of quarter notes, or in the last case, the number of eighth notes per measure.

These tables demonstrate the confusion that reigned in this particular phase of Shaker music for many years. There were also many appeals by letter to Youngs for something more definite on

Title pages of the Shaker theory books. [Upper left: SM504; upper right: BX9789, M9N3a; lower left; BX9789, M9Y8, 1843; lower right: BX9789, M9Y8, 1846.]

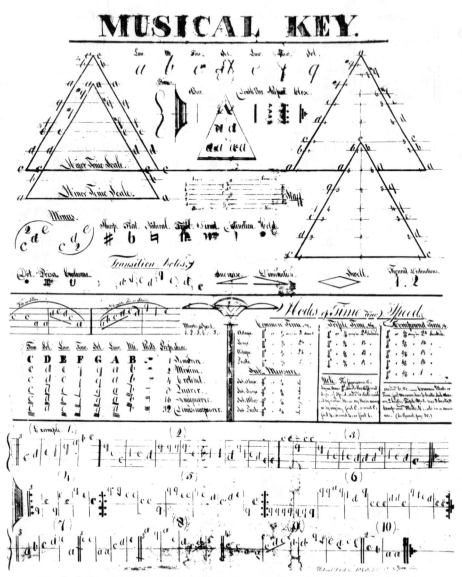

Musical Key; rolled chart used for instruction. [By D. A. Buckingham, Watervliet, New York, October, 1848, SM 507.]

"timing" the tunes, which show that there was little understanding of what the head bishopric was doing in its attempt to establish so-called uniformity in the practice both before and after the printed treatises appeared. Tables of modes are found in several Shaker manuscript hymnals which show agreement in principle with some one of these tables quoted, but a wide variance in details of tempo, names, symbols, and so on.

A pendulum consisting of a string with an adjustable weight, suspended from the ceiling, was suggested in other American tune books as a means of setting tempo, and both Youngs and Haskell give columns for the length of string required to obtain desired speeds. This should have offered little difficulty for any community, but inquiries were numerous concerning the speed of certain types of music or individual songs about which leaders had trouble coming to definite and unanimous decisions. The following opinions have been collected concerning the use of the Improved Modes and are a composite of the following sources: SM320, n.p. [n.d.], SM162, pp. 135–36 (1840), and Youngs' *A Short Abridgement*, pp. 37–38 (1843). This compilation represents only the system of Improved Modes (c. 1840), but should give a fair idea of Shaker tempo for many years previous to this time since Youngs, who was admitted to the Society in 1807, was one of their most prominent musicians and must have known most of the songs.

Table VII. Application of the Modes

Symbols used		Approximate metronome marking*
Even Mode		
Adagio ‖¹ $\frac{1}{8}$ C $\frac{4}{4}$	The slowest funeral songs, solemn songs.	♩ = 80
Largo ‖² $\frac{2}{8}$ ¢ $\frac{4}{4}$ $\frac{2}{2}$	Medium funeral songs, anthems, tunes having regular ♩ ♫ rhythm, "The Messiah," "Gospel Blessing."	♩ = 91
Allegro ‖³ $\frac{3}{8}$ Ɔ $\frac{2}{2}$ $\frac{4}{4}$	Hymns, little prayer anthems, all even timed marches, songs a degree slower than average common hymns, marches, quick dance tunes which go in sub-measure.	♩ = 106
Presto ‖⁴ $\frac{4}{8}$ $\frac{2}{2}$ $\frac{4}{4}$	Hymns, common anthems, common even timed hymns, songs and the greater portion of the anthems	♩ = 128-168

Sub-measures of even mode

					Approximate metronome marking
Sub-adagio	‖ 1	$\frac{1}{4}$	$\frac{2}{4}$		$\quarternote = 80$
Sub largo	‖ 2	$\frac{2}{4}$	$\frac{2}{4}$	Marching accent in anthems not used for march. Hymns, sections of anthems, anthems, quick songs.	$\quarternote = 91$
Sub-allegro	‖ 3	$\frac{3}{4}$	$\frac{2}{4}$	Marching accent used for march, slow marches in common time, quick tunes.	$\quarternote = 106$
Sub-presto	‖ 4	$\frac{4}{4}$	$\frac{2}{4}$	Common marches, *very* quick tunes.	$\quarternote =128\text{-}160$

Triple mode

Adagio triple	‖ 1	$\frac{1}{6}$	$\frac{3}{2}$	Music requiring	$\quarternote = 80$
Largo triple	‖ 2	$\frac{2}{6}$	$\frac{3}{4}$	3 equal timed beats.	$\quarternote = 91$
Allegro triple	‖ 3	$\frac{3}{6}$	$\frac{3}{8}$	Sometimes 𝄞𝄞𝄞 etc.	$\quarternote = 106$
Presto triple	‖ 4	$\frac{4}{6}$	–		$\quarternote =128\text{-}160$

Table VII. Application of the Modes (continued)

Symbols used					Approximate metronome marking*

Compound mode

Adagio	‖ 1	$\frac{1}{7}$	$\frac{1}{6}$	$\frac{6}{4}$	Slowest compound hymn tunes.	$\dotted\quarternote = 53$
Largo	‖ 2	$\frac{2}{7}$	$\frac{2}{6}$	$\frac{6}{8}$	Anthems, medium compound hymn tunes, portions of anthems when they change from even to compound mode.	$\dotted\quarternote = 64$
Allegro	‖ 3	$\frac{3}{7}$	$\frac{3}{6}$	–	Anthems, medium compound hymn tunes, portions of anthems when they change from even to compound mode.	$\dotted\quarternote = 72$
Presto	‖ 4	$\frac{4}{7}$	$\frac{4}{6}$	–	Slow marches, shuffling tunes $\left(\frac{4}{7q}\right)$ "Medium speed of square order shuffle in former days."	$\dotted\quarternote = 86\text{-}106$

Sub-measure of compound mode						
Sub-adagio	𝄴	1	$\frac{3}{8}$ or $\frac{6}{16}$		Common circular march	♩. = 106
Sub-largo	𝄵	2	$\frac{3}{8}$ or $\frac{6}{16}$	All exercising songs & tunes	Square order shuffle	♩. = 128
Sub-allegro	𝄴	3	$\frac{3}{8}$ or $\frac{6}{16}$		Round dance shuffle	♩. = 144
Sub-presto	𝄵	4	$\frac{3}{8}$ or $\frac{6}{16}$		Quick dances	♩. = 172-212

Supplement to compound				
𝄴	5	5) Quick marches 6) Square order shuffle	♩. = 62	
𝄴	6	$\frac{6}{6}$ Round dance shuffle		♩. = 125-150

* From Youngs, *Abridgement*, 1843.

Youngs' mathematics do not always work out accurately; therefore, the modern metronome markings are approximations. If the first measure of compound mode is sung in 2¼ seconds, there will be 26⅔ measures per minute; there are six eighth notes in a measure (♪.+♪.), or 53⅓ dotted quarters per minute; so the 106 beats per minute must be for the value of ♪.

Accent is treated as standard American tune books demonstrate it; Haskell makes the customary remarks about it in his *Musical Expositor* (pp. 28–29) and then proceeds with a discussion of poetic meter comparing musical accents to poetic feet. He seems to be the first Shaker writer to undertake the presentation of this much-needed element in song writing and, in doing so, he presented a table of poetic meters as a basis for the discussion of music measure, somewhat reminiscent of the rhythmic modes of Franco in the twelfth century. The following is Haskell's demonstration of the duple and triple schemes of accent (p. 34):

Two Syllables
A Trochee accented on the first syllable, as lŏvely.
An Iambus accented on the second syllable, as ĕndūre.
A Spondee accented on neither, as ŏn thē tāll trēe.
Three Syllables
Dactyl, accented on the first syllable, as lābŏrĕr.
Amphibrac, accented on the second syllable, as dĕlīghtfŭl.

Anapest, accented on the third syllable, as ŭndĕrtāke.
Tribrac, accented on neither, as cōnquĕrăblĕ.

Shakers evolved sets of solmization syllables as aids to sight
singing, and the following combinations were presented in theoretical writings:

Table VIII. Shaker Solmization Syllables

um	law	lel	oo	lo	la	lu	um	
C	D	E	F	G	A	B	C	Haskell's ms. (1831) [n.p.].
								Also *Musical Expositor* (1847),
law	lel	oo	lo	la	lu	um	law	p. 67.
D	E	F	G	A	B	C	D	
Law	Mee	Law	Sol	Law	Faw	Sol	Law	Youngs' *Short Abridgement*,
A	B	C	D	E	F	G	A	1843 (p. 13). Also D. A.
								Buckingham, chart, 1848.
al	Be	Co	Do	En	Faw	Goo	Al	Youngs' *Ibid.*, 1846 ed., p. 13.
A	B	C	D	E	F	G	A	
(In this same edition someone has written "Do, Re, Mi . . C Do" in pencil								
under C D E . . . B C).								
Do	Re	Mi	Fa	Sol	La	Si	Do	SM502, p. 28 (1871).

Youngs' 1843 treatise presented the "fasola" syllables found
most often in the early American tune book; the other systems
seem to have been original with Haskell and Youngs, but there
is no evidence that they were ever used in the Societies. Books
after this period use the standard Do-Re-Mi system.

Shaker theory after 1850 gradually turned toward the universal
musical practice of "the world." Teachers from neighboring cities
convinced Shaker leaders that they should adopt instruments, part
singing, round-note notation, and music readers about 1870, and
all of the things that had been individual in the Shaker theory
were swept away in a few short years by these revolutionary
changes. Manuscript books containing Shaker theory after the
latter date present the major and minor keys with sharp and
flat signatures, and the controversial "Modes of Time" are not
even mentioned. This change followed a parallel trend in the
American tune books; they too were fast becoming revolutionized, abandoning the modes of time, the old "fasola" syllables,
shaped notes, three-part harmonizations with the melody in the
inner voice, and the introductory sections on notation and theory.
Editions of the tune books became less and less numerous as the
rural "singing schools" gradually passed from the American scene,
and the itinerant singing teacher was replaced by private instruc-
tors and music schools.

Such men as Abraham Whitney, Austin Buckingham, Andrew Barrett, Hervey Eads, Abraham Perkins, Giles B. Avery, Benjamin Dunlavy, Oliver Hampton, Moses Thayer, Thomas Hammond, Joel Shields, and many modest Shakers who remain anonymous, could carry on a lively discussion about theoretical matters, and frequently offered advice to Youngs by letter, which he graciously received. However, writings which concerned music theory came officially from Youngs and Haskell. There is reason to believe that the ideas may in more than one case have emanated from some of these silent workers in the common cause. A letter from Giles B. Avery to Abraham Perkins in 1841 says,

> As you will doubtless be informed by the hand of br. Isaac of the measures we have taken to arrive at a settled and permanent conclusion, concerning the adoption of the new Modes, with the proposed amendments or superstructure of Br. Austin's [Buckingham], it will be needless for me to say much concerning that.[14]

With the passing of the crest of Shaker prosperity after the Civil War era, and the decline of membership, many of the severe rules imposed by the Society were gradually relaxed. Believers' relations with the "world" of necessity became somewhat more free in the struggle to maintain their vast holdings of land. The spiritual manifestations among the Shakers of the 1837–1847 decade with their fantastic happenings and the consequent individuality of expression never returned.

The intense motivation that these manifestations provided a thriving sect at the peak of its life span could not be sustained at such fever heat, and a calm, serene era began in which sincere but routine music was produced. Harmonizations became more correct technically as each successive printed hymnal appeared; Shaker tunes were theoretically like all American Sunday School and revival hymns and no Believer ventured, or needed to undertake, to write a treatise on Shaker harmony.

The following books are devoted exclusively to Shaker theory:
1823 The Patent Gamut or Scale of Music. Wm Little and Wm Smith. A MS copied largely from the tune book of the same title, printed in New London, Conn., 1811. (SM503.)

---

14. Letter from Giles B. Avery, New Lebanon, New York, Sept. 6, 1841, to Abraham Perkins, Enfield, New Hampshire, p. 1. The amendments mentioned, which are of slight consequence, are in MSS. CM358 in The N. Y. State Library: A Treatise on Music; Agreeably to the Plan established and adopted at New Lebanon & Watervliet, N. Y. 1840. Isaak N. Youngs & David Austin Buckingham. 36 pp.

1831 A Musical Expositor. Russel Haskell. Early MS of the printed treatise of 1847 bearing the same name. (SM504.)

1833 The Rudiments of Music Displayed and explained with a Sellected Variety of Lessons and Examples. Isaac N. Youngs. New Lebanon. (MSS., formerly Papers of Shakers 150, New Lebanon, New York; now MT .Y56 case, Library of Congress, Division of Music.)   7

[n.d.] Rules of Music. MS of Youngs' *A Short Abridgement of the Rules of Music* (1833?) (SM505.)

1840 A Treatise on Music; Agreeably to the Plan established and adopted at New Lebanon & Watervliet, N. Y. Isaak N. Youngs & David Austin Buckingham. 36 pp. (MSS CM358 in the New York State Library.)

1843 *A Short Abridgement of the Rules of Music.* Isaac N. Youngs (Bx 9789, M9Y7, 1843.)

1846 *A Short Abridgement of the Rules of Music.* Isaac N. Youngs (BX9789, M9Y8, 1846.)

1847 *A Musical Expositor.* Russel Haskell (SM504.)

1868 A Gradual Series of Lessons in the Science of Music. Exercises selected from a variety of authors, arranged for the School in Enfield, New Hampshire, by James G. Russell (SM500.)

1870 Rules for Learning Music copied in 1870 (same as above). No author. (SM501.)

1871 A gradual Series of Lessons in the Science of Music. Copied by Nancy Eliz Moore, South Union, Kentucky (SM502.)

The following hymnals also contain music theory, singing lessons, exercises, and so on:

SM102 Music theory and vocal instruction (D. A. Buckingham, 1873) (111 pp.).

SM140 Modes of time; Patent Gamut theory; Figure notes explained (pp. 43–47).

SM162 Letter from Isaac N. Youngs on the Modes with tables (pp. 313–18).

SM197 Theory at beginning (7 pp.).

SM242 Musical characters and modes of time (8 pp.).

SM256 Musical Instructor. Singing lessons; exercises (1869) (Whole book [n.p.]).

SM261 Theory of Modes (at end of book).

SM300 Major-minor scales; signature, etc. (4 pp. middle of book).

SM301 Theory and singing exercises (1867) (whole book [n.p.]).

SM317 Modern keys, intervals, triads, etc. (19 pp. at end).

SM320 Theory and improved modes (1824–25?) (13 pp., middle).

5

Technical Aspects of the Shaker Musical Practice

Isaac Youngs wrote from the central ministry in New Lebanon, August 6, 1830, "I have laid out at some time to write a gammut & Remarks on the letteral system, adapted to the use of believers."[1] The manuscript of his "Rudiments of Music" which resulted is in the Library of Congress dated 1833 and, along with Russel Haskell's manuscript for *A Musical Expositor* which preceded it by two years, marks the beginning of the attempt by the head bishopric to establish theoretical uniformity in all musical practice in the several Shaker societies.

The kindly manner of Youngs in his personal dealings with fellow Shakers seems to have made his writings on music theory acceptable to the musicians of the other communities so far as they were able to understand and make use of them. Haskell, on the other hand, was inclined to be dictatorial, and the rather undiplomatic demands he made in matters of notation, tonality, and other details in his treatise and correspondence were not always received kindly by the capable musicians of the other societies.

These two Shaker musicians, backed by the authority of the ministry who were desirous of the utmost uniformity in all things, were among the strong-willed Shakers who felt that much of the musical idiom of their sect could be controlled and directed in the same manner as other routine affairs in Shaker communistic

---

1. Letter from Isaac N. Youngs, New Lebanon, New York, Aug. 6, 1830, to "Beloved brother Andrew" [Houston?], p. 3.

living. Fortunately, many fertile years had already passed before music, the sole outlet for self-expression among Believers, came to ministerial notice as being a possible loophole for nonconformity; and fortunately, even when the leaders did try to organize the typically "folk" expression, there were people who could not obey because they lacked the technical knowledge to follow any theory, and because they had ideas to express which did not fall into any of the categories so neatly set forth by the treatises.

Much of the practice conforms to the theory, and it must be acknowledged that the theorists adopted what was largely early American tune-book usage, at least in part, as a helpful guide for remote communities which had little contact in early days with the central bishopric. While some of the rules were ill adapted to the folk idiom which they tried to serve, the most regrettable part is that interesting technical phases of Shaker music, which were pure folk phenomena, went unnoticed and unclassified by the writers.

The sections of this chapter which deal with tonality, rhythm, form, and composition devices, are based upon a study of two hundred Shaker songs taken at random from the manuscript hymnals. Detailed analysis of the entire body of Shaker music literature is not possible because it consists of many hundreds, probably thousands, of songs; therefore, a cross section or arbitrary sampling best serves the present purpose and the results seem to check favorably with the impression formed through acquaintance with many hundreds of other Shaker tunes not included in the data. The results naturally can in no way be considered conclusive, nor can they pretend to include all of the highly specialized cases. Differences in theory and practice will be noted wherever comparisons can be made, but Shaker theory did not classify or even recognize much of this technical element in music.

The tonalities which Youngs admitted were the major (Ionian), the natural minor (Aeolian), and the melodic minor (the latter also sanctioned by Buckingham), while Haskell arbitrarily condemned the Aeolian form of scale in favor of the Dorian mode; therefore, Shaker authority sanctioned four different tonal systems in the written theory:

C D E F G A B C – (Ionian)

A B C D E F G A – (Aeolian)

D E F G A B C D – (Dorian)

A B C D E F♯ G♯ A — A G♯ F♯ E D C B A — (Melodic minor)

but Shaker music, like other folk music, could not confine itself to such a narrow choice of tonalities. The table on the following page shows the tonal catagories into which the two hundred analyzed tunes fell and the percentages represented by each.

The three (of the four sanctioned Shaker tonalities) — (1), (10), and (16) —total only 47.5 percent of the whole number of tonal schemes and subdivide in each of the three groups into the mode and its Hypo form; neither modes nor their Hypo forms were noted by the Shaker theorists in their writings. Most of the remaining scales are "gapped," and Youngs objected to these scales with notes missing, as he stated in a letter in 1830:

> I observed that James [McNemar] in particular seems to have adopted a new manner, which embarrasses me, so that in perusing the notes, it is hard for me, as I may say, to keep my latitude and longitude! He seems to altogether omit three of the letters ie. d. e. g. so that I know not which note is intended . . . I consider it essential . . . to make use of the 7 letters.[2]

The pentatonic scale— (5), (12), (15), and (19) —which has two gaps, occurs in all of its regular forms except E – G A – C D E (mode 5) and accounts for 13.5 percent of the songs analyzed; (6) and (18) are irregular forms of pentatonic comprising 1.5 percent. Seven tonalities— (2), (3), (4), (11), (13), (14), and (17) —representing 32.5 percent of the songs, are hexatonic or have one gap, while hexachordal (8) with six˙ successive tones, pentachordal (9) with five successive tones, and a tetratonic tonality (7) of four gapped tones are represented.

Both Youngs and Haskell made provision for a change in tonality or a "change of mi" (a new leading-tone) in their theoretical writings, but in actual practice the change seldom took place. Shaker songs followed the general pattern of other simple folk tunes and usually remained in the same tonality throughout. Four songs in the group considered changed tonal centers;two— (21) and (22) —have mutations from one mode to another, and two— (20) and (23) —make such changes between a mode and gapped scale or vice versa.

The two hexatonic scales (11) and (14) are identical, as are numbers (2) and (13), except that the second one in both cases appears transposed. They are presented on the two-pitch levels

---

2. Letter from Isaac N. Youngs, New Lebanon, New York, Aug. 6, 1830, to Brother Andrew [Houston?], pp. 2–3.

Table IX.   Percentage of Tonalities in 200 Songs

Reference number	Tonalities	Classification according to the final illustration in this book: Classification Chart of Tunes	Percentages
(1)	C D E F G A B C		
	Ionian 17.5	Heptatonic ionian, mode 1 A + B	35.5
	Hypoionian 18.0		
(2)	C D E F G A — C	Hexatonic, mode 1 A	16.0
(3)	C D E F G — B C	Hexatonic, cannot be classified	1.0
(4)	C D E — G A B C	Hexatonic, mode 3 A	8.0
(5)	C D E — G A — C	Pentatonic, mode 3	11.0
(6)	C D E — G — B C	Pentatonic, cannot be classified	1.0
(7)	C D E — G — — C	Tetratonic, cannot be classified	0.5
(8)	C D E F G A	Hexachordal, cannot be classified	1.0
(9)	C D E F G	Pentachordal, cannot be classified	1.5
(10)	D E F G A B C D		
	Dorian 2.5	Heptatonic dorian, mode 2 A + B	4.0
	Hypodorian 1.5		
(11)	D E — G A B C D	Hexatonic, mode 1 b.	0.5
(12)	D E — G A — C D	Pentatonic, mode 4	0.5
(13)	G A B C D E — G	Hexatonic, mode 1 A	0.5
(14)	G A — C D E F G	Hexatonic, mode 1 b	1.0
(15)	G A — C D E — G	Pentatonic, mode 1	0.5
(16)	A B C D E F G A		
	Aeolian 3.5	Heptatonic aeolian, mode 2 A +b	8.0
	Hypoaeolian 4.5		
(17)	A B C D E — G A	Hexatonic, mode 2 A	5.5
(18)	A B C — E — G A	Pentatonic, cannot be classified	0.5
(19)	A — C D E — G A	Pentatonic, mode 2	1.5
		Mutations	
(20)	C	Hypoaeolian to C — E F G A B C	0.5
(21)	C	Phrygian to C Hypomixolydian	0.5
(22)	C	Hypoaeolian to F Hypodorian	0.5
(23)		A B C — E F♯ — A to C Aeolian	0.5
			100.0

in each instance in the table because they appeared in this manner in the manuscripts, and represent practice as opposed to theory, or tonalities notated to center around G instead of D and C respectively as given in the Shaker treatises. The actual sound of either tonality would be identical in Shaker performance since the interval relationships are the same in both instances and the person who "pitched" the song started off at any convenient level before harmonium and pitch pipe came into use for this purpose. With the coming of the instruments came part singing, accompaniments, and a general trend toward definite pitch, the same as in the accompanied part songs of other sects.

"Pitching" a song in the religious ecstasy of the dance must have caused occasional embarrassment, since the ranges of Shaker songs are generally wide, and the poor judgment of an untrained Elder or "instrument" could have made the extremes of range impossible to sing. However, this situation has not come to light in accounts of Shaker singing nor has mention been discovered of members possessing absolute pitch. The two hundred songs analyzed have the following ranges:

Table X.   Tonal Range of 200 Songs

Interval of range	Number of songs	Percentage
14th	2	1.0
13th	7	3.5
12th	17	3.5
11th	32	16.0
10th	38	19.0
9th	49	24.5
8th	47	23.5
7th	1	0.5
6th	6	3.0
5th	1	0.5

The greatest concentration is on the range of the ninth, the range the medieval modes usually permitted in vocal composition, and "a melody might go so far as to combine the ranges of the Authentic and Plagal forms"[3] of the modes, which amounts to an eleventh; the range drops abruptly in percentage between the eleventh and the twelfth. Of the total, 13.0 percent of the songs exceed this range, and it is noteworthy that only 4.0 percent of the number fall under the octave range.

While the range of these songs seems generally large for literature belonging to a group of folk performers,[4] the intervals in the melodic line tend to be very small; 76.93 percent of the notes involved do not exceed the major second; skips of a perfect fourth or more become rare. While this is generally true of all folk

---

3. A. Madeley Richardson, *The Mediaeval Modes* (New York, 1933), p. 17. See also Willi Apel, *Gregorian Chant* (London, 1958), pp. 144–52.

4. Cecil J. Sharp states, however, in *English Folk-Song, Some Conclusions* (London, 1907), p. 82, that a characteristic of English folk melodies is their very large compass.

Table XI. Percentages of Intervals in 200 Songs

Number of Intervals	Size of Intervals	Direction	Approximate percentage
2843	Prime	Same level	22.7
2794	Major second	Up	22.3
2837	Major second	Down	22.63
647	Minor second	Up	5.2
512	Minor second	Down	4.1
226	Major third	Up	1.8
303	Major third	Down	2.4
608	Minor third	Up	4.9
970	Minor third	Down	7.8
316	Perfect fourth	Up	2.5
226	Perfect fourth	Down	1.8
101	Perfect fifth	Up	.8
64	Perfect fifth	Down	.5
20	Major sixth	Up	.16
5	Major sixth	Down	.04
12	Minor sixth	Up	.09
10	Minor sixth	Down	.08
12	Minor seventh	Up	.09
6	Perfect octave	Up	.05
7	Perfect octave	Down	.06
12521			100.00

song, the high percentage of small intervals may be due in part to the peculiarities of the Shaker dance, which accompanied so many of the Shaker songs. In spite of the lively "exercises" which involved leaping and whirling, these shuffles, marches, and circular dances which formed the nucleus of the dance ritual were variously described as *"travel . . . what we call marching,"*[5] "a kind of double hop, or a little slip of the foot on the floor,"[6] "rising on their toes" and "keeping . . . step with the music,"[7] and "skipping."[8] All of these phrases suggest a limited physical activity. Curt Sachs classifies dance movements as *closed movement* and *expanded movement,* and says that

---

5. Clara Endicott Sears, *Gleanings from Old Shaker Journals* (Boston, 1916), p. 194.

6. *Ibid.,* p. 193.

7. J. M. Phillippi, *Shakerism, or the Romance of a Religion* (Dayton, Ohio, 1912), p. 24.

8. Leila S. Taylor, *A Memorial to Eldress Anna White* (Mt. Lebanon, New York, 1912), p. 21.

The expanded dance is characterized by a stronger motor reaction, by wider strides, and even by leaps. The chief characteristic of the closed dance is the fixed center of motion to which the limbs come back again and again.

Roughly speaking, peoples whose dances are somewhat expanded use larger melodic steps than those whose dances are more or less closed.[9]

Thus, the predominance of small intervals in Shaker music may throw light on the character of the Shaker dance. Movements on a crowded meetinghouse floor where they "could not all labor at once," but where "a part labored two or three songs, & then stepped by & gave room for the rest,"[10] must of necessity have been of the "closed" variety.

Accidentals as such were rarely written in Shaker music, and there were no chromatic alterations of individual notes in any tonality in the two hundred songs analyzed. Abraham Whitney explained in a letter to Youngs: "In melody there is no flats nor sharps strictly speaking else we must admit of more than seven sounds [the A B C D E F G recognized in Shaker theory]. . . . It is proper however to make use of flats or sharps instead of transposing the key and then have to change back again."[11] In number (23) of the table of tonalities the gapped scale A B C − E F♯ − A is basically the accepted Dorian D E F [G] A B [C] D (in its Hypo form) transposed up a fifth (fourth and seventh steps missing), which alleviates the necessity of a "change back again," or mutation to the Aeolian section which follows it.

9. Curt Sachs, *The Rise of Music in the Ancient World East and West* (New York, 1943), p. 36. By permission of the publisher, W. W. Norton & Company, Inc.

10. Lucy Ann Hammond, Journal—1830; entry, Sunday October 17, 1830.

11. Letter from Abraham Whitney, Shirley, Massachusetts, May 25, 1835, to Isaac N. Youngs, p. 1.

SM270 [n.p.]

SHUFFLING TUNE
(A B C — E F♯ — A, transposed Hypodorian)

In "transposing the key and then having to change back again," the mutation, or change of tonality, would appear as follows for the same tune in Shaker letteral notation:

Since the round note A is "re" in a key with one-sharp signature, and "la" in a key with no signature, the round notes on A at the end of the first line form the mutation by showing that *d* becomes *a* ("re" assumes the properties of "la") on the same pitch level. The *a* enclosed in the square is not to be sung, but shows the pitch into which the preceding note changes.

Change was made from one hexachord to another in medieval solmization by mutation, and the process involved a change of syllables for a given tone. The principle was similar in Shaker music where a change from one tonality to another was sometimes made in a monophonic type of music. Believers' music for some sixty years was purely monophonic, and even for a period after 1845 when Shakers began to combine voices, the parts were like melodies, or the texture was polyphonic in nature, rather than chordal. As shown above, nearly 77 percent of the intervals in the melodic line do not exceed the major second; Donald F. Tovey has pointed out that there are two types of melodies; those primarily built upon conjunct movement along adjacent degrees of the scale, and those primarily built upon disjunct movement which "often tends to produce arpeggio types of melody, i.e., melodies which trace a chord."[12] The former type of melody, predominantly conjunct, appears most often by actual analysis and since Shaker dogma long forbade harmonizations or part singing, the early literature is functionally, at least, not conceived harmonically. Early tunes, it is true, were sometimes taken over from other sects and originally had been harmonized, and recruits from these same sects replenished Shaker membership in all periods and were accustomed to hearing and singing harmonic idiom to some extent. Probably the most difficult features to confine to the harmonic straightjacket are the modal and gapped scales which constitute such a large percent of the Shaker tonalities; the predominance of these tonalities in the literature would tend to preclude most of the harmonic implications which many collectors try to see in all naïve folk music. James F. Mursell wrote concerning this tendency:

If by some miracle we could collect all the melodies human beings have ever created, it is safe to say that by far the greater number would be devoid of all harmonic implications. To be sure we might force harmonic interpretations upon them, as is constantly done today with folk music. But it would do violence to their original constitution and introduce an element certainly foreign to and not even implicit in the intention and experience of their creators. We shall find that harmony depends upon melody, not melody upon harmony; though certainly once a harmonic system has been worked out and come into use it almost irresistibly influences the melodic thinking and construction of all who have become familiar with it.[13]

The intervals in the following march are 11 primes, 37 seconds, and 7 thirds, with few skips to suggest any chord formations.

12. Donald Francis Tovey, "Melody," *Music Articles from the Encyclopaedia Britannica* (London, 1944) , p. 94.

13. James F. Mursell, *The Psychology of Music* (New York, 1937) , p. 102. By permission of the publisher, W. W. Norton & Company, Inc.

Basically Dorian, the tonality (D E — G A B C D) lacks an F, which means that if one were to try to harmonize it and still keep the peculiar flavor of its tonality, the third of the D minor triad would be missing. It is difficult to think of this type of tune as having any harmonic implications inherent in it, although practically any tune can be harmonized in some manner or other with patience and a good, strong will.

SM314, p. 17   MARCH — John Bruce 1812

A hymn like the following,[14] from a printed Shaker hymnal of 1892, with its numerous skips tends somewhat to outline the harmonies innate in the melodic line. The numerals are the harmonies that the Shakers used to harmonize it, and melody and harmony seem to have been conceived with a certain inter-dependence: (See page 143)

Discrepancies between theory and usage in matters of tonality have a parallel in the elaborate system evolved by the Shakers to show the meter and speed in their music, but the application of the details, or rules, of this system enjoyed only modest success in actual practice. Many of the songs were marked C, 4–4, 2–4, 6–8, and so on, like other contemporary American tunes, and the tempo in such cases frequently was not indicated. Occasionally the Shaker symbol for the meter appeared alone, and the number above it which denoted the rate of speed was missing. Which part of this omission resulted from careless copying and which part can be blamed upon lack of comprehension, or upon resistance to new ideas and a real disregard of uniformity, is not clear.

---

14. *A Collection of Hymns and Anthems Adapted to Public Worship* (East Canterbury, New Hampshire, 1892), p. 41.

THE BEACON

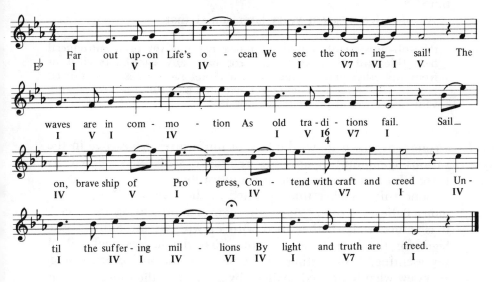

Far out up-on Life's o - cean We see the com - ing— sail! The
Eb   I   V I   IV   I   V7 VI I   V

waves are in com - mo - tion As old tra-di-tions fail.   Sail—
I   V I   IV   I   V I6 V7   I
                                        4

on, brave ship of Pro - gress, Con - tend with craft and creed   Un -
IV   V   I   IV   V7   I   IV

til the suffer-ing mil - lions By light and truth are freed.
I   IV   I IV   VI   IV   I   V7   I

Hervey L. Eads wrote from South Union to Youngs at the central ministry in New Lebanon in 1833:

> according to what authority we have, and our understanding of the same, we are not satisfied, especially respecting the *Moods* of time. We are satisfied as to the different kinds of time, but the *quantity* of time allowed to fill the bar or allowed to the beat is the difficulty.[15]

Meter was clearly understood, but Shaker letters make it seem obvious that because of the intricacies of the system, tempo markings were poorly understood, often not observed, and at best inconsistent in performance.

Youngs wrote another troubled "Brother" in 1840 after the introduction of the "Improved Modes," telling him that they used a sliding ball on a string called a *Mode Ometer* "in order to render the mode more easily understood & applied," but admitting that they cannot keep "the proportionate length of notes" with the same device for the very quick tunes. He suggests that "a little q may indicate a quicker speed" and concedes that "a great

---

15. Letter from Hervey L. Eads, South Union Apr. 22, 1833, to Isaac N. Youngs, p. 1.

portion of our songs given by inspiration are very difficult to time."[16]

Another letter seven years later stated that

> the sub-measure of compound mode has not yet been introduced here [Pleasant Hill, Kentucky], nor have any samples reached us from any other place in the West, it therefore remains to be proved how it will be received here. For my own part, for the sake of convenience, I would prefer to exclude it,[17]

a comment which shows the lack of uniformity in practice in the various communities and the resistance sometimes offered by those who had to master such complications.

Concerning Shaker tunes printed in the *Day Star*,[18] an anonymous Believer wrote: "As to the figures representing the speed, it is immaterial whether used with or without the Sub-measure Sign, for the barring will denote what the ficures [sic] fail of representing,"[19] suggesting, of course, that in actual practice singers knew what happened anyhow, by a glance at the music without having to refer to signatures for the information. Andrew Houston affirms this opinion with a tirade against "16 or 18 modifications of moods," saying that "every tune or song has its 'constitution' . . . and this constitution will always give us the trifling variations that may be attached to each & every song so grouped under a given mood."[20]

Songs given by inspiration were difficult to bar, as was much of a type of Shaker music conceived and sung in free, rubato manner. Frequently in the very early songs, only sections like the middle and end, or ends, of lines were marked with bars:

16. Letter from Isaac N. Youngs, New Lebanon, New York, Sept. 1, 1840, to Brother (?), in SM162, pp. 131–38.

17. Letter from Benjamin B. Dunlavy, Pleasant Hill, Kentucky, Sept. 1, 1847, to Isaac N. Youngs, p. 1.

18. *Day Star* (Cincinnati, 1841–1847).

19. Letter without signature, Watervliet [New York], Jan. 1847, to "Beloved Brother," p. 2.

20. Letter from Andrew [Houston], Union Village [Ohio] Oct. 16, 1841, to Isaac N. Youngs, p. 2.

FLESH AND BLOOD CANNOT INHERIT THE KINGDOM OF GOD[21]

A later version of this early tune appears[22] with bars and rhythmic signatures, showing the Shaker concept of its rhythm:

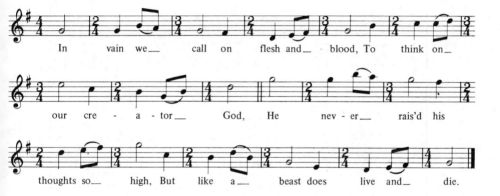

This tune falls naturally into 5–4 measure. In performance, the first notes in each line were probably sung as quarter notes. Such five-beat groupings are rather common in Shaker tunes, and Cecil Sharp says:

> Five-time is a very common measure in English folk-melodies . . . the 5-measure may be a variation of 3-2, due to the impatience of the singer in omitting one of the beats of each of the dotted minims,[23]

21. Tune: Youngs MS Hymnal, SM412, p. 19; words: *Millennial Praises* (Hancock [Massachusetts], 1812) , pp. 255–56.

22. SM314, p. 228.

23. Sharp, *English Folk Song*, p. 80.

an observation which may prove to be one of the best arguments for the English ancestry of much of the early Shaker song literature.

"Beautiful Angel Home." [From the Shaker and Shakeress, *4, no. 12 (1874): 96.]*

Many of the irregularly barred tunes do not fall into recurring groups of any sort, and in spite of the sing-song rhythm of the words in the song quoted below, their regularity has had little effect upon the melodic symmetry of the musical phrases. The words, eight lines of eight feet each, called forth musical phrases of 12 – 8 – 8 – 8 – 9 – 8 – 9 – 8 – beats, criss-crossed by eighteen changes of rhythmic signature.

SM237 [n.p.]

The theorists presented rests for each note value, but in practice rests almost never appeared. Youngs advised against using them to fill out the measure and preferred instead to change the rhythmic signature;[24] neither was done in the last measure of the song, and the rest has here been inserted instead of changing the note value.

Syncopation, although mentioned in theory, did not occur at all in the two hundred songs under consideration, and was a rarity in Shaker music. The accents are so normal in most of the dance tunes that they border on dullness, and misplaced accent,

---

24. Isaac N. Youngs, *A Short Abridgement of the Rules of Music* (New Lebanon, New York, 1843), p. 40.

a characteristic which often forms the distinguishing feature of the music of certain racial or folk groups giving it its peculiar flavor, is seldom encountered. However, word accent is sometimes falsely allied to the musical accent in the worded songs. For this reason Youngs favored leaving the songs with very free rhythm, unbarred, so that the natural accent of the words might serve to suggest the strong musical impulses at the same time. As a rule, the bar was placed before accented or important words, as in the song quoted above, and the frequent change of rhythmic signature allowed the music to follow passages in free verse or prose style much more faithfully than would have been possible with a fixed rhythmic scheme.

Ties were practically nonexistent, although they were discussed in the treatises. As a result of their absence, first notes in all measures were sounded anew, and never were tied to notes across the barline. Long-sustained effects were foreign to this vocal style, which so often served as rhythmic accompaniment to the dance, and a tone seldom exceeded the value of a half note in duration. Notes of longer value usually preceded those of lesser value in the measure or group, except in the case of the frequent grace notes, which were taken as "a short graceful slide," and "the time allotted to them is taken from the notes to which they are attached,"[25] says Haskell. That this actually happened in Shaker singing is doubtful; proof is lacking to deny that it did, but the tendency of untutored musicians now is to put the emphasis on the note which follows the grace note and to take time for the grace note from the beat which precedes it. Grace notes formed no consistent rhythmic patterns, but attached themselves to regular beats according to the whim of the folk singer.

The rhythmic patterns found in the two hundred songs analyzed are recorded in the following tables. Only those rhythms occurring at least twice in a song were considered characteristic. It must be borne in mind that the songs were purposely chosen at random in an attempt to represent the general Shaker song literature; as a result, the number of songs under each rhythmic signature varies. Six songs were either without bar lines or had so many changes of signature that they must be considered a free group impossible to classify otherwise in the tables; they are similar to the two examples just quoted and discussed. One hundred and nine songs are in 2–4 rhythm; the number of appearances of the

25. Russel Haskell, *A Musical Expositor* (New York, 1847), p. 14.

Table XII.   Prevalence of Rhythmic Patterns in Various Meters in 200
Songs Analyzed

(1) Free group: 6 songs without bar lines or with rhythms too diverse to
classify here.

(2) Number of various rhythmic patterns in 109 songs with 2-4 rhythmic
signature.

(3) Number of Various Rhythmic Patterns in 19 Songs with 4–4 Rhythmic
Signature

(4) Number of Various Rhythmic Patterns in 66 songs with 6–8 Rhythmic
Signature

various rhythms in this class is correspondingly large because this rhythmic signature happened to predominate in the two hundred songs chosen. Prevalence of the patterns in these two hundred songs may, or may not, be indicative of their prevalence in the entire literature, but the proportions should be viewed only within the individual rhythmic group as representing the supposed prevalence in that type of measure. Of the remaining songs considered, 19 were in 4–4 rhythm and 66 were in 6–8 rhythm. Songs in 3–4 time are not represented here and are rare in early Shaker literature. Later, more triple-measure songs are to be found.

The first columns of the 2–4 and 4–4 patterns show that parallel rhythms occupy the first seven or eight places of prominence (♩♩♩♩ – ♫.♫ ; ♩ ♩♩ – ♩♫ ; and so on) except for their number of main beats per measure; there are no dotted eighth notes in 6–8, nor do eighth notes precede quarters in triple groups of 6–8. (♫♩) .

Shaker songs have a tendency to begin on a weak beat just before the bar line as follows:

Table XIII. Part of the Measure upon which Initial Note Begins in 200 Songs

Measure	2 - 4				4 - 4				6 - 8					
Beat	1	and	2	and	1	2	3	4	1	2	3	4	5	6
Percentage	24	0	12	64	26	0	37	37	9	0	0	33	11	47
Six songs with free rhythm or no bar lines	Impossible to classify; no bar lines.													

Final notes have a tendency to avoid first beats, and to appear at the middle of a measure instead:

Table XIV. Part of the Measure upon which Final Note Begins in 200 Songs

Measure	2 - 4				4 - 4				6 - 8					
Beat	1	and	2	and	1	2	3	4	1	2	3	4	5	6
Percentage	6	0	90	4	5	0	95	0	3	0	0	97	0	0
Six songs with free rhythm or no bar lines	Impossible to classify; no bar lines.													

These notes, beginning as they do at the middle of the measure, produce a cadence much less positive in quality than those last notes which appeared on the first or strongest beat of the measure. Shaker tunes, however, nearly always reach their final *pitch level* or *keynote* on the first strong beat but need the secondary strong beat at the middle of the measure to satisfy the momentum of the preceding phrase. Dance tunes were repeated over and over until their normal 16-measure length had allowed the members of a Shaker gathering an opportunity to march or dance around a big meetinghouse floor. This popular cadence seems to have been utilitarian, as were most things which survived in Shaker life, since it did not cause any break in the dance by demanding a blunt close when used for countless repetitions. The bounding momentum created in the Shaker dance tunes demanded some such device where motion could be carried on through a final measure, which often becomes static in music that ends with the strong beat; as the following tune demonstrates, this cadence satisfied that need and also made it easy to pick up the initial weak beat with which many such tunes began, when repetitions were made.

SM270 [n.p.]   SHUFFLING TUNE   Watervliet

This Shuffling tune also illustrates the binary form used for the majority of the Shaker dance tunes. Eight measures balance a second eight-measure phrase and either, or both, may have repeat marks or not (Shaker copyists were very careless with their use of these repeat marks.)

Form of Shuffling Tune

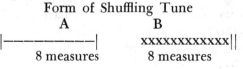

A	B
8 measures	8 measures

Frequently, the second eight-measure phrase is composed of four new measures and four measures of the original idea, as is the March which follows:

SM237 [n.p.]   HOLY GROUND MARCH, 1848

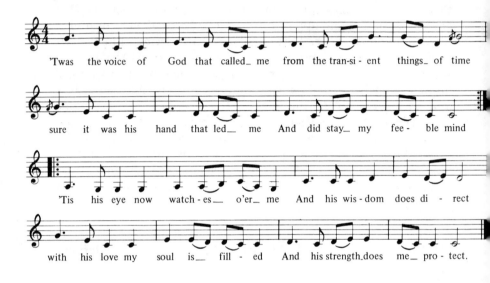

'Twas the voice of God that called_ me from the tran-si-ent things_ of time sure it was his hand that led_ me And did stay_ my fee-ble mind 'Tis his eye now watch-es_ o'er_ me And his wis-dom does di-rect with his love my soul is_ fill-ed And his strength does me_ pro-tect.

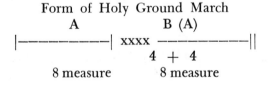

Form of Holy Ground March

Many worded songs that seem irregular at first glance are in the standard binary form. The dance was a powerful influence in regulating form in most Shaker tunes, but some vision songs had texts in "tongues" or prose that defied any standardization. Each song of this type is a case by itself dependent upon the words and free fancy of the Shaker, who may even have added wordless portions after speech failed. The following vision song is based on the descending pentatonic mode (A–G–E–D–C); the tune has an improvised, impromptu quality:

SM267, p. 62   MOTHER'S CALL

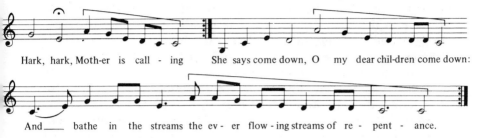

Hark, hark, Moth-er is call - ing   She says come down, O   my   dear chil-dren come down:

And___ bathe   in   the   streams the ev - er   flow - ing streams of re - pent - ance.

"Seen by a company of Spirits in our affter noon meeting Sabath day Oct. 3rd, 1841. They march in solom ranks & sung in a low mile tone for sevrel minits."

Form of Mother's Call.

(varied strophe)

$$\|{:}\ A\ {:}\|{:}\ A^1\ {:}\|$$

The single bar shows the location of the accent at the end and points out the typical Shaker cadence mentioned above. Practically a third (33.0 percent) of the cadences in the songs analyzed anticipate the strong beat of the final pitch level on the weak

(a) SM270 [n.p.]   (b) SM270 [n.p.]   (c) SM270 [n.p.]

(d) SM314, p. 25   (e) SM314, p. 24   (f) SM314, p. 32

(g) SM314, p. 32   (h) SM249, pp. 244–45

beat, either at the end of the measure (a) or before the middle
of the measure (b) while 34.5 percent of the cadences descend
a major second to the final on the strong beat of the measure
(c), or to the secondary beat at the middle of the measure (d).
Progressions of a minor second upward total only 8.0 percent;
6.5 percent go to the first beat (e) and 1.5 percent to the accented
part of the divided second (f). Since neither harmonic minor
with sharped leading tone nor Lydian mode appears in these
two hundred songs, or rarely if ever in Shaker melodies, this ascending half step represents a cadence in what is basically Ionian
(or major) tonality. Larger in proportion is the number of
cadences moving up a major second; 8.0 percent in this category
go to the first beat of the measure (g), and 1.0 percent to the
accented part of the divided second beat (h). This modal close
(up a major second), is found more often in the two hundred
songs analyzed than the cadence suggesting the leading-tone usage
(up a minor second) demanded by harmonic thinking. Only one
tune reached the final on the last part of a measure (the "and"
of two, in 2–4) ; 2.0 percent are without bar lines and are omitted
from these classifications; 13.5 percent of the cadencing progressions approach the final pitch level by skips of varying sizes. The
following table shows the classifications of final cadencing progressions in the two hundred songs:

Table XV. Final Cadences in 200 Shaker Songs

Interval	Direction	Part of measure	Number of songs	Percentage
Perfect prime	same level	to first beat	51	25.5
Minor second	up	to first beat	13	6.5
Major second	up	to first beat	16	8.0
Major second	down	to first beat	60	30.0
Minor third	up	to first beat	3	1.5
Minor third	down	to first beat	1	0.5
Major third	down	to first beat	13	6.5
Perfect fourth	up	to first beat	4	2.0
Perfect fifth	down	to first beat	2	1.0
Perfect prime	same level	to middle	14	7.0
Minor second	up	to middle	3	1.5
Major second	up	to middle	2	1.0
Major second	down	to middle	9	4.5
Major third	down	to middle	4	2.0
Perfect prime	same level	to and of two in 2-4	1	0.5
Tunes without bar lines			4	2.0

The dance imposed eight-measure periods upon much of the Shaker music, and as was previously mentioned, many of the dance tunes have two of these eight-measure periods. Short motives common to both periods often are found which effect an emotional continuity, give organic unity, and add interest to the melodic texture. Idelsohn describes this practice, which exists in all Oriental music as the oriental folk composer's manner of composition:

> The composer operates with the material of these traditional folk motives within a certain mode for his creations. His composition is nothing but his arrangement and combination of these limited number of motives. His "freedom" of creation consists further in embellishments and in modulations from one mode to the other.[26]

This same folk manner of composition is sometimes present in the Shaker tunes, as the following examples show:

SM314, p. 23   MARCH   Luther Copley 1839

SM314, p. 23   MARCH   Eunice Burnham, South Enfield 1834

---

26. A. Z. Idelsohn, *Jewish Music in Its Historical Development* (New York, 1929), pp. 24–25. By permission of the publisher Holt, Rinehart and Winston, Inc.

Occasionally two tunes are found which employ similar motives. These two tunes below are anonymous, as are many Shaker melodies, so the sharing of motive may be characteristic of a personal style or it may be what Idelsohn termed "traditional folk motives within a certain mode." Measures 10 and 14 of the first tune should be noticed; they resemble X, but the unvocal skip of a seventh, G to F, is rare in Shaker hymnology. The range of the tune is a minor ninth within the limits of one measure.

SM249, pp. 166–67   [no title]

SM249, pp. 166–67   [no title]

That part of the procedure which is conscious and artful, and that which is innate folk feeling are impossible to disentangle, and although composition in this manner is not characteristic of all Shaker music, these examples are by no means isolated cases. Such devices as inversion of motive and the use of reiterated melodic figures at different levels in the tunes can be cited, but their use plays no great part in an expression that is basically naïve and untutored; the rare cases in which they are employed seem to be of pure coincidence and do not characterize the body of Shaker songs. They are usually only one measure in length but the following inversion is three notes longer:

SM314, p. 12 JETHRO TURNER'S ANCIENT

Shaker composers frequently illustrated certain words by a florid passage in the melodic line. The chosen words were usually verbs representing sounds or the word "holy." Each musical pattern was entirely different; a word did not call forth a similar or related tonal design each time it appeared, as ideas, objects, or emotions did in Wagner or Bach.[27]

Examples of Musical Illustration of the Word "Sound" in Shaker Hymnals

----

27. Albert Schweitzer, *J. S. Bach*, trans. by Ernest Newman (Leipzig, 1911), 2:49ff.

Examples of Musical Illustration of the Word "Rejoice"
in Shaker Hymnals

Examples of Musical Illustration of the Word "Holy"
in Shaker Hymnals

Miscellaneous Examples of Musical Illustration
in Shaker Hymnals

Much of the fancy represented by these musical illustrations originated in the revival decade of 1837–1847. Shaker imaginations, keenly fired, received songs on gold plates, sacred rolls, and leaf drawings; many words were spelled out; heavenly articles such as the trumpet, sword, spiritual wine, and dove of peace formed a diverse and colorful imagery in song and prophecy; inhibitions were at low ebb, and the credulous Shaker was ready to receive any manifestation which he believed to be from the spiritual realm. One of these manifestations was the "gift" to sing in parts, which the ministry long had forbidden. Although experiments were being tried several years before permission was finally granted to use more than one voice in the worship music, "The Harmony of Angels" by D. A. Buckingham, written in 1843, is generally conceded to be the anthem which inaugurated this new style of music.

Much earlier ("Received June 20, 1833," and "Copied Oct. 1833,") is a three-part song entitled "Ode to Contentment."

ODE TO CONTENTMENT

SM198, pp. 37–38

This ode was written in three voices with the air on the middle staff, as was the common practice in tune books of the period in America. Beginning on the octave A and cadencing with a progression containing two open fifths, this Aeolian tune has many thirds and sixths and several open fifths. Fourths are tempered with the third of the triad which appears above or below it; there is a fondness for seventh chords with third (or fifth) omitted and even parallel sevenths in the ninth measure, but emphasis is primarily upon the third and sixth. Parts cross freely and the concern seems to have been for the three independent melodic lines.

The following tune from the 1845 period places more emphasis upon the fourth, fifth, and octave. While complete triads and consecutive thirds are numerous, there are several cases of parallel fourths:

GOLDEN STREETS

"An advent song from the Spirit world given at Canterbury, N. H."

SM149 [n.p.]

The number of voices in music of this type ranged from one to four individual parts. When one voice was not represented, it united with another part. The lines are quite vocal and independent, crossing freely to give a more interesting melodic contour. What seems at first glance to be the work of a "right-handed" composer at the piano is a real advance towards a concerted vocal idiom even though, by our standards, it is not always entirely euphonious.

Shaker music similar to these two illustrations is limited in quantity and appears mostly between 1840 and 1850. However, the harmonic style was gradually gaining favor in the communities, and with the advent of music teachers from the neighboring cities, and the adoption of harmoniums and pianos bought at the teachers' suggestion, the unaccompanied modal melodies gave way to major-minor tonalities, four-part harmony, and a banal Sunday-school type of hymn heard all over America.

The first hymnal employing four-part harmony in round notes was printed at Albany in 1875 for the Mount Lebanon Shakers. Many of the songs appeared without any harmony but were printed in the round notes that Believers had begun to sing in place of their letteral notation. "Several of the most progressed singers studied the rudiments of harmony, and, under the criticism of able teachers who entered the transient membership list, soon became competent to arrange harmonies suitable for the press."[28] The preface contained a note stating that the hymns were "the product of young Brethren and Sisters of the Order, who, having had no scientific, musical education, have in their arrangement—poetical and musical—chiefly relied upon the teachings of the Spirit."[29]

Harmonizations consist almost entirely of tonic, subdominant, and dominant chords; there are many six-four chords and consecutive fifths and octaves are common. The bass frequently repeats one of the three tones customarily allotted to that part, from six to ten times. Little use is made of first inversions, and the limited vocabulary forbids any great flexibility of parts. The peculiar turn of the early Shaker melodies, rarely conceived with regard for the underlying harmony, frequently made it necessary, when they were subjected to such treatment with the limited harmonic vocabulary, to repeat harmonies over the bar, producing a static, redundant effect. Modulation and chromatics were rarely used, and the tonalities were of necessity monotonous. This is especially true of the first hymnal in which every harmonized tune is in major. The abrupt change from a great variety of modal and gapped scales to major—minor tonality which Shaker music had to make to accept the harmonic idiom, was an un-

---

28. Anna White and Leila S. Taylor, *Shakerism Its Meaning and Message* (Columbus, Ohio, 1904), p. 339.

29. *Shaker Music, Inspirational Hymns and Melodies Illustrative of the Resurrection Life and Testimony of the Shakers* (Albany, New York, 1875), Preface.

natural one forced upon it and void of all normal evolution. The year 1870 seems to mark the coming of the Boston music teachers, the acquisition of the first harmonium or cabinet organ, the end of the common use of letteral notation, the consequent adoption of round-note notation, and the beginning of a five-year transition which led to the publication of a round-note, harmonized hymnal by the Shakers in 1875. Believers took the folk legacy passed on to them by the British Isles and colonial America and enriched it for almost a century, only to have it snatched away in five short years by imported musicians, who, through lack of appreciation for the peculiar pattern of an expression unique with the Shakers, imposed upon them a foreign musical idiom. Both the very special flavor of the tonalities of the unaccompanied music, and the interesting, even fantastic, uses to which it had been put, died suddenly in this abrupt change. What remains of Shaker hymnology after the transition is common to most small Sunday-school congregations in America in the same years. The frontier period and the attendant conditions which fostered revivals, small isolated communities, folk ways, and picturesque traditions had also turned a sharp corner after the war years 1861–1865: communication, travel, education, labor conditions, the newspapers, and the many other forces which dispelled emotionalism in revivals ended isolation, revolutionized American life, and swept away the particular set of conditions that nurtured all folk expression, and, along with it, that part of it which especially concerns us here—a distinctly Shaker music.

6

Performance of the Music

Shakers who remembered Mother Ann Lee said that "the heavenly melody of her voice, in the gift of divine songs, was beyond description."[1] Her brother, William Lee, was also said to have had a remarkable voice, and when he was "under the immediate operation of the power of God," his singing seemed like the music of some sort of superior being.[2]

These Shakers, who were among the first to come to America, recognized the part music played in bringing the minds of devout believers into rapport with the spiritual world, and throughout the history of the societies anthems, hymns, and spiritual songs were used at all important functions. Messages direct from departed members both in English and in "tongues" came to the "instruments," or mediums, couched in a musical setting; songs of welcome and farewell were sung to visiting ministries and important individuals, which intensified the sincerity of the textual expression; funeral hymns bade farewell to Shakers when they embarked upon their journey to the spiritual kingdom; and music accompanied the most sacred Shaker ritual enacted upon the Holy Mount.

Descriptions of the early singing seem to lay emphasis upon volume rather than upon refinement of tone or of any nuance, and such an expression as "his voice was strong," is rather typical of all of them.[3] In the early Kentucky revival "their worship by singing and shouting . . . might have been heard at least to the

---

1. [Calvin Green and Seth Y. Wells], *A Summary View of the Millennial Church* (Albany, 1823) , p. 26.
2. *Ibid.,* p. 42.
3. *A Summary View,* p. 42.

distance of two miles," but "their various songs, and perfect
harmony in singing, shouting, &c. rendered the meeting very
solemn."[4] Harmonious singing and great solemnity, in the camp-
meeting and revival atmosphere which sired early Shaker music,
depict something very different from what those words suggest to
the worshipper of the twentieth century who is accustomed to
trained choirs and professional soloists. The emotional appeal
which frontier religion made to the sturdy settler, who had limited
cultural resources, came largely from hearty group singing rather
than from any choral effects by a small and highly specialized
choir. Appeal to the Holy Spirit was direct and personal, both
through verbal testimony and exhortation, and hymn singing.
Choir, soloist, and preacher acted less as an intermediary between the worshipper and God than in the more sophisticated
urban communities and regions which had been settled for a
longer period. Words which the frontier folk sang were largely
in their own idiom and understood by all; the stern warning
against the unrighteous way of life and the promise of reward
for the chosen few frequently filled fifteen or twenty verses with
vivid pictures of the terrors of hell and the enticements of heaven.
Vigorous participation in the singing was often accompanied by
violent bodily exercise which heightened the religious experience
for the individual, who shouted, leaped into the air, shook in all
his members, reeled, whirled, and not infrequently fell cold and
stiff in a trance that lasted for hours or days. Music and gesture
combined to bring about a highly emotional state where mass
hypnosis and hysteria as well as self-hypnosis found ideal surroundings in the crowds of simple, devout folk eager to snatch at any
suggestion which they thought of divine origin.

The Shakers were not the only group who were "exercised"
in their worship; Schismatics, New-Lights, Methodists, Presbyterians, Baptist Merry-Dancers, and most of the sects which found
favor on the frontier accompanied some of their music with
physical activity, especially in times of revival. What had been
an unorganized "free-for-all," and promiscuous leaping and shouting with Shakers in England and the early years in America,
became "shuffling and step manner" about 1791.[5] The organiza-

    4. Richard McNemar, *The Kentucky Revival* (Cincinnati: printed; Albany: re-
printed, 1808) , p. 118.
    5. Clara E. Sears, *Gleanings from old Shaker Journals* (Boston and New York,
1916) , p. 183.

tion of these physical motions into a dance, which still seems to have been very free in form and speed and given to many variations in this early stage, caused the Shakers to be severely criticized by the other sects, since it suggested secular dancing and marching used in less reputable connections, and now employed in the worship of God. The early Shaker hymn writer revealed the close-knit texture of song and dance, communal and spiritual experience all rolled into one composite whole,

> We love to dance, we love to sing,
> We love to taste the living spring,
> We love to feel our union flow,
> While round, and round, and round we go,[6]

welded together by the ecstatic state "while round, and round, and round" they went.

While Shaker song composition was not a communal process in its initial stages (in conscious composition, adaptation, or inspirational writing), Shaker song preformance *was* communal for the most part, and with few exceptions must be approached in this light if its true spirit is to be grasped. A solo voice sang the "inspirational" songs in trance, but once they were learned and written down, they were sung by the community. Two things, both probably lost to us forever, are essential in faithfully recreating a Shaker tune and bringing to life the cryptic pages of the Shaker hymnals; one concerns the utilitarian aspect of the song, the other, the psychological aspects of the communal mind. Since conditions cannot be supplied at will to meet either of these peculiarities, the most elusive and subtle element of all performance—the spirit, the conviction, the *raison d'être*—must be supplied vicariously by literary account and imagination.

A concert performance of a communal song that originally involved hundreds of sincere Shakers, sincere in their convictions to the point of denying themselves all worldly pleasures, who went about "stamping out sin" as they sang, and drawing imaginary bows to let fly arrows against the devil of the flesh, produces not a fanatical religious fervor today as it once did, but only an incredulous mirth. The use for which the song was originally intended, as well as the conviction in the minds of Shaker singers,

---

6. *Millennial Praises* (Hancock [Massachusetts], 1813), p. 70.

is a thing which can only be "staged" at best and which results
in a self-conscious performance. It is not possible to reenact the
performance of certain Shaker music which has a decidedly impromptu quality, interspersed with Shaker mysticism that even
a believer could not repeat precisely at will. A Harvard journal
tells of a leave-taking by visitors from another community:
"Thursday we arose and after we had eat our Breakfast, the
cooks came in to see us a few minutes and bid us farewel, on a
sudden two of them became inspired, and we had many blessings
pronounced upon us by singing and talking in tongues and singing and talking in english."[7] Speaking with "tongues" and inspired speech in English were here mixed with song, which had
as its mission both social sentiment and spiritual blessing. This
composite of the musical, spiritual, and social with the "gift of
tongues" was further complicated by the addition of the dance
in most cases of Shaker performance. Bodily exercise fired the
worshipers with an enthusiasm and religious frenzy that made
suggestions from strong-willed Elders equivalent to a divine com-
mand. Under such conditions strange ceremonies developed, self-
consciousness vanished, and the ardent Shaker behaved in a way
that must have astonished a believer as much in his calmer
moments as it did the nonbelievers who witnessed it. An excerpt
from a letter exchanged between ministries in 1824 records a performance as fantastic and colorful as that of any opera, and one
full of psychological implications.

> Some time past on the sabbath, the whole Chh. west branch, and
> all that were in chh. relation, assembled at the meeting-house—we
> gave them liberty to worship God—They all marched out into the
> street, brethren & sisters together in a body—they began to march in
> these words. March on, March on, O ye little band;
>> March on, march on to the heavenly land;
>> For God will reward us with peace & good love,
>> And give us a place in the mansions above, &c &c.
> The strong singers, brethren & sisters, went forward & lifted up
> their voices. The trumpeters followed after to sound the alarm in
> God's holy mountain. (I do not mean artificial trumpets, but the
> power of God) and the boys and girls playing in the streets of the
> new Jerusalem. They marched down south to the cross road below
> the south house; they then wheeled about, and came to the north
> house, strewing their garments by the way, as they did when—Christ
> rode to Jerusalem, sounding all the time, so that they were heard for

---

7. Betty Grove, John O. & Sally L., Journal, Harvard, Massachusetts, Aug. 31,
1840: entry of Sept. 10, Thurs.

miles. . . . I suppose there was about 300 in the street full of life and power, and sounded the gospel all the way. There was a number of the world [nonbelievers] in the street at the same time, and they were confounded.[8]

Notice that *the Ministry* "gave them liberty to worship God." The marching and singing set the emotional tenor and the singers beheld imaginary trumpets, while "the boys and girls [adult Shakers] playing in the streets of the new Jerusalem." imitated the biblical characters and incidents they imagined, accompanied by a terrific din of singing "300 in the street . . . were heard for miles." "In conditions of instability the subconsciousness has a tendency to bring to the surface normally regressive and concealed characteristics, in which emotional elements predominate . . . these would be of childish origin,"[9] and in a state of ecstasy "the higher judicial and regulative mental functions are almost entirely inhibited," and "the suggestion of being another person has all the effect of such a suggestion during the hypnotic state."[10] With such a highly wrought emotional state, a tonal effect must have resulted that would be difficult to recapture in performance by a cultured group of singers more than a century later.

Shaker song was of this uninhibited revival style until after the spirit manifestations of 1837–1847. Philemon Stewart was for many years one of the Shakers who kept the religious and emotional ardor in Shaker singing at white heat; however, the wildly exuberant quality gradually gave way to a calm, peaceful type of worship, and after 1850 a quiet march, to which believers waved their hands slightly as they kept time to the hymn, constituted the main part of the ritual.[11]

At the regular worship in the Shaker meetinghouses, a few of the best singers were usually placed in a group in the center while the dancing and marching took place around them. There are many accounts of the ritual telling about the singing and dancing over a long period of years, and they show that the number of singers varied greatly, depending upon the supply available. The

8. Letter from David [Darrow], Union Village, Ohio, July 31, 1824, to the Ministry, p. 2.

9. George B. Cutten, *Speaking with Tongues* (New Haven, 1927), p. 162. By permission of the publisher, Yale University Press.

10. Cutten, *Speaking with Tongues,* p. 86. By permission of the publisher, Yale University Press.

11. Sears, *Gleanings from Journals,* p. 273.

rigorous physical activity of the dancing made it necessary to withhold a few of the strongest voices so that these singers could maintain a good solid musical texture and sound rhythm for the dancers without themselves becoming winded. Some songs were sung without dancing or marching and were known as "stand-still songs"; these latter melodies did not need the firm, steady beat required for dancing and appear to have been taken with much greater rhythmic freedom, but for "exercising" songs the best singers still "placed themselves in the center of the room, in two ranks, the one facing the other, sisters facing sisters, and brethren facing brethren, with the spit box in the middle."[12] for the convenience of those who became sick from the violent whirling,[13] and the dancers performed their countless variations of figures based upon the circle, oval, and square around them.

The elder or the "instrument" who was speaking "pitched" the song, or began to sing, announcing the pitch which would decide the key for the song to be sung, and then others joined him in singing. A journal of 1827 has the following typical entry: "April 29, 1827. After he ceased speaking Joel pitched a song & we went forth in the circular march, & marched the Gospel Baptism Anthem. The cross bearing company sounded, & trampled old nature all down to the ground."[14] At times the singing was "entirely drowned" by the fury of the stamping and the "roaring out" against the sins of the flesh.[15] Older members too feeble for the exertions of these rapid dances sat around the meeting room[16] and occasionally the violent exercise proved to be too much for an overtaxed heart: "Hezerkiah Mary departed this life Feb. 18th 1821 on Sabbath . . . labored two songs . . . but never breathed again."[17] Singing must have had to be loud to be of any benefit to the dancers in the lively meetings, when shaking, "hallooing," "zealous & loud speaking," and "warring" were going on. It is

---

12. David R. Lamson, *Two Years' Experience Among the Shakers* (West Boylston, 1848) , p. 86.

13. *Ibid.,* p. 88.

14. Alonzo Giles Hollister, The Book of Moses, etc., containing an Extract from Elizabeth Lovegrove's Journal, 1827, p. 261.

15. *Ibid.,* p. 336.

16. Sears, *Gleanings from Journals,* p. 298.

17. Letter from the Canterbury Ministry to the Harvard Ministry, Apr. 10, 1821.

easy to believe the account in the same entry of a journal that
noted: "In their marching, they make quite a sound on the floor
as they step, such a body of people."[18] It is a compliment to
Shaker builders that a building so full of people leaping and
marching in the same rhythm was able to stand without collaps-
ing; they foresaw the possibility that it could collapse, so that
meetinghouse floors were especially constructed with an understanding of the spring in the flooring, and allowance was made for
this elasticity in their structure.[19] Acoustical properties of the
meetinghouses were also subjects of experiment in an effort to
eliminate echo and improve singing conditions, and after a curtain was hung to stop the reverberation of the sound, a journal
of 1825 records: "We then all seated our selves and sing the free
volenteer while the brethren were making preparation to let the
curtain down. After the ceremony was performed we sung some
more."[20] Twelve years later the problem was still being investi-
gated and a journal reads:

> The Chh. & Second family attend meeting at the meeting house
> last evening for the purpose of ascertaining the benefits (if any) of
> the sounding board which has just been made, & suspended over
> the ranks. it is a floor made of ⅜ stuff nailed on to some ribs: is 16
> feet 8 inches wide & 35 feet long weighs 625 lbs. We test it by much
> reading, singing, & speaking, & try to find where the best place is
> for it on the part of echo; by raising & lowering it & standing in
> different parts of the room reading the same words in every change
> in order to perceive the variation of sound at different heights of
> the board. We think it helps the sound essentially & generally feel
> much pleased with it.[21]

The leaders were the only Shakers who ever took a hymnbook
into meeting and all singing in the worship was done from memory.[22] In the first days of Shakerism in America the tunes were few

18. Thomas Hammond, Church Journal, Harvard, 1816–1872; entry, Sat. Oct. 3,
1846, pp. 92–93.
19. Letter from Lorenzo D. Grosvenor, South Groton, Massachusetts, Dec. 13,
1855, to Giles [B. Avery], pp. 1–4.
20. John DeWitt, Journal; entry: Wed., May 27, 1825.
21. Giles B. Avery, Daily Journal: entry: Thurs., Apr. 27, 1837.
22. Anna White and Leila S. Taylor, *Shakerism Its Meaning and Message*
(Columbus, Ohio, 1904), p. 337.

and well known, and easily sung from memory; without a system of notation the believers were forced to memorize and retain great numbers of songs until the 1820 period. The quantity of songs multiplied rapidly at this time, because after 1816 many believers began learning to read notes and to write music. Details of Shaker dogma changed continually as well as details of ritual, rendering both words and song styles obsolete. Old songs dropped out of active use and those found at one period in the hymnals were replaced by a flood of new ones in each successive period; however, the number at all times remained so large that much effort was required to learn and keep up the active repertoire. A notebook kept in the middle of the 1837–1847 spiritual manifestations gives a list of thirteen "Songs Sung in one Singing Meeting to learn & relearn," showing the tremendous labor of practicing and reviewing which this phase of the worship necessitated, and also how the repertoire was retained.[23]

Singing from memory as the believers did was bound to cause the same variation in the song literature that takes place in all folk literature. These many hundreds of Shaker tunes were in manuscript until 1852, when the first hymnal was printed with tunes,[24] and the majority of them never did get into print. Copyists who collected hymns for their individual manuscript books wrote down the version they had been singing or had heard sung in their community. A visiting ministry wrote upon hearing the singing in another community: "they sung some & we some. E[lder] Br. seemed to think that our singing was much in the sense & manner they sung," and later, "she also thought that our singing was something in their manner."[25] *Something* in their manner; they do not say, *identical.* An Eldress from the head bishopric at New Lebanon, New York, wrote in her journal while visiting the society at South Union, Kentucky, in 1889: "Attend family singing meeting this P.M. The manner of singing does not accord with the East although most of the songs originated here in Mt. Lebanon but could hardly be recognized the time tune

23. Giles B. Avery, Notebook 184–, p. 62.

24. *A Sacred Repository of Anthems and Hymns* (Canterbury, New Hampshire, 1852).

25. Thomas Hammond, Church Journal, Harvard, 1816–1872; entry: Oct. 4, 1846, pp. 108–9.

and even the words changed."[26] Two versions of the "Fellow Travellers" show by the manner in which they were notated how they had been sung by the copyists or the communities where these copyists lived. As in most cases of this sort, definite data are not available concerning dates, scribes, or communities except that the second version came from Kentucky; the first version is possibly from Shirley, Massachusetts:

The variation in the rhythmic concepts of these two versions, which is typical to some extent of all folk singing, is scarcely less marked than the variation in tempo must have been in the performance of Shaker tunes. An early Shaker manuscript from the Harvard society says that after Mother Ann's death in 1784 most of the dances were very slow, but that "this was not always so, for although they began their dances quietly, the pace quickened as the ardor increased, but the difference from the old method was, that now, *however fast the dance became* [my italics] there was rhythm throughout."[27] This situation probably is characteristic of much of the Shaker music used for the dance during its entire history, since physical activity increases the speed of the pulsebeat and, even in the case of most trained musicians, at the same time increases the rate of tempo. In a conversation concerning the tempo of Shaker songs, Ricardo Belden of the Hancock, Massachusetts Society said (August 23, 1946) : "It was a common practice to sing them faster than they were written" in the Enfield Society. Abraham Whitney must have recognized something of the futility of trying to demand exact tempi from "folk" performers of the dance, when he wrote in defiance of their own elaborate Shaker system of precise modes: "If a tune be properly divided into measures it is very little consequence to me whether it be marked with any particular mode of time or not [Shaker mode included both rhythmic signature *and* rate of tempo], especially traveling Songs."[28] Even hymns and anthems were often "labored" or danced, and must have been subjected to a certain degree of emotional quickening of the tempo. One Shaker hymnal added the words "Largo & Presto" to the nine modes of time "so

---

26. Eldress Harriet Bullard, Journal of a trip to the southern and western societies, Mar. 22–May 29, 1889 [n.p.].

27. Sears, *Gleanings from Journals*, p. 182.

28. Letter from Abraham Whitney, Shirley, May 25, 1835, to Isaac N. Youngs, p. 2.

FELLOW TRAVELLERS

SM255 [n.p.]

SM314, p. 243

Come on fel-low trav-'lers to Zi-on we're go-ing the cost we have count-ed, the score is com-plete; The world with its beau-ty still dark-er is grow-ing From which we for-ev-er in-tend to re-treat.

We'll press thru all storms to the man-sions of glo-ry, where tri-als & suf-f'rings will find us no more. We then with de-light will re-peat the glad sto-ry, And join the bright cho-rus of thou-sands be-fore.

that the musicians may sing the tune as much quicker or slower as they choose,[29] an indication, again, that folk practice was not to be dictated to on matters as basic in the music as the religious emotion which inspired it.

Tunes that were not intended to be marched or danced often had a very free rhythmic structure and the performance must have been equally free and rubato, as in the case of the following song with its many changes of rhythmic signature:

THE SEALED PROMISE

SM237 [n.p.]

Phillips Barry wrote that the Shakers must have sung rubato because of these irregularly barred songs, "as do many of our best folksingers in the Northeast. The style is very old, no doubt; it is a feature of Hungarian and South Slavic as well as of British folksinging. That the Shakers had it proves again that for the melodies of their hymns, they drew on the fund of traditional British folkmusic."[30]

The above example also illustrates the Shaker practice regard-

---

29. SM197, p. 5.

30. Phillips Barry, "Notes on the Songs and Music of the Shakers," *Bulletin of the Folk-Song Society of the Northeast* 1 (1930):7.

ing the grace note; Isaac Youngs wrote that "when there is merely a short graceful slide of the voice, the diminutive note is written,"[31] but a consideration of the fondness of all revival and camp-meeting singers for "whooping" effects when they "get religion," makes it seem reasonable to believe that whooping more nearly describes what actually happened in a good "Shaker high," or lively meeting, than "merely a short graceful slide." Such effects common to all revival singing often were notated in Shaker hymnals, and although not usually written out, were used in the hymns of most other sects.

The tendency of the folk singer to slide up to notes, to add passing tones, and generally to embellish a melody was also a part of the Shaker practice. A phrase like the following demonstrates the passing tones which the Shakers added, and which folk singers are apt to insert unconsciously as one of the devices to facilitate

32

33

getting the next pitch. The Shaker singer or singers here also changed the A into G (the last note but one), so that instead of having to sing a second and then an awkward fourth in moving from B down to E, the melody became two descending thirds (B–G–E), which is easier to sing. Effects much like the prepared appoggiaturas of the learned harmonic music were frequently

31. Isaac N. Youngs, *A Short Abridgement of the Rules of Music* (New Lebanon [New York], 1843), p. 27.

32. William Walker, *The Southern Harmony and Musical Companion* (New York, 1939 [orig. ed. 1835], p. 41. By permission of the publisher, Hastings House, Publishers, Inc.

33. SM412, p. 6.

inserted by the singers when they delayed going down to a customary pitch until after the strong beat, and examples varied like the following are common when multiple versions of a song are to be had:

SM314, p. 233

Singers frequently moved to a new pitch before the regular beat of the customary version of a song, producing the following standard variation in the melodic line, a variation which seems again to have resulted from the eagerness of the singer to be prepared to sing the next pitch accurately, especially when the melodic progression involved a leap.

SM63, p. 120

SM194, p. 110

34. *Ibid.,* p. 7.

It is common for notes to shift beats and assume a new place in the measure, as in the case of the C and D in the following two examples.* The change in the last measure may be the result of harmonic feeling upon the part of the singer or community; the

SM314, p. 225

last measure in the X version which is from a very early hymnal was possibly adapted by the Shakers from outside sources, and suggests a dominant harmonization; the Y version, written down some thirty years later at a time when Shakers did not sing parts, shows little regard for harmonic implication when a change of harmony might be expected over the bar line.

Another phenomenon of Shaker melody, although rather infrequently found, is the complete shift of the tonality of a tune from one mode to another in various versions; an unconscious change in mode in the performance of folk musicians is mentioned as a commonplace by Cecil Sharp[36] and Jackson[37] in their folk-song collecting. However, Russel Haskell, the prominent Shaker theorist, insisted upon the use of the Dorian mode instead of the Aeolian mode. Haskell's insistence may have influenced the making of such changes and thus removed them from the realm of unconscious phenomena in singing to conscious ac-

---

35. *Ibid.*, p. 17.

36. Cecil J. Sharp, *English Folk-Songs, Some Conclusions* (London, 1907), p. 125.

37. George P. Jackson, *Spiritual Folk-Songs of Early America* (New York, 1937), pp. 115, 50. By permission of the family of the late Dr. George Jackson.

"Messenger." [From the hymnal Shaker Music *(Albany, 1875), p. 51.*

ceptance of musical dictatorship. In his treatise *A Musical Expositor,* Haskell converts tunes to illustrate his arguments, and he also sent four Dorian tunes to Austin Buckingham in a letter, with the comment, "Perhaps you have observed that I insert d sol and not a law for the first governing sound in the minor key. I always do so, whether I insert the music in letteral notes, or any other: for I certainly know it to be the only right method, whatever may be said to be contrary."[38] The instance quoted below shows a tune fundamentally Hypoionian in the first case (a hymn book of 1839–1842), which in the second hymnal (1856 or later) had been copied, for we must presume it was being sung at that time, in a mode fundamentally Hypodorian:

---

38. Letter from Russel Haskell, Enfield, Hartford County, Connecticut, Sept. 25, 1834, to Austin Buckingham, Watervliet, New York, p. 2.

HIDDEN MANNA

SM417, p. 41 1839–1842

SM314, p. 248

This is not the customary change made by conscious theory in Haskell's book or letter, but "The Voyage to Canaan," found in Hypoaeolian in SM412 copied by Youngs, has been changed to Hypodorian in SM314, p. 235, and also in Haskell's *A Musical Expositor*, pp. 80–81.

We cannot be sure what the Shaker singers did about raising and lowering certain notes as they sang, notes which were not so designated in the score. This process, which always goes on to some extent in folk singing, was known as *musica ficta* in the Middle Ages, and its very prevalent use was one of the contributing factors leading to the breakdown of the medieval modes and their replacement in general musical practice by the major–minor system of tonality. A Shaker hymnal written in 1834 gives evidence that certain notes *would* likely be altered according to this practice if they were difficult to perform when it states that

> The distance from one letter, or note to another that is, from a to b from b to c &c. ascending or descending is always the same, unless there is some sign to show that a certain note should be contracted or raised a half tone; but this is not often if ever necessary in vocal music; for there are not many voices able to perform the task, when the sign [an accidental] is inserted, unless the voice would naturally fall into it, & if so, they would not avoid it if the signs were omitted.[39]

Such passages as the following might be difficult for many unskilled singers, and the pitches marked above the note, not in the score, could have slipped into the performance:

In progressions down a whole step and back, like G–F–G or A–G–A, the middle note was often altered as was a B between two notes on A; the middle note in the former case was sharped, while in the A–B–A progression, the singer often lowered the B. In the last example quoted, the relationship between the B flat and E constitutes an augmented fourth or tritone, which was known throughout the Middle Ages as the *diabolus in musica;* it is difficult to sing and was long forbidden. The situation was sometimes corrected by singing the E flat, but it does not seem probable that

---

39. SM197, p. 4.

it would happen in this case, when the E had just been sounded twice in a song that definitely begins in C major. The scantily recorded and nebulous history of *musica ficta* makes any discussion of the practice highly speculative; this one does not pretend to more accuracy than any other so devoid of definite data.

Early Shaker music was, to summarize, highly emotional in style; considered very vital even by the first Shakers to their peculiarly energetic, uninhibited type of ritual in establishing rapport with the spiritual world; most unusual in its utilitarian and psychological aspects; and given to all of the variations of rhythm, pitch, and tonalities found in general folk-song performance. Successful re-creation of a Shaker performance depends upon an understanding of these spiritual, utilitarian, and psychological conditions, which will probably never be duplicated precisely, and also upon an understanding of the manner of singing practiced by the "folk" of whom the Shakers were a part. In folk singing each performance is highly individual, and at the same time "the summation of an infinite series of individual recreative acts."[40] The folk singer is a "latent creative artist, who will re-create what he has learned"; his memory sometimes fails, but his version of the song is to him the only correct one,[41] and his version is but one single step in the long series of changes the song and singing undergo. A notated folk song is like one single "still" picture extracted from a long moving-picture film—a complete unit by itself but fully understood only when viewed in the light of a long and ever-changing sequence of pictures which precede and follow it. Folk singing, likewise, is subjected to a fast-changing social milieu which shifts the emphasis placed upon it in family, community, country, or racial group, and the story of Shaker music and its performance concerns itself with this change in social custom.

When singing teacher Abraham Whitney joined the Shakers at Shirley in 1816, Believers were almost without musical training and were singing both the denominational hymns that their members brought with them from other religious sects and the secular dance tunes commonly known at this period in their part of the country. In this sense their literature was a part of the general American folk music of the times, largely British in

40. Philips Barry, "Communal Re-creation," *Bulletin of the Folk-Song Society of the Northeast* 5 (1933) :5.

41. *Ibid.*, p. 4.

ancestry, and taken into a ritual that included dancing, marching, and gesturing as religious parallels to the secular party games and rustic dances of their neighbors.

Musical instruments were forbidden by the early society; no harmony or part singing was employed, and when the early hymn writer beckoned Shakers with

> Come Brethren, tune your notes of praise,
> And Sisters, your shrill voices raise,[42]

it was to join in a unison melody to which, if there were no words as in the case of many Shaker dance tunes and "wordless songs," they sang "loo, loo, loo,"[43] "lal lal la, lal lal lal la," etc.[44] or "something like the following: lo lo lo liddle diddle dum, te hoot te hoot te diddle te hoot, &c.,"[45] according to various reports.

After 1818 several Shakers had learned enough about writing music to make the exchange of music between communities possible, and to increase considerably the output of original music. An interest in education began to be manifested among the societies in 1823 under the leadership of Seth Y. Wells of the central ministry at Mount Lebanon, and in 1833 the recommendation "that twenty or thirty minutes be devoted each day to singing" was made at Canterbury[46] and soon resulted in the establishment of singing schools in all of the societies.

Russel Haskell's *A Musical Expositor* (MSS. 1831) was published in 1847, and Isaac Youngs' *A Short Abridgement of the Rules of Music* had two printings in 1843 and 1846; the early haphazard system with its naïve, instinctive creation and performance was heading toward man-made rules and conscious control, but still had a ten-year period of fever heat in the revival of 1837–47 where emotions seem to have won out over a coldly calculated theory of music.

The singing meetings which were organized early in Shaker history were much like choir practice in any other religious group. The "Millennial Laws"[47] of 1821 (revised 1845) demanded that

---

42. *Millennial Praises*, p. 61.
43. Thomas Brown, *An Account of the People Called Shakers* (Troy, 1812), p. 143.
44. Phillips Barry, "Heavenly Display," *Bulletin of the Folk-Song Society of the Northeast* 1 (1930):6.
45. Lamson, *Two Years' Experience*, p. 98.
46. White and Taylor, *Shakerism*, p. 338.

"no one should sit cross-legged, nor in any awkward posture in the time of any meeting for worship, and in union, or singing meetings there should be at least five feet distance between the seats of brethren and sisters, when there is sufficient room to admit of it" (Sec. V, 19, p. 40). Another law commanded that "all should . . . attend to the reading of the hymn or anthem to be sung in meeting, which should be read in retiring time" (a period reserved for meditation after the evening meal) (Sec. II, 2, p. 30). There was concern for the singing even in this very early period, but rehearsals which were conducted by those in the societies who were most proficient in music, and not by professionals from "the world," as non-Shakers were called, must still have been little more than a memorizing period for songs that were to be sung without any books in the Sunday meetings.

In 1848 a journal entry records: "About 300 of the worlds people attended the public meeting."[48] Shaker meetings became one of the greatest shows in America, and Americans from far and near and distinguished foreign visitors went to see this spectacle of song and dance. Even from the earliest days, visitors had come in great numbers to the Sunday meetings and the Shakers had realized the value of publicity if a group of celibates were to go on replenishing their ranks. Dances and songs were practiced assiduously until they are reputed to have been astounding exhibitions of precision. High standards of performance must have been the definite goal of this list of refinements from a notebook of the 1840 period:

Things to be considered in singing.
　1st Suitable pitch notic to give worshippers warning.
　2. Suitable freedom of sound by the full & free opening of the organs.
　3rd Proper accent.
　4. Proper stress
　5. Proper sliding, crescendo & dimuendo
Be prudent of Character & time.

---

47. Millennial Laws, or Gospel Statutes & Ordinances adapted to the day of Christ's Second Appearing by Father Joseph Meacham & Mother Lucy Wright. Aug. 7, 1821. (Revised Oct. 1845.)

48. David A. Buckingham, Journal B., Church or 1st Order, Watervliet, New York, 1848–1854; entry: June 25, 1848.

A place for everything and everything in its place.
A time for everything and everything in its time.[49]

Buckingham wrote "The Harmony of Angels" in 1844, which was the signal for the beginning of part writing and part singing among the Shakers. Many other such anthems appeared about the same time, and while all were feeble attempts at harmonization, they meant the beginning of the end for the old type of Shaker music. A sophistication had set in which demanded music teachers from Boston,[50] Pittsfield,[51] and neighboring cities to teach Believers in the different societies to sing part music, and to produce a type of singing which would meet a new set of ideals for performance.

A feeling began to develop that the Shakers should have some sort of musical instrument for accompaniment, and an entry in a diary of 1869 states that "Giles goes to Albany to get some teeth stuffed & get information concerning making a sounding board for a monochord, [possibly for setting the pitch] and try to learn what kind of an instrument will do best for our singers."[52] The following year, at the suggestion of the singing teacher from Boston, a melodeon, or small cabinet organ was purchased at Canterbury,[53] and within a few years all of the societies had an organ or piano for accompanying the singing.

Printed song books were brought from "the world" to teach the singers to read notes,[54] which meant that Shaker letteral notation was used but little after this period (c. 1870) and that Believers were subjected to hearing many of the Sunday-school type of songs from the outside which tended to neutralize any individuality Shaker music might have had in the earlier years.

Duet and quartet singing developed, cantatas were sung, pipe organs were installed, and the small orchestra made its appearance.[55] The Canterbury Quartet of Shaker sisters finally went out into the world to sing concerts of Shaker music. The first concert seems to have been at Pittsfield, New Hampshire, in August, 1894,[56] and in 1897 they sang in "Gloucester & will sing at the Poland Spring House. . . . This is a venture, but possibly they may

49. Avery, Notebook, 184– [n.p.].
50. White and Taylor, *Shakerism*, p. 338.
51. Giles B. Avery, Diary (1876); entry: Thurs., Nov. 30, 1870.
52. Giles B. Avery, Diary (1869); entry: Sat., Feb. 27, 1869.
53. White and Taylor, *Shakerism*, p. 339.
54. *Ibid.*
55. Letter from Anna Case, Sabbathday Lake, Maine, Nov. 1, 1933, to Walter [sic] M. Cathcart, Cleveland, Ohio.

bring back about as much gold as though they went to Klon-dike."[57]

Thus came about the series of events that changed Shaker music from a folk manifestation, which was probably as distinctive of an individual folk group as any other in our American scene, because of its utilitarian purpose and peculiar psychological implications, to an expression typical of almost any small American community with Sunday-school singing and a modest village choir.

The earlier tunes were always in monophonic style and often were modal; the interest in part singing, and the subsequent study of harmony by Shaker musicians, confined the modes largely to major and minor and often reduced the free rhythmic structure to a trite regularity of phrase. While instrumental accompani-ment was long confined to rehearsal, its equal temperament must have affected the intonation of the singing and have tended to point out any personal variation in performance which character-izes all folk singing.

The emotional states which vitalized the performances in the early "Shaker high" meetings gave way to calm, calculated sing-ing. A meeting in 1880 brought forth the comment, "Exercises few and formal in these days very generally among Believers."[58] The ritual lost its distinctive, fantastic trappings, and self-con-scious Shakers no longer sang their songs in the fields, or while sweeping out sin in a "cleansing" ceremony, or while throwing their clothing to the four winds in a march that left the spectators "confounded." Spiritually and technically there had been a complete metamorphosis in Shaker hymnody, but the Shakers had foreseen and provided for this eventuality when they wrote in the preface to the first printed hymnal: ". . . these hymns, wher-ever they may be sung by Believers, must be limited to the period of their usefulness: for no gift or order of God can be binding on Believers for a longer term of time than it can be profitable to their travel in the gospel."[59]

56. White and Taylor, *Shakerism*, p. 339.

57. Letter from Elder Henry C. Blinn, East Canterbury, New Hampshire, Sept. 3, 1897, to Elder Joseph Holden.

58. Giles B. Avery, Diary (1880) ; entry: Sun., Feb. 1, 1880.

59. *Millennial Praises, Preface*, p. iv.

7
Song Types and Analysis

It is difficult to classify Shaker songs either according to title or definite musical traits. Similar titles often reveal no distinguishing musical features common to a supposed category of tunes, and similarity of musical feature is no proof that the tune will fall into a definite category according to title.

Perusal of nearly five hundred Shaker manuscript hymnals shows that Shakers made no strict classification of their song literature according to type. Individual copyists frequently collected, and placed together in one hymnal, shuffles, quick dances, funeral hymns, and songs which were being received currently by inspiration, such as "Roll songs," "Shepherdess Songs," or "Gold Plate Anthems." One is tempted to see among these copyists those Shakers who would have been the coin, stamp, and Indian arrowhead collectors of the non-Shaker world, gratifying that same universal urge through the sole activity in Shaker life in which such vanity could still go undetected.

Except for a few early years when Shaker tunes had been wordless, the worded and wordless songs existed side by side for a century and a quarter. Some dance tunes had words and some were wordless, and the same may be said for songs given by inspiration, for hymns, anthems, so that categorical grouping cannot be made upon the basis of worded or wordless tunes. Anthems, hymns, extra songs, and even the dances and marches, appear with such a variety of rhythms that rhythmic structure cannot be used to group or classify the literature. The Shakers themselves were not always certain of the category of an unlabeled tune so far as names were concerned, when either rhythm or tempo were the only guiding factors. Tonalities, as in the case of all music produced by folk musicians, were not confined to any single title, style, group, or community, but cut across all such artificial bar-

riers and formed the general musical vocabulary of all who produced songs. Diaries and journals reveal that the ritual changed
constantly over the several decades of Shaker history, and even
differed in the various communities at any one given date, in
spite of the desire of the central ministry for uniformity. These
accounts also show that the order of ritual was often extemporized
by the elder who "felt" to sing, or "had a gift" to "labour" tunes
in all manners of succession, a fact that only confuses the would-be
chronicler of this characteristic of Shaker life, and offers no aid
to classification. The symmetrical form of the two eight-measure
phrases used in most of the Shaker dances is also used in many of
the hymns, anthems, and so-called "extra" songs, while songs with
this regularity of form intended for dancing, as well as those with
unbarred or very free rhythm which were not put to this use, cut
across the sections of worded and wordless songs without regard
for titles.

Music, like everything else in the Shaker community, had to
be useful, and except that it appeared in such great quantities at
certain periods that not all of it could be learned, used, or even
written down without great inconvenience to an already busy people, succeeded in meeting these utilitarian demands. The utilitarian requirements, however, were not constant, but were subject to
change according to the growth and evolution of the fanciful
aspects of the ritual of the sect, as the author of the preface
(p. iv) to the first printed hymnal, *Millennial Praises,* foresaw
in 1813 when he said that Believers were not to be "confined, in
their mode of worship, to any particular set of hymns . . . and
that the spiritual songs of Believers, as well as every other part
of their worship . . . must be limited to the period of their usefulness."

The great common denominator which underlies Shaker music
in all of its phases and periods, holding it together as a distinct
body of folk expression, is its utilitarian nature, rather than its
titles, forms, tonalities, or rhythms. Any other criterion of classification would be an arbitrary one, and might well include tunes
wrongly grouped or overlapping, under headings which baffled
even the Shakers themselves, for we find some anthems called
hymns and some shuffling tunes called round dances, while still
others come under any one of several such categories.

The songs used in this chapter have been chosen to illustrate
the most prevalent musical types found in the Shaker hymnals,
and to show the functional purposes music served in the Shaker

communal life. Preference has been given so far as possible to those songs which, according to account, were used most frequently, and to those songs which accompanied the special practices which were peculiar to the Shaker sect and made its worship one of the most spectacular phenomena in the rural life of nineteenth-century America.

Metronome markings are derived from the Shaker symbols, and are based upon the table of modes in chapter 4; when such information did not exist in the manuscript, it has been supplied from the Shaker practice as stated in this same table, and will be enclosed in brackets. Occasionally, when there is neither indication of tempo by the composer nor any hint of the type of song it may have been considered to be by the Shakers themselves to help group it by the table, the statement of Andrew Houston to Isaac Youngs that "every tune or song has its 'constitution'" which helps determine its tempo, and his statement in the same letter, ". . . how can it be expected that we shall all sing a given tune the same speed,"[1] have been used as guide and authority for the liberty taken in suggesting the tempo in the brackets.

To facilitate comparative study in two parallel and closely related fields, the system for the classification of tonalities and the accompanying chart have been taken from George P. Jackson's excellent work, *Spiritual Folk-Songs of Early America*. Both the system of classification and the chart were devised for Jackson by Hilton Rufty. Rufty describes the system as follows:

> In identifying the modal character of the "gapped" tunes I have deemed it advisable to proceed by an entirely arbitrary method, free from any sort of theoretical connotation. Should a missing tone be presupposed to make either a major or minor, perfect or imperfect, interval with the tonic, there arises at once ambiguities of modality. For purposes of harmonic treatment it is quite necessary to decide upon which particular mode a gapped tune suggests, but in studying the purely melodic aspects it is reasonable to accept the tune as an entity, considering it in its actual tonal structure and not with regard to its possible modal permutations. To accomplish this purpose I have evolved a chart, based on methods used by Cecil J. Sharp in his *English Folk-songs from the Southern Appalachians*, which for the great majority of tunes in this collection is an adequate system of classification. The arrangement of the chart is very simple: there are five columns, each beginning with one of the five pentatonic

---

1. Letter from Andrew [Houston], Union Village [Ohio], Oct. 16, 1841, to Isaac N. Youngs, New Lebanon, New York, p. 2.

scales. Immediately below each pentatonic scale are four Hexatonic scales which are formed by the addition of the missing tones, singly and in their variable positions. The system permits these variables to be read in terms of natural and flatted tones. Lastly in each column are three regular heptatonic modes which are the outgrowth of supplying both missing tones simultaneously and in variable combination. The gaps in the pentatonic and hexatonic scales are indicated by slurs and the numerical positions from the tonic of the missing tones. The supplied missing tones are indicated by black notes, and in fitting any given tune to any scale on the chart I have endeavored where possible to let these black notes indicate the weak tones. Since it was possible so far as the *actual tonal structure* of the tunes was concerned, to have a choice in the placing of them, the device of indicating weak tones was a happy solution to a more careful classification. Above each tune in this book I have indicated the modal and, following this and in parentheses, the tonal pattern of the tune with the heptatonic scale as a norm, that is, treating gapped tunes arbitrarily as broken-down Heptatonic tunes. A Roman numeral indicates a major or perfect interval with the tonic; an Arabic numeral a minor interval. In event of augumented or diminished fourths or fifths, I have used conventional signs. A gap is indicated by a dash.[2]

Because the folk practice in notation is rare, if not unique, with this body of literature, the seventy-one songs quoted in this chapter have been transcribed exactly as they were found in the Shaker manuscripts. Many practices, such as the unorthodox Shaker use of repeat marks, the disregard for time values in notes in the beginning and final measures, the lack of a new time signature where a measure suddenly has one beat more or less, all these, which seem baffling at first glance but which are easily comprehended by any trained musician, have been retained, because they give invaluable insight into the folk notation.

---

2. George P. Jackson, *Spiritual Folk-Songs of Early America* (New York, 1937), pp. 15–16. By permission of the family of the late Dr. George Jackson.

Marches

No. 1

FATHER WILLIAM'S 1782
Heptatonic aeolian, mode 2 A + b (I II 3 IV V 6 7)   ♯³ (♩=106)
SM314, p. 9

This is one of the earliest of the Shaker tunes. It was preserved by memory, and later copied in the Shaker manuscript hymnals. Father William Lee, the natural brother of Mother Ann Lee, came from England with the original group of eight Believers and was known for his "strong" voice. He died in 1784, two months before Mother Ann.[3]

No. 2

MARCH. SUNG ABOUT THE YEAR 1790
Hexatonic, mode 2 A (I II 3 IV V − 7) ||³ (♩=106)
SM314, p. 20

---

3. David R. Lamson, *Two Years Experience Among the Shakers* (West Boylston, 1848), p. 4.

Like Father William's March, this one was retained from memory and written down after the Shakers began to notate their songs in the 1815–1820 period. No composer is given and it is possible that this may have been an adapted secular march, since visitors often heard the Shakers sing secular dance tunes in these early years.

Solemn Songs

The earliest reports of Shaker singing mention that they sang in a solemn manner, and for a number of years after 1791 "to stand in their ranks and sing solemn songs without words was often the principle manner of worship."[4] Since these were not dance songs, the rhythm was usually of a very free nature. Solemn songs continued to be written and sung as late as the 1830–1840 period (SM314, pp. 217–19), but the three which are given here were "Sung by Mother Ann while in the body" (before 1784).

No. 3

Heptatonic ionian, mode 1 A+B (I II III IV V VI VII)

$\natural^2$ ($\downarrow$.=64)

SM51, first page [n.p.]

_____
4. Clara Endicott Sears, *Gleanings from Old Shaker Journals* (Boston and New York, 1916), p. 183. By permission of the publisher, Houghton Mifflin Company.

No. 4

Heptatonic aeolian, mode 2A+b (I II 3 IV V 6 7)
$$||^4 \quad (\; \downarrow =128\text{--}168)$$
SM51, first page [n.p.]

No. 5

Heptatonic ionian, mode 3 A+b (I II III IV V VI VII)
$$||^4 \quad (\; \downarrow =128\text{--}168)$$
SM51, first page [n.p.]

No. 6

ANCIENT FUNERAL SONG

Hexatonic, mode 3 A (I II III — V VI VII)   [♩=80]
SM171, pp. 206–7

This is one of the oldest of the many Shaker funeral songs, dating back to 1784, and was composed by Father James [Whittaker] who came from England with Mother Ann Lee. The tunes at this period were wordless, but in later years Shakers sang "Our Brother's (Sister's) gone to his (her) eternal home.—Let us prepare to follow him (her) be righteous & be Holy" to this melody.

No. 7

WORDS OF THE SAVIOUR

Hexatonic, mode 3 b (I II III IV V VI –)   [♩=91]
SM171, p. 174

Come, saith the Sav - iour, come all   ye who have de - ny'd your -

selves   took   up   your   cross   and   fol - low - ed   me.

Come   and I___   will   show   you   the   glo - ries of   my   king - dom;

come   and___   I   will   crown_   you   to_   be ___ heirs of___   them.

Final tribute was paid to many of the Shakers by individual songs to be sung at their funeral. The hymn above was written for the funeral of Abigail Cook, September 29, 1845.

No. 8

THE LAMB'S WAR

Hexatonic, 7th missing, cannot be classified but obviously aeolian
(I II 3 IV V 6 —)   [♩ =128–168]
SM413, first page [n.p.]

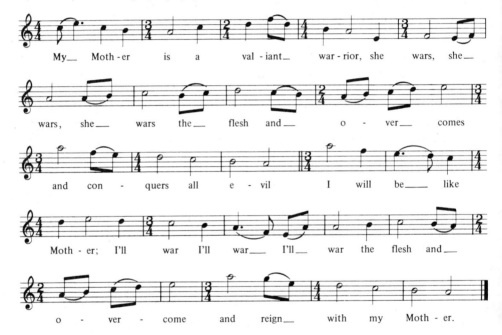

My__ Moth-er is a val - iant__ war-rior, she wars, she__

wars, she__ wars the__ flesh and__ o - ver__ comes

and con - quers all e - vil I will be__ like

Moth - er; I'll war I'll war__ I'll__ war the flesh and__

o - ver - come and reign__ with my Moth - er.

Shakers sang "The Lamb's War" in loving memory of Mother Ann Lee, and accompanied their singing with gestures at the words "she wars" and "I'll war." They stood in a line, or sometimes sat, as they sang, making a violent motion with both hands similar to a man mowing. This anthem, as it was called,[5] was Daniel Wood's, and was one of the earliest to be motioned.[6] This

5. William J. Haskett, *Shakerism Unmasked* (Pittsfield, 1828), p. 187.
6. Isaac N. Youngs, Journal, Papers of Shakers, No. 42, 1815–1823.

MS was found without key signature. When signatures were not available in other early MSS, later copies were found to prove the tonality. None was found for this song but it is quoted here because of historic interest. It may have been sung in Dorian or Ionian mode instead of Aeolian as here presented, or possibly in all three, since a change of mode was not an uncommon practice.

No. 9

THE GOSPEL TRUMPET
Hexatonic, mode 3b (I II III IV V VI —)   [♩=128–168]
Tune: SM412, p. 12   Words: *Millennial Praises,* pp. 107-9

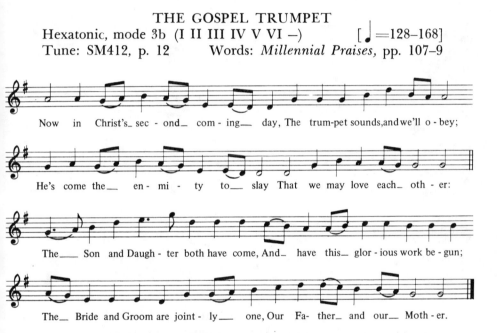

Now in Christ's_ sec - ond_ com - ing_ day, The trum-pet sounds,and we'll o - bey;

He's come the__ en - mi - ty to__ slay That we may love each_ oth - er:

The___ Son and Daugh - ter both have come, And_ have this__ glor - ious work be - gun;

The_ Bride and Groom are joint - ly __ one, Our Fa - ther_ and our__ Moth - er.

The singing of hymns had become a custom by the summer of 1807, and this type of music replaced the wordless songs prevalent in the early years. In the evening, a hymn was sung and the Square Order Shuffle was danced; "Gospel Trumpet" was said to have formed an important part of the worship.[7] No tempo markings were indicated, nor did bar lines appear in these earliest hymn tunes. Most of them were in the style of the solemn songs then prevalent and were probably the "mournful" tunes

7. Anna White and Leila S. Taylor, *Shakerism Its Meaning and Message* (Columbus, 1904), p. 331.

travelers reported hearing the Shakers sing. The absence of bars permitted the necessary flexibility of rhythm in the performance.

No. 10

MOTHER'S CHILDREN

Hexatonic, mode 3b (I II III IV V VI −)   [♩ =128−168]
Tune: SM412, p. 15   Words: *Millennial Praises,* pp. 188−89

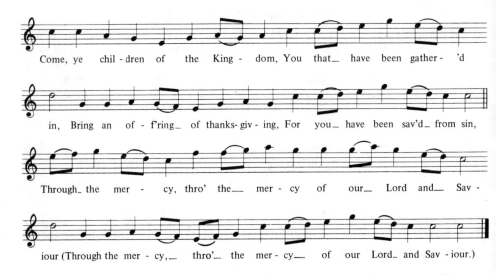

Come, ye chil-dren of the King - dom, You that_ have been gather - 'd

in, Bring an of - f'ring_ of thanks-giv - ing, For you_ have been sav'd_ from sin,

Through_ the mer - cy, thro' the_ mer - cy of our_ Lord and_ Sav -

iour (Through the mer - cy,_ thro'_ the mer - cy_ of our Lord_ and Sav - iour.)

This was the first hymn sent to Ohio from Mt. Lebanon with the notes, in 1815.[8] It had been customary to exchange only the words before that time; the tune either had been a well-known one, or was taught to the Shaker singers by the visitor who sang it from memory.

---

8. Isaac N. Youngs, Journal, 1815–1823; entry: May 9, 1815 (in Library of Congress) .

No. 11
THE EARTHQUAKE

Heptatonic ionian, mode 3 A+b (I II III IV V VI VII)

♮³ (♩. =72)

Tune SM314, p. 228   Words: *Millennial Praises*, pp. 178–79

Lift your heads ye once af-flict-ed! Let your eyes with joy be-hold

What the proph - ets long pre-dict-ed, What the Son of God fore-told.

Now Je-ho-vah fills his tem-ple, Thence his glo - ry shines a-broad;

There his saints with rev - 'rence trem-ble, And con-fess that he is God.

Variants
SM412

3. While his last loud call he utters,
Nature can no more be still;
All creation moves and flutters,
In obedience to his will.
When his power is to be proved,
To convince the stupid soul,
If he says, "O earth, be moved!"
Lo, it rocks from pole to pole!

4. While the judgement is advancing,
   Satan's kingdom to destroy,
   Fields and forests fall to dancing,
   Dwelling houses crack for joy;
   Rivers heave and swell like Jordan,
   Water fowls ascend the air;
   Soon this earth shall loose her burden,
   All creation does declare.

The first Shaker hymns, composed largely in the West in Ohio and Kentucky, chronicled early Shaker history and at the same time served as propaganda for their religious belief.

A series of earthquakes ("14 in number") occurred in Ohio between December 16, 1811, and February 11, 1812, and a Shaker wrote that it "shook fowls from their roosts, and made the old cabbins Crack and lose their pinting &c. it also made the frame of our meeting house as strong as it is, Crack like a bed-stade."[9] The Shaker poet saw in this happening an act of God which he could turn to use to teach a good lesson, and the following year the words of a hymn based upon it appeared in the *Millennial Praises* as a part of the first printed Shaker hymnal.

No. 12

THE LIVING BUILDING

Heptatonic aeolian, mode 2 A+b (I II 3 IV V 6 7) [♩ =128–168]
Tune SM412, p. 14   Words: *Millennial Praises*, pp. 158–59

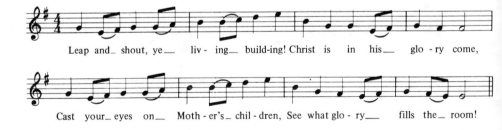

Leap and shout, ye living building! Christ is in his glory come,

Cast your eyes on Mother's children, See what glory fills the room!

---

9. Letter from Daniel [Moseley], Union Village, Warren County, Ohio, Feb. 19, 1812, to Richard Spier, p. 1.

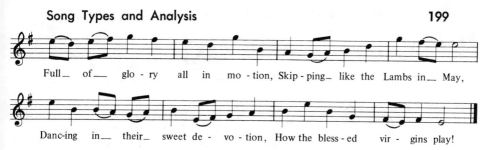

Full_ of_ glo - ry all in mo - tion, Skip - ping_ like the Lambs in_ May,

Danc-ing in_ their_ sweet de - vo - tion, How the bless - ed vir - gins play!

Variants
SM314, p. 227

Although coming from the *Millennial Praises* of the 1807–13 period, the words of this hymn foreshadow the spirit of "Mother's skipping children at play," found so frequently much later in the texts of the fanciful vision songs. The barring is from the SM314, p. 227 version of the tune.

No. 13

TYPICAL DANCING

Heptatonic aeolian, mode 4 a+b (I II 3 IV V 6 7)

$\|^4$ ($\bigsqcup$ =128–168)

Tune SM255 [n.p.]   Words: *Millennial Praises,* pp. 24–26

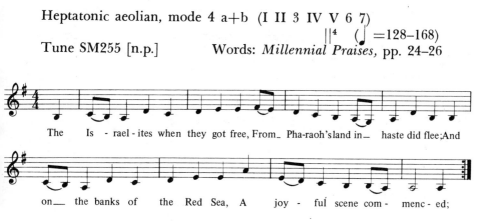

The Is - rael - ites when they got free, From_ Pha-raoh's land in_ haste did flee; And

on_ the banks of the Red Sea, A joy - ful scene com - menc - ed;

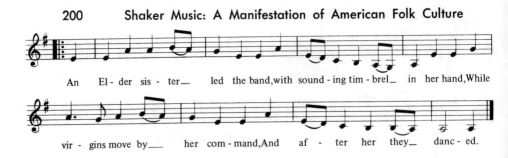

An El-der sis-ter— led the band, with sound-ing tim-brel_ in her hand, While vir-gins move by__ her com-mand, And af-ter her they_ danc-ed.

This poem is found in MSS as early as 1809[10] defending the Shaker ritual dance against a hostile public by quoting a long list of Scriptural references to dancing. The similarity of the cadencing measures at the middle and end of this hymn is typical of most of the tunes accompanying the *Millennial Praises* texts, and likewise of hundreds of non-Shaker religious tunes which were used in early nineteenth-century America.

No. 14

A DIALOGUE BETWEEN JACOB AND ESAU

Heptatonic aeolian, mode 2 A+b (I II 3 IV V 6 7)   [♩•=106]
SM255 [n.p.]   [♩•= 53]

Jacob:
The war is now pro-claim-ed the bat-tle is be-gun I'm bound for full sal-va-tion With world and flesh_ I'm done I'll keep you at a dis-tance to die it is__ your doom I'll nev-er shed a tear for you but

---

10. SM391, pp. 11–12.

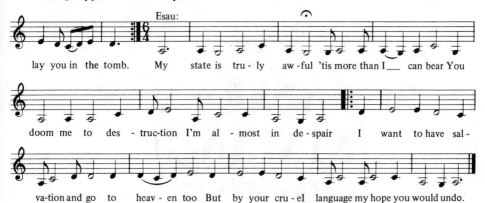

Esau:

lay you in the tomb. My state is tru - ly aw -ful 'tis more than I__ can bear You

doom me to des - truc-tion I'm al - most in de - spair I want to have sal -

va-tion and go to heav - en too But by your cru - el language my hope you would undo.

> Come all who hate Old Esau & Jacob's cause defend,
> See Jacob's faithful struggles on Esau don't depend;
> Poor Esau's weak and feeble, and his armour & his shield,
> Is sure to fall in battle and he will have to yield.

Jacob: Heaven is not intended for such a wretch as you
> There is a place prepared for all old Adam's crew
> I want none of your snuffles your talk will all be vain
> I doom you to destruction with your old brother Cain

Esau: O listen to my story and hear me plead my right
> See what I've suffered with you don't bring me to the light
> I want to be concealed dont bring me to disgrace
> I want to have salvation when I have run my race.
> (7 other quatrains)

Shaker dialogue songs were quite numerous in the 1820–1830 decade, and seem mostly to have come from the Societies around Dayton; Richard McNemar and Isaacher Bates wrote some of them, but this one is not signed. SM397 (1823), contains six such songs, and the second printed hymnal[11] contains five poems written in this manner. The rhythmic pattern in the second half is rare in Shaker music.

11. Philos Harmoniae [Richard McNemar], *A Selection of Hymns and Poems; For the Use of Believers* (Watetvliet [sic], Ohio, 1833) .

Artifacts [courtesy The Western Reserve Historical Society Museum],
Shaker Singing Meeting signs, and homemade pens for lining music
paper.

No. 15

TRUE BELIEVER'S HEAVEN

Hexatonic, mode 3 b (I II III IV V VI −)   [♩=128–160]
SM413, p. 23

O___ my__ El - ders, O my___ El - ders, you look like the

heav - ens, you act like the heav - ens, you___ are the heav - ens!

Where__would be my heav - en, if I was not with you.___

I ___ should have no heav - en, if I could·not see___ you.

"Second time sing Brethren instead of Elders; Third, sing Sisters."

Betsey Bates

Substitution of words in different verses of the early American
revival hymn made the learning process a simple matter for the
untutored frontier worshiper. This hymn is a rare example of
that usage among the Shakers which doubtless stems from revival ancestry. (Compare words of "Hebrew Children"[12] which
substitutes "twelve apostles," "holy martyrs," and so on for "Hebrew children" in successive verses.)

---

12. William Walker, *The Southern Harmony and Musical Companion* (New
York, 1939 [orig. ed., 1835]) , p. 266. By permission of Hastings House, Publishers,
Inc.

Instruction chart in vocal culture. (Broadside mounted on board.)

No. 16

A RUB FOR OLD SLUG

Heptatonic aeolian, mode 2 A+b (I II 3 IV V 6 7)   [♩.=72]
SM144, p. 71

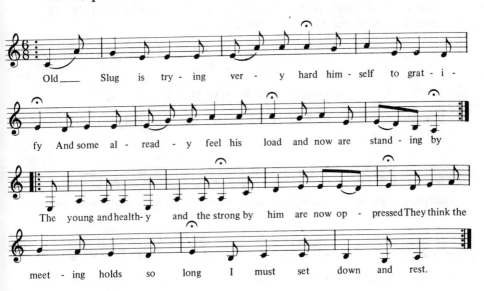

Old___ Slug is try - ing ver - y hard him - self to grat - i -
fy And some al - read - y feel his load and now are stand - ing by
The young and health- y and the strong by him are now op - pressed They think the
meet - ing holds so long I must set down and rest.

I now have marched a Song or two
And that will do for me
I've nothing further now to do
O dear how tired I be
But Father cries ye Stupid Souls
Arise Arise and Shake
Come free Yourselves from Slugs
    control
His bands is [sic] peices break.

With Strength of Soul & body too
Come forward work with zeal
And be not satisfied til you
The power of God do feel
For this is flowing flowing free
And all who are awake
May come with equal liberty
And freely now partake.

There was no place in the Shaker community for the idle, self-centered individual. Richard McNemar's poem "Slug," published in the 1833 hymnal,[13] describes this well-known character as a stupid, lifeless soul,

---

13. Philos Harmoniae [Richard McNemar], *A Selection of Hymns and Poems*, p. 162.

Whose object is to live at ease,
And his own carnal nature please,
Who always has some selfish quirk,
In sleeping, eating, and at work.

The song "from Father Isacher Canterbury 1843" is in the same
vein as McNemar's poem. The holds at the end of each line are
reminiscent of the German chorale tunes.

No. 17

PINCH'D UP, NIP'D UP

Pentatonic, mode 3 (I II III — V VI —)   [♩=128–168]
SM198, p. 93

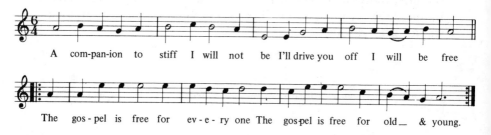

"Old Stiff," like Old Slug, was another Shaker character; Stiff
represented pride, and many songs were inspired by this war on
pride.

No. 18

A COMPANION TO OLD STIFF I WILL NOT BE

Heptatonic aeolian, mode 2 A+b (I II 3 IV V 6 7) [♩.=86–106]
SM234, p. 23

Old stiff you have no bus-iness here 'Tis time that you be gone

I'll give you a dis-mis-sion here So now— be-gone— be-gone.

The manuscript hymnal from which this song was copied is dated 1827–1828. It is common practice in Shaker tunes to omit half a measure (as is done here after the fifth bar), without any change in rhythm signature. Notice the climax on the A in the last measure but one, used nowhere else in the song, and reserved for this purpose. Such climaxes are not a regular feature of most Shaker tunes.

No. 19

GREAT I LITTLE i,

Heptatonic aeolian, mode 2 A+b (I II 3 IV V 6 7) [♩=128–160] SM403, p. 40

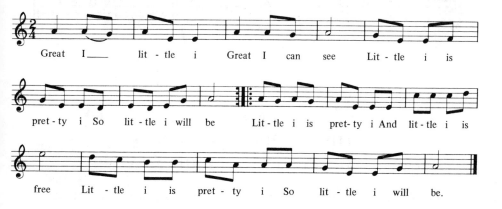

Great I—— lit-tle i Great I can see Lit-tle i is

pret-ty i So lit-tle i will be Lit-tle i is pret-ty i And lit-tle i is

free Lit-tle i is pret-ty i So lit-tle i will be.

There were numerous songs against self-pride, or "Great I." Inherent in the communistic principles of the Shakers was this doctrine which demanded that self be forgotten, and that the individual assume an anonymous role in the social structure through humility.

No. 20

MOTHER

Heptatonic aeolian, mode 2A+b (I II 3 IV V 6 7) [♩=128–168]
Tune, SM314, p. 226   Words: *Millennial Praises,* pp. 78–82

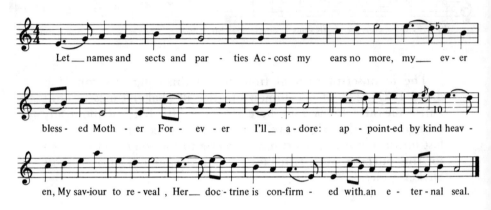

Let __ names and sects and par - ties Ac-cost my   ears no more, my __ ev-er

bless-ed Moth-er For-ev-er   I'll __ a-dore: ap-point-ed by kind heav-

en, My sav-iour to re-veal, Her__ doc-trine is con-firm-   ed with an e-ter-nal seal.

Variants
SM412, p. 9

No. 21

THE PRECIOUS WAY OF GOD

Heptatonic ionian, mode 3 A+b (I II III IV V VI VII)
[♩=128–168]
Tune SM314, p. 227   Words: *Millennial Praises,* pp. 118–21

How __ pre-cious is the__ way__ of__ God, now in the   new cre-a-

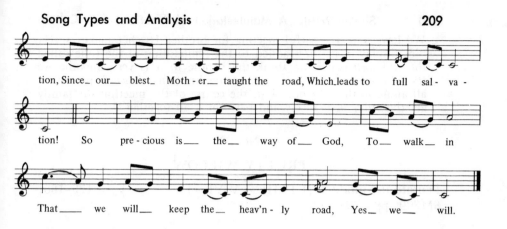

tion, Since_ our_ blest_ Moth-er_ taught the road, Which_leads to full sal-va-

tion! So pre-cious is_ the_ way of_ God, To_ walk_ in

That_____ we will_ keep the_ heav'n-ly road, Yes_ we_ will.

An order was sent to all of the Shaker communities that every Believer in the land should unite at the hour of six o'clock on the evening of February 29, 1835, in singing the two hymns, "Mother" and "The Precious Way of God," in celebration of Mother Ann's birthday.[14]

No. 22

STUBBORN OAK

Heptatonic aeolian, mode 4 a+b (I II 3 IV V 6 7) [$\downarrow$ =128–168] SM413, [n.p.]

I will not be like the stub-born Oak, but I will be like the wil-low

tree; I'll bow & bend un-to God's will, & I will seek his mer-cy_ still.

The stubborn Oak was symbolical of pride and self-interest, while the "limber Willow Tree" represented humility. There were many songs about these two opposed traits symbolized by the Oak and Willow trees. A manuscript journal records in an entry dated Sunday, August 16, 1835:

_____
14. Giles B. Avery, Journal (1834–1836); entry: Sun., Feb. 29, 1835.

We have a very cheerful meeting for brother Issacher makes a very nice display of gestures added to the remoddling of the tune called the stubborn oak & we think the handle to it is very smoothe we try to learn to motion it after seeing him sing dance & motion it all alone to show us how & in the course of the meeting the family get the order of it nicely and perform it all together.[15]

No. 23

PRETTY WILLOW

Pentatonic, mode 3 (I II III – V VI –)   [♩ =128–160]
SM209, pp. 135–36.

Shall I stand like the Oak un - bend - ing When all a - round me in mo - tion is set,

Or shall I be like the sup - pli - ant Wil - low Rath - er than the tall tree stand - ing e - rect.

Ah rath-er would I be like the pret-ty wil - low Bow-ing and bend-ing in Mother's simple way

Reeling in-to free-dom turning from all e - vil Read-y and will-ing each call to o - bey.

This is another motioning song. There is a bit of musical representation in the words "bending" and "willow," where the two slurred notes give the "limber" effect.

---

15. *Ibid.*, entry: Aug. 16, 1835.

ACTION SONGS

No. 24

Heptatonic ionian, mode 3 A+b (I II III IV V VI VII)

$\sharp\sharp^4$ ($\downarrow$ 128–160)

SM111 [n.p.]

Shake shake shake off Leave all death be - hind you, Break break

break off Eve - ry band that binds you La - bor for the gifts of God For

they will make you free free Tra - vel in the nar -row road Of low hu-mil - i - te te.

Shakers were fond of songs in which the words called for action. Party games were popular in rural America until very recently, and their prevalence may have been responsible for a parallel in Shaker song literature where certain words were acted out, producing shaking, bowing, bending, turning, skipping, and many other similar gestures to embellish the ritual.

No. 25

Hexatonic, mode 4 b (I II 3 IV V — 7)   [$\downarrow$ =128–168]
Shaker Letters, North Union, June 16, 1852, p. 4.

I love to see a liv-ing soul, A - live in their de - vo - tion Quickened with the power of God

Free in ev - ery mo - tion I love to see them bow and bend, I

love to see them turn-ing Though mor- ti - fy - ing con - de -scend,With them I'll be u -nit - ing.

No. 26

Pentatonic, mode 3 (I II III — V VI —)   [♩.=125–150]
SM176 [n.p.]

O how I love to skip and play In in - no-cent de - vo - tion, I love I love this

pret - ty way I love to be in mo - tion. *(The latter half is wordless, and was*

sung with "la" or "loo."

No. 27

Hexatonic, mode 3 b (I II III IV V VI —)   [♩.=125–150]
SM184 [n.p.]

Scip, scip like fawns up - on the moun-tain's height Gather-ing love   gather-ing love

gather-ing ho - ly Moth - er's love.

The long skips in measures 1–2, and again in measures 11–12, are unusual in Shaker songs.

No. 28

Hexatonic, mode 3 A (I II III — V VI VII)   [♩ =128–160]
SM198, p. 68

Come life Shak-er life Come life E - ter - nal Shake shake out of me All that is   car - nal

I'll play a nim-ble step   I'll   be a   Dav - id   I'll shew Mi-chael twice how he be-hav - ed.

No. 29

UNION SMOKE SONG

Hexatonic, mode 3 A (I II III — V VI VII)   [♩. =72]
SM198, p. 58

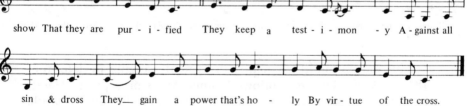

How   love - ly are God's peo - ple who have like gold been tried Their ver- y   coun-te-nan - ces

show That they are   pur - i - fied   They   keep a   test - i - mon   - y A - gainst all

sin & dross   They— gain   a   power that's ho -   ly By vir - tue   of the cross.

"The above verse is from the young Sisters in the second family
N. Lebanon to the young Sisters at S. Union Ky, to be sung the
3rd Sunday in Oct. 1835 in our union smoke."

Although men and women were not allowed to hold conversation except in the presence of other Shaker brethren or sisters,
they did have union meetings at which both sexes sat and talked.
In the period before the use of tobacco was forbidden to all

members under forty years of age (1841), women as well as men smoked pipes at these gatherings[16] and the preceding song increased the general sociability in at least one such smoking meeting.

No. 30

ALL GLEAN WITH CARE

Heptatonic ionian, mode 3 A+b   (I II III IV V VI VII)

SM288, p. 273[17]

$\|^4$ ($\downarrow$=128–168)

SM291, pp. 121–22)

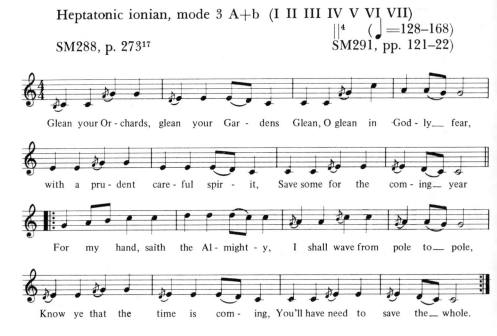

Glean your Or-chards, glean your Gar - dens Glean, O glean in God - ly__ fear,

with a pru - dent care-ful spir - it, Save some for the com - ing__ year

For my hand, saith the Al - might - y, I shall wave from pole to__ pole,

Know ye that the time is com - ing, You'll have need to save the__ whole.

This song is found frequently in hymnals ranging in date from 1835 to 1890. The text follows Mother Ann's precept of "Hands to work, and hearts to God," and her constant admonitions while on earth to be prudent with God's gift that Shakers might have sufficient to offer the poor. Here is the musical mirroring of the Shaker religious economy upon which the Society was founded.

---

16. Thomas Brown, *An Account of the People Called the Shakers* (Troy, 1812), p. 360.
17. Also SM167, p. 56; SM293, p. 152; SM295, p. 81; SM291, pp. 121–22.

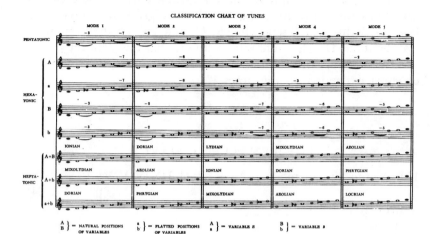

Classification Chart of Tunes. [From Spiritual Folk-Songs of Early America *by George P. Jackson (New York: J. J. Augustin), opposite p. 254.]*

No. 31

A MARCH FOR INSTRUCTION

Tetratonic, cannot be classified (I — III — V VI —)

SM80, [n.p.]

♯ (♩=106)

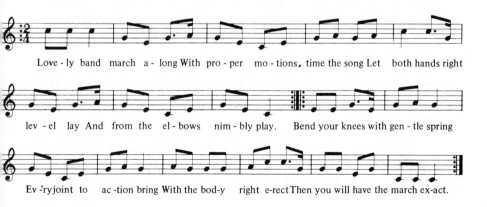

Love - ly band march a - long With pro - per mo - tions, time the song Let both hands right

lev - el lay And from the el - bows nim - bly play. Bend your knees with gen - tle spring

Ev - 'ry joint to ac - tion bring With the bod - y right e - rect Then you will have the march ex - act.

This is a fine example of Shaker utilitarianism. These concise directions for performing the March were given in a text set to four easily learned pitches (C, E, G, and A) , or the pentatonic scale without D. The tune was so simple that the Believer's mind was free to apply this self-instruction as he went, with a minimum of effort expended on the notes.

No. 32

THE PENTECOST MARCH

Heptatonic ionian, mode 1 A+B (I II III IV V VI VII)

♮² (♩ =64)

SM314, p. 217

The names of the customary Shaker dances may be found with a great many qualifying adjectives varying a standard type. These variants are for the most part in name only, and were intended for some special occasion, or to add interest and variety to the private family gathering. In such instances little difference can be detected musically in these offspring of a common type and neither the music nor the dance variant is said to have gained entrance into the public worship ritual, but to have remained private family manners of "laboring." A list of such variants prominent in the 1837–1847 decade was noted as follows: "Winding March, Lively Line, Changeable Dance, Double Square, Mother's Star, Cross and Diamond, Mother's Love, Elder Benjamin's Cross, Finished Cross, Lively Ring, Moving Square, Square and Compass, Celestial March. Many others might be added."[18] These particular titles have not been found preserved in the music of these manuscript hymnals, however.

No. 33

CHECK TUNE

Hexatonic, mode 3 b (I II III IV V VI —)   [♩=128–160]
SM272, p. 48

No. 34

CHECK SONG

Heptatonic ionian, mode 3 A+b (I II III IV V VI VII)
                                                 [♩=128–160]
SM272, p. 49

Here is a rarely encountered example of the tie in Shaker music.

18. Henry Clay Blinn, *Manifestations of Spiritualism among the Shakers* (East Canterbury, New Hampshire, 1899), p. 31.

No. 35

GARRET'S TURNING SONG

Pentachordal, cannot be classified (I II III IV V — —)

$[\text{♩}=128-160]$

SM272, p. 15

No. 36

STATIONARY QUICK DANCE

Hexatonic, mode 2 b (I — 3 IV V 6 7) $[\text{♩}=128-160]$

SM269, p. 19

No. 37

SHUFFLING SONG

Heptatonic ionian, mode 3 A+b (I II III IV V VI VII)

$\sharp^3$ ($\text{♩}=106$)

SM127 [n.p.] (Part III—Shuffling Songs)

I want to shake with   in - dig - na - tion   I want to shake with   earn - est zeal

I want to give my   soul sal - va - tion The   power of God O   let me feel.

Bow - ing & bend - ing in   pret - ty free - dom Turn - ing & twist-ing in the gift of love

Breth - ren & Sis - ters   pure & love - ly,   Let us join the hosts a - bove.

See Cr. W.W. 66.

Shuffling tunes were in duple measure; they were usually notated in a 6–8 scheme, but are found with 2–4 and 6–16 signatures
too. When they were not labeled, even the Shaker musicians
confused them with the Circular or Round Dances. As a letter of
1833 states: "here is a tune . . . which we, in our manner would
have made out a shuffling tune, if he [Haskell] had not wrote
above it, 'Circular Dance.' "[19] Some shuffles had words and some
were wordless. Wordless songs were known among the Shakers
as "noted songs."

No. 38

MOTHER'S WAY IS EASY (SHUFFLING SONG)

Pentatonic, mode 1 (I II — IV V VI —)   ♩² (♪.=128)
SM36, p. 261

Moth - er's way's an   eas - y way, Moth-er's way is   ho - ly Come let us joy - ful -

ly o - bey her ho - ly ho - ly   call - ing.

19. Letter from Hervey L. Eads, South Union, Kentucky, Apr. 22, 1833, to Isaac
N. Youngs, p. 2.

No. 39

SHUFFLING TUNE

Heptatonic aeolian, mode 2 A+b (I II 3 IV V 6 7) [♩.=128]
SM270 [n.p.]

No. 40

ROUND DANCE

Pentatonic, mode 3 (I II III — V VI —) [♩.=144]
SM197, p. 71

O I love I love to be with the in - no - cent__ free O I love I

love to see the sim - ple and the liv - ing liv - ing.

The terms Round Dance and Circular Dance seem to have been employed synonymously. It is easy to see how this dance could be confused with the preceding shuffling tune if it were not labeled.

No. 41

ANGEL'S SHOUT. Letter from Benjamin Dunlavy, Pleasant Hill, Kentucky, April 9, 1852, to Isaac N. Youngs, New Lebanon, New York, p. 8.

Major triad, cannot be classified (I — III — V)

A Shaker wrote from Pleasant Hill, Kentucky, in 1842:

It is not uncommon, when the bell rings for meeting, for the shouting to commence and continue till we assemble ready for singing. This is a mild and beautiful shout received from Mother, called the "Angel's Shout." Below are the sounds. [Copied above]

No. 42

SHOUTING SONG

Heptatonic ionian, mode 3 A+b (I II III IV V VI VII)

[♩=128–168]

SM106, p. 4

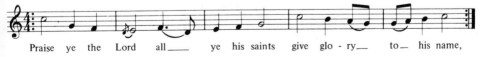

Praise ye the Lord all ____ ye his saints give glo - ry ___ to ___ his name,

Raise your hands shout to— God   Sing prais - es   to   his   name   Shout

Samuel Spooner wrote this song in September, 1837, at the very beginning of the decade of spiritual manifestations which produced so many fantastic happenings among the Shakers. There were other similar songs produced in the late months of this same year, and all have a shout upon a long note at the end of a phrase as a distinguishing feature.

No. 43

MOTHER ANN'S COUNTING SONG

Heptatonic ionian, mode 3 A+b (I II III IV V VI VII)

⫟⁴ (♩ =128–160)

SM3 [n.p.] (middle)

Now— I   will   sing   to   you   one   line,   One—   two, three, four,

five,___ six,   sev - en, eight, nine.   I__ now will   sing   to   you one more

1,   2,   3,   4,   and— now   I   sing   one   more you   see,

1,   2,   3.   When_   all   is   done_   then   you   will

see,   And   think   of   me   your   Moth - er   An - ne   Lee.

Songs whose texts include counting or numbers are frequently encountered in the Shaker hymnals, but the textual significance is usually more rhythmic than instructive. (Compare such counting songs as "Two, four, six, eight, Johnny caught a little snake;" "One little, two little, three little Indians;" "One, two, button my shoe," and other counting game and country songs long common in American life.)

No. 44

VENY VEN FROM EIGHT TO TEN

Heptatonic ionian, mode 3 A+b (I II III IV V VI VII) [♩.=106]
SM69 [n.p.] (middle)

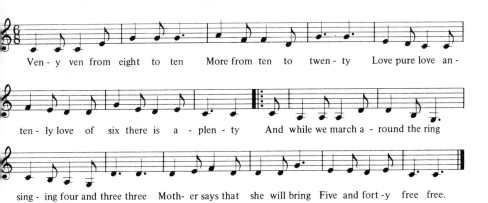

Ven - y ven from eight   to   ten   More from ten   to   twen - ty   Love pure love an -

ten - ly love   of   six there is   a - plen - ty   And while we march a - round the ring

sing - ing four and three three   Moth- er says that   she will bring   Five and fort -y   free   free.

No. 45

COUNTING SONG

Heptatonic lydian, mode 3 A+B (I II III IV V VI VII)

[♩.=106]

SM140, pp. 39–40

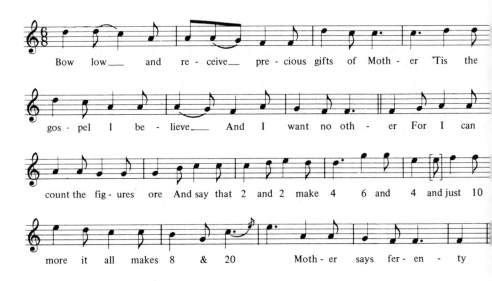

Bow low___ and re - ceive___ pre - cious gifts of Moth - er 'Tis the

gos - pel I be - lieve___ And I want no oth - er For I can

count the fig - ures ore And say that 2 and 2 make 4 6 and 4 and just 10

more it all makes 8 & 20 Moth - er says fer - en - ty

From Lebanon 2nd family 1839.

2	"This is the
2	way the sum
4	is done."
6	
4	
10	
28	

No. 46

A TRUE LESSON WRITTEN UPON A SEAL

Heptatonic ionian, mode 3 A+b (I II III IV V VI VII)

$$\frac{3}{7}$$ (♩.=72)

SM3 [n.p.]

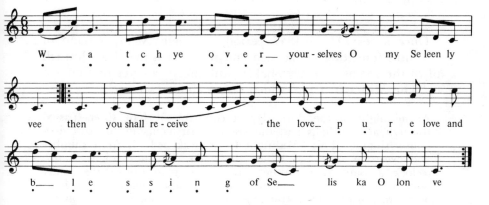

W___ a t c h ye o v e r___ your - selves O my Se leen ly

vee then you shall re - ceive the love__ p u r e love and

b__ l e s s i n g of Se__ lis ka O lon ve

"2nd Order Jan. 8 1841."

Many of the songs given by inspiration spelled out part of the
text; in such instances, a dot was placed under each letter of the
word. This device, like the numbers in the counting songs, probably gave the inspired singer an opportunity to think ahead and
keep a flow of speech to sustain his melodic gift.

No. 47

THE MIDNIGHT CRY

Hexatonic, mode 1 b (I II — IV V VI 7)   ♮² (♩.=64)
SM255, p. 9

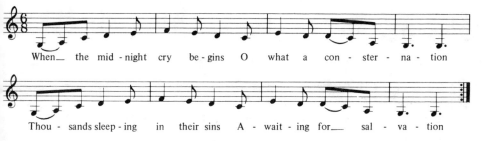

When__ the mid - night cry be - gins O what a con - ster - na - tion

Thou - sands sleep - ing in their sins A - wait - ing for__ sal - va - tion

Once a year (1837–1847 period) for eight years, a band of mediums consisting of six men and six women marched through all of the rooms in every Shaker building in a ceremony known as "The Midnight Cry," which lasted about two weeks.

> At midnight of the third day, a company of four sisters passed through all the halls and the sisters' apartments in the dwelling-house, singing. This "Midnight Cry" awakened all from slumber and everyone arose and joined the ranks. The next night at two o'clock, a company of brothers and sisters again aroused the family who at three A.M. gathered in their chapel and engaged in an hour of active worship. This strange alarm had a wonderful effect on the minds of those thus suddenly aroused.[20]

Words to this hymn which they sang are found in Shaker hymnals as early as 1809 (SM391, pp. 7–9) and until the 1845 period. The same text with a different tune appears in Walker's *The Southern Harmony* (p. 32) of 1835.

No. 48

A KITCHEN VISIT

Hexatonic, mode 3 b (I II III IV V VI –)   ♩ (♩=106)
SM187, p. 18

------

20. White and Taylor, *Shakerism*, pp. 234–35.

and be glad O be sim-ple and be free for ye are_ my pret-ty lit-tle com-pan-
y. And__ now says Moth - er re - ceive ye
yea re - ceive ye my love and bless - ing for my
love and bless - ing shall rest up - on you__ all.

"From Mother Lucy to those that work in the kitchen. By H.G. June 19th 39."

Several Shaker sisters cooked and waited upon the communal tables for a period of one week, and at the end of this time were relieved by other members.[21] "A Kitchen Visit" is typical of a class of song sent to reward a specific group for faithful perseverance in spiritual and physical labors.

No. 49

ENCOURAGEMENT FOR MOTHER'S SWEEPING INSTRUMENTS

Pentatonic, mode 1 (I II — IV V VI —) ||⁴ ($\bullet$=128–168)
SM93, p. 117

Fear not O ye lit - tle ones__ Fear not to do
your Par - ent's__ will Co low se ne__ ven do
Bow down Thy spir - its and be hum - ble and low.

21. Thomas Brown, *An Account of the People Called Shakers* (Troy, 1812), p. 360.

"Given by Father James December 20th 1841."

Like the preceding song, this "gift" is for the chosen group. Shakers are reported to have been embarrassed by some of the fantastic rites they were called upon to perform, and this notice from the spiritual world is evidently intended to reassure the sweepers, who went through the motions of sweeping out sin, of the propriety of the Parental revelation.

The Gift of Tongues

Many of the songs in this category were purported to have come from spirits in foreign lands, and to have been given in a great variety of languages.

No. 50

CHINESE

Pentachordal, cannot be classified (I II III IV V − −) [♩=106]
SM140, pp. 251–52

The inscription with this song says that it was "learned from a Chinee 1842." It is pentachordal and has an interesting phrase structure in which the normal four-measure phrase is cut short one beat each time. Five-rhythms are not uncommon in Shaker tunes, but any regular grouping in sevens is rare.

No. 51

AN AFRICAN SONG

Pentatonic, mode 3 (I II III — V VI –)   [♩.=86–106]
SM148, pp. 38–39

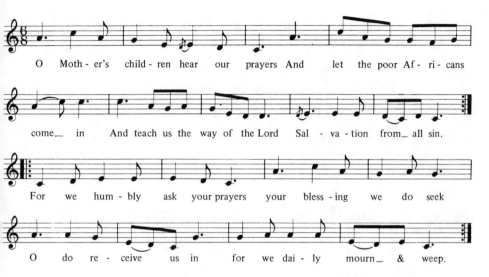

O Moth - er's child - ren hear our prayers And let the poor Af - ri - cans

come_ in And teach us the way of the Lord Sal - va - tion from_ all sin.

For we hum - bly ask your prayers your bless - ing we do seek

O do re - ceive us in for we dai - ly mourn_ & weep.

"The foregoing Song was sung by some Africans from Sucatoo
in Africa Decem 21, 1842. Given at Silan."

This song is given in English, but the visionist heard it sung
by Africans as the inscription above reveals, and interpreted it.

No. 52

MADAGASCAR SONG

Heptatonic ionian, mode 3 A+b (I II III IV V VI VII) [♩=80]
SM389

Ma go za on a moo-de O with hear to full of bu-be O Be - cause I know dat Mas-sa O will

bles- se O poor me me O

A combination of "tongues" and English, which lapses into American Negro dialects.

No. 53

LEN-A-VA RU RA VA

Heptatonic mixolydian, mode 1 A+b (I II III IV V VI 7)

[♩ =80]

SM198, p. 92

Len   a   va   ru   ra   va   se - e-ack   a   dack   a   ne   U - ron

don - a - von   sa - ra   ack - a - ne - na   I   O   ock - a - see   Let - a - ve

let - a - ve   U - ro   rock - a - see   Sa   ra   ack   a   ne   na

No interpretation accompanies this rhythmic song in "tongues." It was given at the central bishopric in New Lebanon in 1839.

No. 54

INDIAN SONG

Hexatonic, mode 3 A (I II III — V VI VII)   ♮⁶   (♩. =125–150)
SM32 [n.p.]

Te   he   te haw   te   hoot-it-y hoot   Me   be Moth-er's   good-y   pa-poose Me

ti - ny   one dant   te   id-idy um   Cause   me   to whit-y's   here   can come

Hi - de - di - de   ti - did-le   O   Round & round   &   round   me   go   Me

leap   me jump   me   up   & down   On   good whit - y   shin - y ground.

A letter of 1843 says that "the native spirits have been increasing their number amongst us for two months past. Some of the Turks, French, and Irish are frequently here, and sometimes 3 or 4 different nations and tribes at a time." Four hundred Indians joined the Shakers in the spirit world at this same period[22] and sent many songs to the "mediums" in the 1837–1847 decade. It is a typical early jig-tune in spite of its supposed origins.

No. 55

VUM VI, VIVI VIVE

Hexatonic, mode 3 b (I II III IV V VI —)   ♯³   (♩ =106)
SM38, pp. 182–83

---

22. Letter from Lovely Vineyard to the Ministry, Feb. 9, 1843, p. 1.

Vum vi, vi - vi vi - ve   vi - ve vi - ve vum vi   vi - ve vi - ve vum vi   O

vum vi   vi - ve vi - ve   vi - ve vi - ve vi - ve   vum vi   vi - ve vi - ve   vum vi O

The manuscript hymnal from which this song is taken claims that it was "Sung by Mother Ann while on earth at Petersham," which would date it as of 1781.[23] The words are similar to others attributed to Mother Ann and her natural brother William Lee while on earth.

No. 56

THE VOICE OF GOD

Heptatonic ionian, mode 3 A+b (I II III IV V VI VII)

SM138, pp. 195–96

(♩ = 106 and 80)

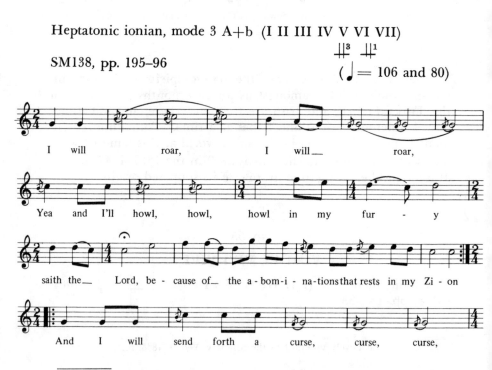

I   will   roar,   I   will __   roar,

Yea   and   I'll   howl,   howl,   howl   in   my   fur - y

saith the __   Lord, be - cause of __ the a - bom - i - na-tions that rests in my Zi - on

And   I   will   send   forth   a   curse,   curse,   curse,

23. Clara Endicott Sears, *Gleanings from Old Shaker Journals* (Boston and New York, 1916), p. 40. By permission of the publisher, Houghton Mifflin Company.

yea, I will send forth a   heav-y   curse, up - on the in-hab-i-tants that dwell in her.

"Sept. 1841. Given at the first order C.H.H."

The 23rd of September was designated by revelation in 1843 to be set aside for cleansing the Shaker outbuildings and yards. Once a year for a period of ten years, the families arose at four o'clock, assembled in the meeting house, and sang the song entitled "Voice of God." This was a day of fasting when no meat was eaten, and supper consisted of bread and water. A band of singers chosen from the brethren and led by the Elders passed in solemn procession through every room of the Shaker workshops and outbuildings, repeatedly singing this same song. At the words "curse, curse, curse," the Elders stamped their feet with indignation, and the procession stopped, that all might shake at any spot where they believed "any filthiness" had been committed. In the afternoon the procession marched through the fields, singing the same song and repeating the same ceremonies.

A band of sisters led by the Eldresses went through the sisters' workshops, nurse rooms, and laundry with the same ceremonies and singing the same song in the forenoon. In the afternoon the procession passed through the yards and around the buildings and continued singing it. All singers "roared" or "howled" at the mention of those words. Those who did not sing spent the day cleaning and repairing Shaker property.[24]

Mountain Meeting Songs

In 1842 an order came by divine inspiration to establish a holy mount on a hilltop near each Shaker community. A clearing was made and in the center of a grassy plot was constructed a hexagonal enclosure with a low fence which constituted a spiritual "fountain." Dressed in spiritual garments which were visible only to the mediums or elders and eldresses, the Shakers marched to this mountain twice yearly to enjoy imaginary feasts of fruits and fine foods, to drink wine, to receive individual rewards, and to bathe in the imaginary fountain. Singing, dancing, and prophetic visions accompanied these fantastic rites, and the three songs below were among those used in this sacred ceremony.[25]

---

24. David R. Lamson, *Two Years Experience Among the Shakers* pp. 105–6.
25. *Ibid.*, pp. 56ff.

No. 57

O SEE THE LOVELY SAINTS OF GOD

Heptatonic ionian, mode 3 A+b (I II III IV V VI VII) [♩ =106]
SM99 [n.p.]

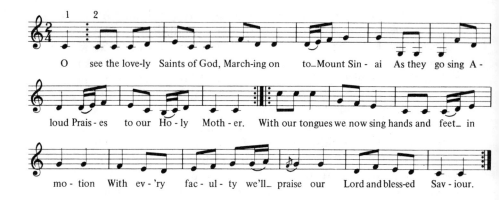

O   see the love-ly Saints of God, March-ing on   to—Mount Sin - ai As they go sing A -

loud Prais - es   to our Ho - ly Moth - er. With our tongues we now sing hands and feet— in

mo - tion With ev - 'ry   fac - ul - ty we'll— praise our   Lord and bless-ed Sav - iour.

The inscription with this song reads: "This Song will be sung
by the holy Angels, as we march up to the holy Mountain.
Learned April 24th, 1842 1st Order."

No. 58

HOLY FOUNTAIN

Hexatonic, mode 3 b (I II III IV V VI −)
(♩ =128–160)   ♯♯♯♯⁴ (♩ =128–160, and ♩. =64)
SM99 [n.p.]

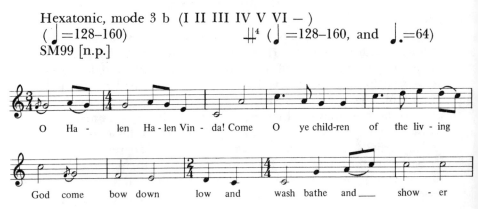

O   Ha -   len Ha - len Vin - da! Come   O   ye child-ren   of   the liv - ing

God   come   bow down   low and   wash bathe and — show - er

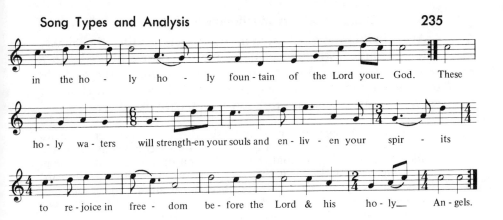

in the ho - ly ho - ly foun-tain of the Lord your_ God. These
ho-ly wa-ters will strength-en your souls and en-liv-en your spir - its
to re-joice in free - dom be-fore the Lord & his ho-ly_ An-gels.

Shaker brethren on one side, and sisters on the other, approached the sacred fountain as the order was given out to bathe in its holy waters. They proferred towels and sponges to each other and went through the gestures of aiding in scrubbing one another.

No. 59

SONG OF THE PROPHET JEREMIAH

Heptatonic ionian, mode 3 A+b (I II III IV V VI VII)

SM99 [n.p.]

Be - hold! Up-on this ho - ly_ Mount The Lord has placed a liv - ing_
fount Where crys-tal wa-ters nev-er_ dry Al - tho' up - on the moun-tain high.
Come vir-gin_ souls your Pitch-ers_ fill In_ faith go_ forth these wa-ters_ spill But
let each one mark well_ the_ lot, They sprink-le on, yea ev - 'ry spot.

After bathing symbolically in the waters of life, the Shaker elder announced to the assembly that a measure of seed and a vessel of water was to be found beside the fountain; the seed was to be sown and the water was to be carried on the left shoulder while making the gestures of sowing. A participant wrote:

> So we pass through the motion of shouldering our water, take up our measure of seed, and form ourselves into a column at the north side of the meeting ground, facing the South; and in concert begin to swing our hands, as in the act of sowing. We all move forward and sow as we march across the meeting ground, and beyond till we come to a fence, when we wheel about, take the water from our shoulder, and water the ground as we march back.[26]

The inscription with the song states that it was "Learned of the Prophet Jeremiah's little Angel called Core an Seal, April 23rd 1842. To be sung at the fountain on the day of the Passover just before going forth to water the land."

Shepherdess Songs

No. 60

MOTHER ANN'S PLUMB CAKE

Hexatonic, mode 3 b (I II III IV V VI —)   ♯³   (♩=106)
SM133, pp. 9–10

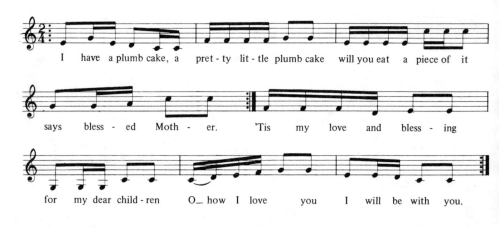

I have a plumb cake, a pret-ty lit-tle plumb cake will you eat a piece of it

says bless-ed Moth-er.   'Tis my love and bless-ing

for my dear child-ren O— how I love you I will be with you.

---

26. *Ibid.*, p. 64.

In 1843 and 1844, Mother Ann sent many songs to individuals through the spirit known as the Shepherdess. The Shepherdess had been a keeper of sheep while on earth, and represented herself as having the same occupation in the spirit land.[27] Elder Ebenezer Bishop received the song from her at New Lebanon, October 9, 1843, and it is a notice from the spirit world in the form of a "reward"; imaginary, to be sure, to us today, but very real to a sincere Shaker of the 1843 manifestation era.

No. 61

SINCERE PRAYER

Hexatonic, mode 3 b (I II III IV V VI –) ||[4]   ($\downarrow$ =128–168)
SM133, pp. 37–38

O— Lord my— God I— pray to— thee In— trib - u - la - tion— strength-en— me And when threat-ning— dan - gers— round me— roll O— Lord O Lord do help my— soul For— while I trav - el— here be - low These— rag - ing winds will ev - er— blow, but O my God thou— art my— friend and do my lit - tle— bark de - fend.

The Shepherdess remembered Stephen Baker with a song, too, at the Holy Mount, New Lebanon, November 13, 1843. It is

---

27. Blinn, *Manifestations of Spiritualism*, pp. 45–46.

almost altogether 5-4 measure, and unlike the fanciful one which
precedes it, is in the form of a prayer.

Songs For Individuals

Songs were given to good Shakers as a special notice from the
spirit world, through the inspired "mediums." Pointing out individuals for such marks of favor is in sharp contrast to the usual
Shaker policy of anonymity in all things, which removed even
the composer's name from most of the hymns.

No. 62

MARY ANN BATES

Hexatonic, mode 3 b (I II III IV V VI —)   (♩=128–160)
SM262, p. 38

Pure gos-pel love, pure gos-pel love is what I will have and
love-ly sim-pli-ci-ty is what I will la-bor for Ob-tain it I will, Obtain it I will Yes I will have— it and make it my own.

No. 63

ANNA SLATERS

Hexatonic, mode 3 A (I II III — V VI VII)   (♩=128–168)
SM262, p. 76

I have plac-ed in— your fore-head A bright star I've seal-ed you for— mine,

And I'll give to— you a robe— to— wear, Of—— my pure love di - vine.

No. 64

NANCY WELLS

Heptatonic aeolian, mode 4 a+b (I II 3 IV V 6 7)

SM262, pp. 41–42

Watch— ye watch— ye and be read - y to meet— me, for—

low! I will come at noon - day. Fear— not fear— ye

not For with my hand I will lead you on And—

safe - ly I'll guide your lit - tle Bark be-yond this vale of sor - rows.

Extra Songs

A Shaker hymnal of 1848[28] states that the Shakers had "not far
from one thousand little anthem like songs" which were usually
called Extra songs because they were sung mostly to fill in the
interval "between exercises & speaking" and that while some had
been learned and sung, not all of them were performed. The tunes
have no characteristic meter or tonality, and the texts cover a

---

28. New Lebanon, New York, "Inspirational Writings," Songs & Anthems given
in Mother's Manifestation, Jan. 30, 1848 [n.p.]

widely diverse subject matter. Notice the skip of a minor seventh (measures 2–3) in the first song, which is most unusual in Shaker melodies.

No. 65

THE FIG TREE

Hexatonic, mode 4 A (I II — IV V VI 7)   ‖   [♩=128–168]
SM107, pp. 43–44

O Come! O come, come a - way, Where the Fig Tree for - ev - er is bear - ing, Where the flocks and the herds are so pleas-ant and gay, And the des - ert a sweet smile is wear - ing. And the wild-er-ness re-stor-ed to her glo - ry, The tongue of the dumb sweet-ly sing - ing, O— grave! O grave! Where is thy vic - to - ry O— Death! Where— is thy— sting.

"From South Union 1840."

No. 66

WEAPONS KEEN

Pentatonic, mode 3 (I II III — V VI —)
$♮^3$ (♩.=72 and $\sharp^4$ ♩= 128–160)
SM70, p. 133

O hap - py, hap - py I do feel I love the way of

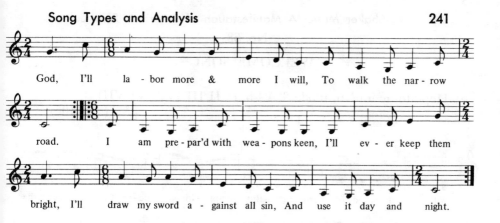

God, I'll la - bor more & more I will, To walk the nar - row

road. I am pre - par'd with wea - pons keen, I'll ev - er keep them

bright, I'll draw my sword a - gainst all sin, And use it day and night.

"Sung here [New Lebanon] by Willard Johnson, 1849."

No. 67

ANNA MATTHEWSON'S FAREWELL

Hexatonic, mode 3 b (I II III IV V VI —)   [♩=91]
SM171, p. 186

I ____ leave my ____ bless - ing for you all My ____ peace my com-fort-ing

love; My ____ Moth - er calls & I ____ must go, fare - well,

fare - well, Heav - en is my hap - py home. Fare - well.

This is another funeral song, "Learned in a dream Ap. 5th '51," and sung at Anna Matthewson's funeral. Records show that she died January 9, 1852, so this song was not composed or given by inspiration at her death as were many others.

No. 68

WELCOME SONG[29]

Heptatonic ionian, mode 3 A+b (I II III IV V VI VII)

$\sharp^3$ (♩ =106)

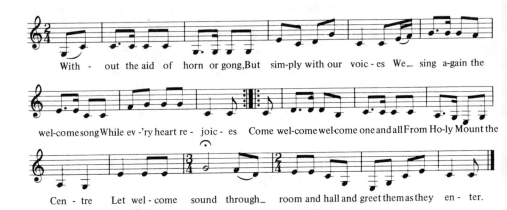

With - out the aid of horn or gong, But sim-ply with our voic - es We— sing a-gain the

wel-come song While ev -'ry heart re - joic - es Come wel-come wel-come one and all From Ho-ly Mount the

Cen - tre Let wel - come sound through— room and hall and greet them as they en - ter.

The letter accompanying this song explains the use to which it was put in greeting visitors:

> This will inform you that our good friends arrived here this after-
> noon about 5½ P.M.—all in good health and spirits—According as
> you wrote B. Henry Blynn that we must not sound our horns or
> Gongs or ring the bells on their arrival we done just as you directed.
> But several of our singers happened to be in the office hall when
> they arrived about four and twenty in number and sung the following
> words.

No. 69

A FAREWELL SONG

Hexatonic, mode 3 b (I II III IV V VI —)
SM197, p. 105

$\frac{6}{4}$ (♩. = 53)
(♩ =106)

Fare - well fare - well where ev- er you go where ev - er you dwell Moth - er will be

---

29. Letter from David Parker, Shaker Village, New Hampshire, September 20, 1854 to Giles B. Avery, New Lebanon, New York, p. 1.

Similar to the songs of welcome, which Shaker singers performed for arriving visitors from other communities, were the songs used to bid them farewell. Note the effective use of the descending third on the word "Farewell."

No. 70

ACROSTIC

Hexatonic, mode 1 A (I II III IV V VI —) $\natural^5$ ($\dot{\downarrow}.$=106)
SM381, p. 121

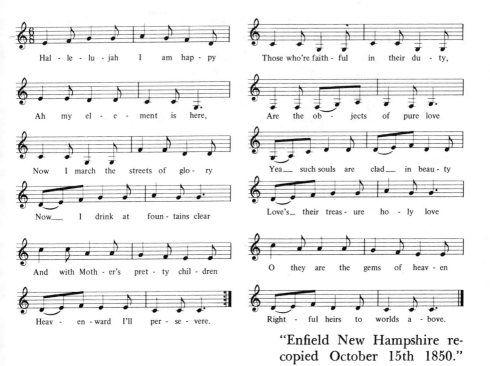

"Enfield New Hampshire recopied October 15th 1850."

This rare type of Shaker song constitutes a special notice to an individual, and is in the form of an acrostic upon the name of Hannah Taylor. Dating back to Greek and Latin classical literature, the acrostic must be considered as conscious literary composition and with few, if any, parallels in American folk music. Notice that it is dated 1850, after the great emotional decade of 1837–1847, when the literature was beginning to lose its distinct Shaker flavor and turn toward part singing and the many other outside influences which beset it during this and following decades.

No. 71

LIFE, LIFE, ETERNAL LIFE

Hexatonic, mode 4 b (I II 3 IV V — 7)   [♩=91]
SM94 [n.p.]

Life, life e - ter -nal life,   Is a heaven born treas- ure   Live live the spir - it cries

live to God for - ev - er.   Death and dark-ness flee a - way   Guilt & con- dem -

na - tion   There's no room for   you to stay   In the new_ cre - a - tion.

8

Conclusions

Practically all characteristics of Shaker music had a parallel in the non-Shaker musical life of America. The first tunes used by the original Shakers who had come from England were from the British Isles, and were largely secular in nature between 1784 and 1807. English secular tunes, likewise, had crept into the music of most of the other American religious sects shortly after 1770. The Shakers often adapted both words and music from these other sects until the 1820 period, a fact that accounts for the close-knit relationship of Shaker music to the general hymnology of rural America in the first four decades of its existence.

The Great Revival of the first years following 1800 which swept the American frontier regions gave birth to a new kind of religion which preached salvation for the common man and which shook itself free from the more sophisticated doctrines and rituals it had inherited from Europe and the urban communities of our own Eastern seaboard. The common man wanted no intermediary of elaborate ritual, pageantry, soloist, or choir to intercede for his soul, but made his approach simply and directly to a personal God in language and music which he himself used and understood. The very principles upon which Shakerism was founded made the Shaker part and parcel of this simple, rural life, and the revival atmosphere, which set the tenor of Shaker dogma and music, also set up the same general ideals for belief and simple musical expression among Schismatics, Baptist Merry Dancers, New Lights, and all of the other similar groups of folk in rural America at the time. Shaker converts came largely from these groups, and the music often served either Shaker or non-Shaker by a change in text that allowed for the Shaker belief in the evils of the flesh and a dual Godhead.

The folk of rural America all sang innumerable religious tunes from memory until a period roughly around 1840. Booklets of religious words made the rounds of revival groups in all of the frontier denominations during these early years, making it difficult or even impossible to give credit to any one sect for originating any definite hymn. The tunes were subjected to the constant variation which takes place in the literatures of all folk groups until standardization set in with the printing of many of the tunes near the middle of the nineteenth century. Early Shaker manuscript hymnals likewise contained only words, and the notation of tune became common in manuscript only after the 1830 period, with the first printed tunes in 1852.

The psychic phenomena of the Great Revival were common to most frontier religions, and recurred sporadically throughout the nineteenth century with other American religious groups, at first with Merry Dancers, New Lights, and Schismatics who had the "jerks" and fell cold and lifeless and prophesied or spoke in tongues, and later by Mormons, Spiritualists, Ranters, Holy-Rollers, and many other smaller groups under different guises. The distinctive achievement of the Shakers in this phase of their development derives from their ability to overcome these uncontrolled physical movements, at first by substituting such actions as handshaking and dancing for the "jerks" which they later incorporated into a regular voluntary worship ritual. Furthermore the "gift of tongues," known also to other groups, had an accompanying tune which frequently was received at the same time as the jargon by the Shakers.

The shaped notes and singing schools gave the non-Shaker folk singer a new means of retaining the body of song literature which had become too vast for his memory. Parallel to both of these aids came the Shaker notation and the Shaker singing meetings, which served the same purpose among Believers as in "the world" of non-Shakers. Both had sought a simple means that would replace the difficult notation of learned music and would give the untutored singer of these folk tunes his pitches by association with various shaped notes or letters.

The singing school and the body of song, chiefly religious in nature, which it fostered, gave the people of nineteenth-century rural America their only cultural outlet and means of self-expression, and the meetings served as social functions for a rural populace which had little else to entertain it. In the Shaker community music was the only realm in which fancy had any play or through which self-expression could venture forth under guise of divine inspiration and not be curbed unduly by watchful Elders who were eager to replace all individual action by conformity to the strict rules of the group or community.

What appears at first to be a rather highly developed and unusual system of theory for a folk group is, as Youngs and Haskell both admitted, largely based upon other American tune books in use in rural singing schools of the time, and is for the most part, only information concerning symbols of notation to aid in sight singing and notating music, since Shakers long had no printed hymnals containing hymns setting forth their special religious teachings. These needs for instruction in sight singing and for hymns teaching religious doctrine were both satisfied in the case of the other sects by the printed long-ways tune books on the market, but these printed tune books would have been of little use to the Shakers in teaching their peculiar doctrines of dual Godhead and celibacy.

Folk ways are stronger than the man-made theories which were presented in the introductory pages of the early American tune books, and with both Shaker and non-Shaker the real folk practice was rarely touched upon in the theoretical writings, except in the case of the most fundamental matters. Tonalities presented were not adequate to cover modal, pentatonic, and the other various gapped scales. Much of the rhythm in performance was so free that many tunes were long left unbarred. It was not uncommon for an earlier tune to be sung in different modes by different singers before printed notation finally tended to standardize tonality. Passing tones, a sliding up or down to anticipate the approaching pitch in a large skip, and variations of both a melodic and rhythmic nature, were part of the folk singer's individual manner of performing any tune that kept the whole literature in a state of constant change. This was true in Shaker music and that of other contemporary American religious or folk groups, and is true of all bodies of folk literature at all times. Multiple versions of a tune in the Shaker manuscript hymnals show that these points all existed in Shaker music and varied greatly with date and the community in which the tune was sung and copied. The tardiness of printed hymnals in the Shaker sect (1852) maintained folk practice longer for the Shakers than it did for other sects whose music had been standardized more quickly by printed tunes which perpetuated one version in practically all hymnals. The fact that Shaker songs were for so many years monophonic also kept them in their original modal state longer than those of some other folk groups, which in some cases are known to have been changed from Dorian to Aeolian, and further to harmonic minor, to permit the necessary sharped leading-tone in harmonization. However, for the few hundred songs harmonized and printed by the Shakers, there were many other hundreds which were never printed or harmonized, and which retained many of the earlier characteristics until after the Civil War period.

The special flavor of Shaker music results from its utilitarian aspects. Organically, it did not maintain an especial independence from the general American spiritual folk song, having most of the same characteristics of tonality and rhythm, and other distinguishing features found in the songs of the many religious groups in rural America in the same period. The special uses to which the Shaker sect put this music, however, make it a distinctive and unique body of folk literature, which served an original and fantastic ritual. Most of these tunes were closely allied to the dance, as folk music traditionally had been since remotest times, and in practically all places where it existed. It served the Shaker ritual by teaching the strange Shaker dogma that Mother Ann Lee was the Bride of Christ, and that the flesh was the root of all evil; it accompanied the Shaker welcome, the farewell, the funeral, cleansing and sowing ceremonies in shop and field; in it were couched special messages from the spirit world and the granting of special rewards to individuals; it produced a psychological state among its frenzied dancers which transformed the community into a humble and awed group, willing to follow the strong-willed Elders without question; its strains roused sleeping Shakers at midnight and struck terror to the hearts of those who harbored secret sin; it attracted hundreds of non-Shakers to a sabbath worship which was spoken of as one of the greatest shows in America by people who came to be entertained but not infrequently were converted.

The music was closely woven into the texture of Shaker living and is with difficulty divorced from it. So long as the Shaker communal scheme of existence remained an entity to itself, haughtily denying its members contact with the outside world, the music was of this functional nature and maintained its vitality. The coming of harmony, printed hymnals, musical instruments, professional singing teachers, and constant contact with a non-Shaker business world, necessitated by the changing social conditions in rural America after the Civil War period, changed

Shaker music into a colorless, methodic sort of expression similar to the average rural Sunday-school music of any American community and stilled the real Shaker voice that had sung lustily for a century.

Collation of the Manuscript Hymnals

Of the many collections of Shaker manuscript hymnals consulted in the preparation of this book, the largest is located at The Western Reserve Historical Society, 10825 East Boulevard, Cleveland 6, Ohio, and is a part of the extensive collection of Shaker manuscripts including church records, diaries, journals, letters, account books, recipes, drawings, maps, and so on, assembled by Dr. Wallace H. Cathcart over a period of many years, as the Shaker communities closed and such data became available.

Of these manuscript hymnals, there are 430 volumes numbered consecutively from 1 to 430 with SM classification, three folders of loose-leaf music listed under SM Miscellaneous, Container 19, Folders 2, 3 and 4, and seven volumes numbered SM500 to 506 of Shaker music theory. All SM numbers are from this collection of The Western Reserve Historical Society. Recent work done at the library of the society will also provide classification according to community and date.

Other collections which were consulted, and which are collated alphabetically under the various libraries or localities, have the call number of these collections when they are catalogued.

The hymnals range from 6 to 321/2 centimeters in height, with corresponding diversity in length and number of pages. A few volumes are ordinary copy books or school notebooks and ledgers, but the majority of the hymnals were bound in leather by such skilled artisans as Henry DeWitt, Isaac Youngs, and Giles B. Avery, and constitute superb examples of the bookbinder's art. The unadorned appearance of the books is explained by the Millennial Laws, which stated that "Believers are allowed to make plain bound books, for writing hymns, Anthems, &c. or for journals, records &c. &c.—. But superfluously marbled books, or paper, are not allowed to be used, or made among Believers."[1]

---

1. Millennial Laws (MSS Volumes of Covenants Constitutions, Millennial Laws and Ordinances for Communities NT, 1826–1888 undated, Container 2, Volume 6), Sec. XI, pp. 1, 55.

Copyists appear to have been chosen for their fine penmanship as well as for their knowledge of music. Except in a few rare cases, the pages are neatly and beautifully written. Titles are often embellished with decorative pen work, and SM 257 and SM268 have the original pencil sketching for the florid pen work, which shows that in some cases it was done lightly in pencil and later traced in ink. The handwriting and styles of notation (see chapter 3) differed widely over the century and a quarter of the history of the Shaker sect. Books begun at a specified date were often continued by several different hands and not finished until some decades later. Still other books were copied throughout by a single hand and were definitely dated on each flyleaf, showing that they were copied in a few weeks.

The earliest hymnals contained only the words. After the 1825 period when music also began to be noted in these manuscripts, the notes usually appeared at the beginning and the verses were written below. Throughout the 1825–1835 decade the words appear indiscriminately above or below the tune, or with or without the notes. About 1835, when the standard small-letteral notation had gained a firm foothold in most of the communities, the words began to appear directly above the notes to which they were to be sung, a practice which continued down to the last manuscript hymnals.

The free exchange of music between communities, and the anonymity of many of the copyists, add to the confusion of dating the hymnals or locating them by community. Many manuscript hymnals were the result of the combined efforts of several Shakers; some were passed on to friends at the death of the copyist and had been a temporal possession of the individual in spite of Shaker communistic principles which forbade most private ownership; some hymns were copied into books by visiting Shakers from other communinties as tokens of friendly esteem; some tunes were written down from memory years after the period of their creation and given with the remembered date of their first appearance; some follow a definite date chronology, some do not; a few contain songs grouped under such headings as shuffles, extra songs, quick tunes, and anthems, but most hymnals follow no plan at all and the order of the tunes seems to depend upon the caprice of the copyist: some songs were "tuned" in one community and the words came from another Shaker colony; a hymnal like SM28 [n.p.] (near end) states that a song is "From Watervliet I suppose," showing the vagueness of the copyist concerning the origin of these tunes and verses. The picture is a confused one, and while many of the manuscripts have such identification as "Shir." (Shirley) written on the flyleaf in pencil, sometimes hymnals and other Shaker papers were moved from one community to another as a society was forced to abandon its activities and send its remaining members to live in more prosperous Shaker groups.

Part of the hymnals have title pages with data concerning community, date, copyist, and contents; more often this information is lacking, and the words or tune begin immediately. To identify such books, the first words to appear have been used, and constitute either the first title or first line. Dates are given when they exist; otherwise the range of the dated hymns is given in brackets as being significant information but not necessarily relevant as far as the date of the copying of the individual hymnal is concerned. If there are unnumbered pages preceding and following those with numbers, that information is given in brackets as follows: [3] 198 [5]. For convenience in locating the manuscript, the height is given in centimeters. The type or types of notation most prevalent are given in code when it is possible. The abbreviations used are as follows:

[f.t.]—first title, when there is no given title for the whole book
[f.l.]—first line in the book, when it does not constitute a title
n.d.—no date
n.p.—no pagination
SL—small-letteral notation
RN—round-note notation
CL—capital-letteral notation
PN—patent-note notation
NN—numeral notation

The Western Reserve Historical Society, Cleveland, Ohio

SM1   Believer's Choice [f.t.], n.d.[1836–71 range of dated hymns], n.p.[175 hymns with confused numbering], 17¾ cm., SL.

SM2   Hollisters Hymn Book Written in the Fall of *1852*. [At end: "Finished December 12th 1852."], [10]217[1]pp. [172 and 177 omitted in the numbering], 17¾ cm., SL.

SM3   Extra Songs Short Anthems &c—G.B.A[very]., 1839–50, n.p. 17 cm., SL.

SM4   We will sustain the Structure [f.l.], n.d.[several songs

dated 1876], n.p.[about half of book blank], 17¼ cm.,
Belonged to Lorenzo D. Prouty, Shirley, SL.

SM5   Zion of God [f.t.], n.d.[hymns dated 1845–49 period; religious writings dated 1904–05], 17¾ cm. Hymns; no music.

SM6   Give me the treasure that cannot be sold[f.l.], n.d.[hymns dated 1876–87], [1]181[153]pp.[many empty pp. near end], 17½ cm. Flyleaf: "Frances Demsey, Harvard," SL.

SM7   3rd Book of psalms . . . Commenced November 1851. [Back flyleaf: "Finis March 13th 1853"], [10]278 pp. [145, 231 repeated; 235 skipped], 18 cm., SL.

SM8   Down in the lovely vac no ve [f.l.], n.d.[hymns dated 1874–82], n.p.[blank pp. at beginning and end], 18¼ cm., SL.

SM9   The Harmony of Angels, Wisdom's Valley, Dec. 30, 1844, 11[3]pp., 12½ cm., [D. Austin Buckingham,] One- two- and three-voiced writing; colored 5-line SL.

SM10   A Colection of Hymns and Spiritual Songs. Improved in our general Worship . . . September 1824, [6]86[2]pp. [p. 71 skipped], 19 cm., RN.

SM11   Hymns and Poems by Eunice Wyeth Copied by Eunice Bathrick in 1865. [8]179[9]pp., 20½ cm., SL.

SM12   Good Faith [f.t.], [10]170[4]pp.[and many blank pp. at end], n.d.[hymns dated 1840–52], 19¾ cm., 5-line SL; SL.

SM13   A Collection of Class and Extra Songs in General use In our Sacred Worship. Begun to be written 1848 By Orren N Haskins. [Last hymns dated 1851], [12]332 pp.[54–55 cut out], 16½ cm., SL.

SM14   A Collection of songs given Mostly By Inspiration. Begun to be written May 28th 1843. Rhoda Blake. [Last dated hymn: October 5th, 1845], [8]208 pp., 16¾ cm., SL.

SM15   Come Sweet Conviction [f.t.], n.d.[first hymn dated 1869; last one 1871], [2]96[4]pp., 16½ cm. Flyleaf: "Chancy Dibble", SL.

SM16   A Collection of Hymns and Extra Songs. Written in New Lebanon. By Sarah Bates. Begun in Novr—1850 [Hymns dated as late as 1869], [2]172[8]pp.[many blank pp. at end; table of contents, 5 pp. in back; 152, 153 repeated; 170 omitted], 16½ cm., SL.

SM17   Hymn Book with Music, n.d.[dated from 1837; many given in the period of Spirit Manifestations], [8]161[1] pp.[71–76 missing; cut out], 17 cm., SL with and without lines.

SM18   Consecration Give me thy heart [f.t.], n.d.[Last hymn: "Finished this Book, Sabbath, July 4th 1869"], [6]194 [12]pp., 17½ cm. Flyleaf: "Thomas Hammond, Shaker Society Harvard Mass."], SL.

SM19   The Lovely Band [f.t.], n.d.[only dated songs in 1843–47], n.p.[more than last half blank pages], 13¼ cm. PN; SL; 2-line staff; 1-line staff.

SM20   A Beautiful Home [f.t.], n.d.[p.289; "Finished Oct 27th 1843"], [24]289[2]pp.[confusion and duplication after p.209], 13 cm., SL.

SM21   Brigt Joys [f.t.], n.d.[At end: "Finished in the Year 1859"], [18]208[4]pp., 13 cm., SL.

SM22   Voice from Heaven [f.t.], n.d.[hymns dated from 1841–54], [10]105[4]pp.[and many blank pp.], 13½ cm., SL; 2-voice, 1-line letteral.

SM23   A Mother's Hand [f.t.], n.d.[hymns dated 1841–54], [10] 66[13]pp. [and many blank pp.], 13¾ cm., SL.

SM24   Verse book No. 3rd Gifts of the Spirit for Spiritual exercises. Commenced to be written here sometime in 1847. [22]260[8]pp. [142 omitted in series but not missing; 148 repeated; 246, 244 confused], 13½ cm. John Lockwood's book, SL.

SM25   Anthems Collected and Transcribed By & for Benjamin Lyon commenced Jany 1840. [12]179 pp. [and many blank pp. at end], 13½ cm. Music for 6 songs only, near the end, SL.

SM26   I am coming I'm coming saith Jehova [f.l.], n.d.[hymns dated 1843–48 period], [18]309[1]pp.[62, 108 omitted but not missing], 13 cm., SL.

SM27   A Collection of Anthems Given mostly by Inspiration; As rewards and encouragement, for Mother's true children; also for worship. Transcribed by Rhoda Blake. n.d. [hymns dated between 1841–48; "In the year of our Lord 1848 I finished this book. R. W. B."], [14]308pp. [279–298 cut out], 13 cm., SL; 2-voice song, 1-line.

SM28   A Choice Selection of Songs Of the best Quality written by Henry DeWitt New Lebanon Beginning Jany 1852. [2]111[165]pp. [two sections of blank pp. in the middle], 13 cm., SL.

SM29   A Collection of Songs of Various Kinds, Used for Singing, Extra Tunes in Meeting. Written by Henry DeWitt. Beginning September – 1849 Mount Lebanon. [Latest date 1854], [4]281[11]pp.[80, 81, 146 repeated; 189 omitted; 2 pp. without numbers between 209–210], 12¾ cm., SL.

SM30   I see the prize the lovely prize [f.l.], n.d. [first song 1851; at end: "Finis Oct. 26, 1856 N. Lebanon N. Y."], 21 [240]pp.[11, repeated], 12½ cm., SL.

SM31   Travel on, travel on, O every good believer come [f.l.], n.d. [date range of hymns 1854–70] [2]221[69]pp. [blank pp. near end and informative index, classified; 2, 205 omitted but not missing], 12½ cm., SL.

SM32   O Mother help me help me to overcome [f.l.], n.d., n.p., 12¾ cm. Leather case with broken lock, SL.

SM33   In the cross I've placed my faith[f.l.], n.d.[3 dated hymns range 1835–39], n.p., 10½ cm. Flyleaf: "Presented to Louisa M. Crocker By Eliza Avery," SL.

SM34   Ann Eliza Scriven's Song Book: New Lebanon, Columbia Co. 1855. A Present from Ann Buckingham, Watervliet, November 1855. [1854–72 period], n.p., 10½ cm., SL.

SM35   Sacred Poems. Written by D. A. Buckingham. [Cover title: Hymn Book of Sacred Poems], n.d. [hymns 1840–52 period], [5]439[7]pp. [197 omitted], 8¼ cm., SL; 1-line; 5-line; without lines.

SM36   A Choice selection of Hymns Anthems And Spiritual Songs. Adapted to the Use of belivers writen by Moses. W. Thayer of Union Village Ohio 1st Order Aprile, 3, 1852. [At end: "Finish'd May 23, 1852"; inside cover: "Sanford Russell's Book Written here the 30th of October 1852"], [2]282pp.[2 extra pp. between 15–16], 10¼ cm., SL.

SM37   A Choice Selection of Sacred Hymns Sung by Believers in Christ's Second Appearing By Laura Dole Groveland 1860. [14]382[10]pp.[101, 161, 176–177, 278–279 omitted], 17½ cm., SL.

SM38   Holy & Divine Songs Given for the Encouragement of Mothers Children on Earth. Transcribed by Hannah Blake. August 17th 1842. [Last date 1845], [10]189 pp., 17 cm., SL.

SM39   Freedom and Simplicity [f.t.], n.d.[hymns dated 1841–45], [18]95[149]pp., 17 cm., SL.

SM40   Anthems of Joy And Songs of thanksgiving Received from the bountiful Stores of Heaven. . . . Selected and Transcribed by Nancy Dow. September 7th 1842. [Dates extend to 1847], [14]218 pp., 17 cm., SL.

SM41 Musical Band [f.t.], n.d.[5]242[1]pp., 16½ cm. Hymns; no music.

SM42 Millenial Praises; Being a collection of Gospel Hymns Improved in Sacred Worship . . . written by Garret K. Lawrence, 1829. [10]246[2]pp.[160 by Lawrence], 16½ cm. Hymns; no music.

SM43 Celestial Hope [f.t.], n.d.[dates range 1840–52], 248 pp. [2 pp. inserted between 99-100 and 113–14; 122 omitted; p. inserted between 144–45; 155 omitted; 156–59 repeated; 163–64 confused; 198, 202 omitted; 205–10 torn out; 222, 229, 232 omitted; 242–44 missing], 17 cm., SL.

SM44 A Collection of Spiritual Songs . . . Rhoda Blake, 1847–50, [8]129[80]pp.[121 omitted], 16¾ cm., SL.

SM45 Scratch Book No. 2. [cover title], n.d. [hymns 1839–41], 23[85]pp., 16¾ cm., SL.

SM46 A Collection of Anthems & divine Songs. Given from Heaven To the children of Zion . . . Selected & Transcribed by Louise Sears January 1st 1844. [Hymns as late as 1852], [6]176 pp., 16¾ cm., SL.

SM47 A Collection of Precious Treasures and Heavenly Presents Given by Divine Inspiration at the Church, first Order New Lebanon Since Dec. 7th 1838. Collected and Transcribed [cut out], [6]237[13]pp. 17 cm. Hymns, poems, spiritual writings; no music.

SM48 A Welcome for the Canterbury Ministry [f.t.], n.d. [hymns range 1840–65], n.p., 16¼ cm., SL.

SM49 Love Divine [f.t.], n.d.[Flyleaf: "This collection of Shaker hymns thought to be written 1825–40."] Enfield, Conn., [6]130[8] pp. [125–128 missing], 16¼ cm., [Flyleaf; "Marion Marshall Shaker Station Connecticutt Age 105"]. Hymns; no music.

SM50 Crown of Life Eternal [f.t.], n.d.[dated hymns range 1840–42], [8]228 pp. [12 occurs three times; 2 pp. inserted between 55–56], 16 cm., SL and 1-line SL.

SM51 Tunes not Originating in this Society, Copied in the year 1857. [Date on back cover 1866], n.p., 16 cm., SL.

SM52 For Eldress Ruth Landon [f.t.], 1843, [10]55[9]pp.[132 songs], 16¼ cm., SL.

SM53 Hymns Chh. Mount Lebanon, N. Y. No. 2. 1864. [p. 127: "77 Hymns in this Book 1864 April 10th Sab."],

[6]127[1]pp., 16¼ cm. Hymns; no music.

SM54   The Gospel is lovely, the gospel is pure [f.l.], [Flyleaf:
        "Songs composed and copied about the year 1840. Writer
        of this book unknown."], 92[1]pp.[53–56 missing; p.
        inserted between 91–92], 15½ cm. One tune only; SL.

SM55   Anthems Being a Collection of nearly all, given since
        the beginning, with the Tunes Affixed. Collected, and
        Transcribed By Giles B. Avery. n.d.[dates of anthems
        range 1812–69], [10]147[9] [and many blank pp. at end],
        14 cm., SL 5-line and 1-line.

SM56   A Collection of Anthems Improved in our General Wor-
        ship: Written & pricked for the purpose of retaining
        them, by Henry DeWitt. Beginning Feb 8th 1840 New
        Lebanon Co Couy St. N. Y. [At end: "Finis Feb. 1845"],
        [14]303[4]pp.[193, 290 repeated; 291 omitted], 15 cm.,
        SL.

SM57   Anthems Ancient & Modern Improved in General Wor-
        ship Writen 1856. [18]164[9]pp.[and many blank pp.
        at end; 55 omitted; 59, 60 repeated; a stray p. 92 inserted
        between pp. 90–91; 125 repeated], 13¾ cm., SL.

SM58   A Collection of Anthems and Spiritual Songs: Improved
        in our general Worship. Arranged in order, as they came
        forward. From June, 1811. [8]69[1]pp.[blank pp. at end],
        13½ cm. Words; no music.

SM59   Anthems Given by Inspiration to the Children of Zion
        Collected & Transcribed by Giles B. Avery, n.d. [Flyleaf:
        "May have been begun in 1841. Certainly not earlier."]
        [Anthems dated 1841–43], [12]223[9]pp., 13½ cm., SL.

SM60   . . . hath called me, so lay up a store when time is no
        more. [part of broken f.l.], n.d.[dates range 1848–52],
        n.p., 18 cm., SL.

SM61   In Songs of Adoration Praise and Supplication, we write
        our voices in the Song that shall have no end; Selah!
        . . . Hannah Blake. April 1850. [1849–53 date range],
        [28]372[4]pp.[42, 43 repeated; 2 pp. inserted between
        73–74], 12¾ cm., SL.

SM62   Anthems, and Songs of Praise and Thanksgiving. Given
        for the use of the Holy Church of God . . . Selected and
        Written by Phebe Smith, Mar, 1843. [Date extends 1843–
        47], [10]247 pp. [blank pp. at end; 45–48 repeated; 139–
        152 missing; 188 repeated; 191 omitted; 223–226 torn
        out], 13 cm., SL.

SM63 I have adorned thee Jerusalem [f.l.], n.d.[dates of hymns range 1854–62], [4]241[48]pp.[2 pp. inserted between 169–170], 12¾ cm., SL.

SM64 Mothers Babes [f.t.], n.d.[range 1842–54], [22]35[75]pp.; many blank pp. at end and some in the middle, 12½ cm., SL.

SM65 The Tree of Life [f.t.], n.d., n.p., 14½ cm., SL.

SM66 A Collection of Spiritual Anthems, Given by Inspiration; As Rewards & encouragements For Mother's faithful children . . . Written by Eliza Avery and Rhoda Blake Jan. 11th 1840. [1838–43 period], [8]272pp., 14 cm., SL.

SM67 Heavenly and Divine Songs. Received from the fountain of Everlasting Goodness . . . Selected & Transcribed By Augusta Lannuier. January 10th 1841. [extends to 1846], [16]222[55]pp.[161 repeated], 12¾ cm., SL.

SM68 A collection of Verses anthems & tunes &c &c of almost any description. Written by Giles B. Avery. n.d.[range 1835–38], n.p., 11½ cm., SL

SM69 With triumphant songs of gladness[f.l.], n.d.[1839–1845 range], n.p., 11 cm., 5-line SL; 1-line SL; SL.

SM70 A Collection of Spiritual Songs: Commonly called Extra Songs; improved in our Sacred Worship. Written by Isaac N. Youngs. 1845 and onward. [last date 1860], [22]322[10]pp.[124–125 omitted], 10½ cm., SL.

SM71 A Vancenevone of Comfort [f.t.], n.d.[dates range 1839–49], [4]170[61]pp.[79–82, 105–122, 135–136 missing], 20 cm., SL.

SM72 A collection of Hymns and Anthems mostly received by inspiration and suitable for Millennial worship. n.d. [1857–65 date range], [4]50[103]pp.[many blank pp. at end; 14 repeated], 20½ cm., SL.

SM73 William, Charles, Brackett's Anthem Book. Watervliet Dec. 10th 1839. (Flyleaf), [1839–42 date range], [8]164-[4]pp., 20 cm., PN; 5-line SL; SL.

SM74 City of Light [f.t.], n.d.[hymns range 1873–86], 188[4]-pp.[2 pp. inserted between 26–27; 31–38, 79–86, 93–94, 121–140, 143–144, 159–172, 178–180 missing], 20 cm., SL.

SM75 Beams of Glory [f.t.], n.d.[only dates on hymns 1848–71], [16] 46[62]pp. and many blank pp., 19¾ cm., Grey cover, SL.

SM76   Beams of Glory, n.d.[hymns range 1848–71], [16]45[39]-pp. and many blank pp. at end, 19¾ cm., Brownish cover, SL.

SM77   A Selection of some of the Sweet Songs of Zion, where-with we praise ‘the God of our Salvation . . . 1851. [8]279[3]pp., 19¾ cm., SL.

SM78   Heavenly Joys[f.t.], 1823, [4]101[6]pp.[blank pp. at end; 2 pp. inserted between 5–6; 71–74 missing.] 19¾ cm., Flyleaf: "Nancy Orsment's Book 1823." Hymns; no music.

SM79   Beatuty full Gods habitation [f.l.], Flyleaf, "This collection between 1860 & 68 Mostly Mt. Lebanon," [1]239-[2]pp.[52–55 cut out]. 19¾ cm., SL.

SM80   Safe Hiding Place [f.t.], n.d.[hymns dated 1861–62], [16]-27[75]pp.[many blank pp. at end], 19½ cm. Flyleaf, "Hymns written by Joanna Randall," SL

SM81   Ye who've forsaken home & friends [f.l.], n.d.[hymns range 1858–61], n.p. 19cm., SL.

SM82   Our Days on Earth [f.t.], n.d.[Flyleaf, "various periods 1835 to 1860"], n.p., 18¼ cm. SL.

SM83   A Choice Collection of Sacred Holy & Divine Songs. Improved by the Believers in Christ's Second Appearing . . . Transcribed by Gabriel Thompson ‘March '52 A.D. Groveland, N.Y. [12]163[94]pp.[blank pp. at end,; 13 and 101 omitted], 17¾ cm., SL.

SM84   A Small Hymn Book Written by Eleanor Bottom. In 1828 Aged 16 years, [4]72pp., 17¾ cm. Hymns; no music.

SM85   Anthems & Hymns used in Ohio & Kentucky. Perhaps the earliest, n.d., n.p., 17¾ cm. Hymns; no music.

SM86   Invatation To Souls [f.t.], n.d.[range of hymns 1858–70], [18] 32[2]pp.[more blank pp.; three series of paginations] 19[3]pp., 17½ cm., SL.

SM87   Slow March [f.t.], 1870[1867–73 period], [28]70pp.[many blank pp. at end; 8 pp. of music in the middle], 17½ cm., [2 loose mimeographed song-sheets in back of book], SL.

SM88   Pour forth the testimony [f.l.], n.d.[hymns 1889–1909]., n.p. 17 cm., SL.

SM89   The Savior's Universal Prayer [f.t.], n.d.[1845–52 period], [14]259[1]pp.[195 repeated; 214 omitted], 17½ cm., SL.

SM90   Anthems of Joy and Thanksgiving Praise and Adoration

... Compiled by Emily S. Williamson June 11th 1846. [Cover title: Anthems Vol. II], [8]147pp.[38 omitted], Bound with "A Collection of Short Songs. Compiled by Emily P. Wilkinson June 11th 1846" [8]145pp.[12 and 33 omitted; 128 repeated], 17½ cm., SL.

SM91   ... heavenly hosts and wait a little [partial f.l.], 1853, [hymns range 1839–42], [8]159[1]pp.[blank pp. at end; 47 and 114 repeated], Flyleaf: "Andrew Fortier Mar. 1853," 16¾ cm., SL.

SM92   A March [f.t.]["Hymns" on title cover], n.d.[1839–46 period], [4]105[42][pp. cut out; blank pp. at end; 21 omitted; 95 numbered 96; duplicate pp. 103–5 follow 112], 16¾ cm., SL.

SM93   Reflections on Mother Anns Birthday [f.t.], n.d.[hymns 1840–46], [14]183[10]pp.[many blank pp. at end], 17 cm., SL.

SM94   Round Manner; Hymns: cover-title [f.t.], n.d.[range 1866–70], n.p., 16½cm. Flyleaf, "Chancy Dibble," SL.

SM95   A Hymn Book S.B.[part of title-page cut out], n.d., [6]148[8]pp. [p. 90 omitted; pp.130, 135–6 repeated], Flyleaf, F.S. Wicker, 17 cm., Hymns; no music.

SM96   Zion the City of God [f.t.], n.d., [10]190[2]pp., 16¾ cm. Flyleaf, "Ann Maria Graves," SL.

SM97   I'll take my gospel sword in hand [f.l.], n.d.[1834–37 period], [32]151[3]pp. [62–63 repeated], 16¾ cm. SL.

SM98   Anthems Transcribed by Sarah Simons January 1841, [2]191[2]pp. [27–28 missing; 51–58 missing; 117 skipped], 16¼ cm., SL; 5-line SL.

SM99   Like the nightengale in spring to my Mother I will sing.[f.l.], n.d.[hymns 1841–44 period], n.p. 16 cm., SL.

SM100 Isaacher Bates' Book 1835, n.p., 15¼ cm. Front cover loose, SL.

SM101 A Book of Anthems & Spiritual Songs: Written by Lucina Risley. First Order, Union Village November 20th 1847, [hymns to 1834; letters at end 1875], [2]119-[24]pp.[blank pp.], 15¾ cm., SL.

SM102 Music Book Variety. D. A. Buckingham, 1873, [16]110 pp., 14½ cm., RN; two-three- and four-part RN; PN; NN; SL.

SM103 The parting hour O has it come [f.l.], n.d.[mostly 1853], [2]47[89]pp.[many blank pp. at end], 12¾ cm., SL.

SM104   The Saviour's Voice [f.t.], n.d.[1843–63 period], [16]111-
         [20]pp. [many blank pp. at end; 100–109 unnumbered],
         13 cm., SL.

SM105   Anthems, of Praise and Thanksgiving, Given for the use,
         of the Holy Church of God. Selected, and Written, by,
         Phebe Smith Dec.^{br} 1839. [1839–42 period], [16]208pp.
         [pp.24, 84 repeated; 2 small pp. bound between 156–7;
         unnumbered p. between 196–7; 202 omitted]. 13¼ cm.,
         SL.

SM106   O love it is a heavenly treasure[f.l.], n.d.[1837–40 period],
         [12]88pp.[many blank pp. at end]. 11 cm., SL.

SM107   Praises to the Lord [f.t.], 1854[mostly 1852–59 period],
         [12]70[223]pp.[23–26 missing; 66 skipped], 11½ cm.,
         SL.

SM108   The New Years Gift 1821 [f.t.], n.d.[1821?], [4]161pp.-
         [14–15 repeated; p. between 30–31 not numbered; p. 37
         repeated; 2 sealed pp. between 83–84; 101 omitted; 158–
         159 omitted], 12¼ cm., SL; 1-line SL.

SM109   A Book of Hymns and Spiritual Songs; Adapted to the
         present faith of Believers in Christ's Second Appearance.
         Begun to be Written Octr 8th 1821, [2]102[10]pp., A
         loose leaf hymn at p. 40, 20¼ cm. Words; no music.

SM110   Very old Collection copied hymns Enfield Brother
         [cover title], n.d., n.p., 20½ cm. Hymns; no music.

SM111   O Mother I am thankful I'm thankful I was called [f.l.],
         n.d.[hymns 1840–50 period], [8]23[131]pp., 19½ cm.
         Paper in several colors, by sections, SL; 5-line SL.

SM112   The Invincible Band [f.t.], 1856, [22]103pp.[blank pp. at
         end], 19 cm., p. before p. 1: "This book belongs to J. W.
         Copley and was given by him On the 9th day of March
         1856." SL.

SM113.   Mercy Stout Her Book; South Union [July] 30, 1843,
         [16]95[59]pp., 19 cm., SL; 5-line SL.

SM114   A Collection of Hymns and Spiritual Songs, Improved in
         our general Worship. New Lebanon November 16 1828
         Giles B. Avery [cover title, "Hymn book No. 1 G. B.
         Avery"], [10]135 pp., 19 cm., SL; 1-line SL.

SM115   Arise Ye slumbring and awake [f.l.], n.d.[hymns range
         1865–71], n.p., 19 cm. Flyleaf, "Willie Bennett Columbia
         Co New York", SL.

SM116   Gospel Blessings [f.t.], n.d.[2]43[43]pp.[blank pp. at end;

21–26 missing], 18¾ cm., pp. cut out 3 different places. Hymns; no music.

SM117 Love Union and Peace [f.t.], n.d.[hymns near end dated 1836–37], [2]215[8]pp.[p.215 repeated], 19 cm. Flyleaf "Written by D. A. B[uckingham] Chh. Watervliet," PN; SL; 5-line SL.

SM118 Hymn 1st For the New Year 1833 [f.t.], n.d.[nearly all hymns dated 1835; last one 1841], 86[2]pp. [49–50 missing; 55–56 missing], 18½ cm. Hymns; no music.

SM119 O strenthen me my God I pray [f.l.], n.d.[hymns dated 1867–70], [6]127[19]pp.[13–14 omitted; 44 omitted; 46 repeated; 60 repeated; 62 omitted; 71–74 omitted], 18 cm., SL.

SM120 In the rough rugged path of progression [f.l.], n.d.[most hymns dated 1860–62; older ones at end], [6]222pp.[107–108 missing], 18 cm., SL.

SM121 Praise the Lord Sing praises Unto his name [f.l.], n.d. [hymns dated 1868–70, [10]11[101]pp., 19 cm., SL.

SM122 Awake my Soul [f.t.], n.d., n.p., 17¾ cm. Cover-title, "MSS Hymns and Poems. Awake my Soul. . . ." Four poems; no music.

SM123 A present from Timothy Randlett To Mathew van Deuson April 25th 1852, n.p., 18 cm., Cover title, "MSS. Shaker Hymns—Fervant Desire . . ." SL; 4-part SL.

SM124 Ensign of Freedom [f.t.], n.d.[hymns dated 1845–47], n.p., 17¾ cm., Cover-title, "MSS. Book of Shaker Hymns. . . ." SL; 1-line SL.

SM125 A Funeral Hymn [f.t.], n.d., 14pp.[pp. 1 and 2 missing], 17¾ cm. The only dated hymn is 1833. Hymns; no music.

SM126 The Morning Dawn [f.t.], n.d.[hymns dated 1877–78], n.p., 17¼ cm., SL.

SM127 I'm thankful for my Zion home [f.l.], n.d.[range 1835–76], [12]141[204]pp. [45–60, 65–68 missing; 2 pp. inserted between 87–88; 113–114, 131–140 missing], 17¾ cm., Title page, "Bro. Samuel S. Butler Hymn Book"; on back, "Grnd" [Groveland], SL.

SM128 Written by Eldress Antoinette For the Social Gathering, 1866 [f.t.], n.d., n.p., 17¾ cm. Religious writings and hymns; no music.

SM129 Fear God [f.t.], 1854, [6]112[6]pp.[confusion of pagination first few pp]., 17¾ cm. Hymns; no music.

SM130   Rock of Ages [f.t.], n.d.[6]92pp.[many blank pp. at end; 2 pp. inserted between pp. 25–26; pp. 49–70 cut out; many numbered pp. blank], 17½ cm., SL.

SM131   In the role of humility [f.l.], n.d.[hymns range 1855–61], n.p., 17½ cm. Many pp. cut out near back and in middle. SL.

SM132   A Collection of Spiritual Hymns From Various Authors . . . n.d.[dates near end 1862–67], [12]183[14]pp., [7–8 missing; 18–26 missing; 95–100 missing (cut out) ; p. inserted between 141–142; 2 pp. inserted between 162–163], 17¼ cm., SL.

SM133   Many of the following Songs were received in spirit from the Shepherdess, Who was sent by Mother Ann. in 1843 and 4. The rest, extra songs of Praise . . . [Philemon Stewart], 1846[range of dates 1843–47], [14]229[1]pp. [121 repeated, 177 omitted], 17¼ cm., SL.

SM134   Tributes of Respect [f.t.], 1830, [12]233[3]pp., 17½ cm. Flyleaf, "Elizabeth Lovegrove's Psalm or Hymn Book A.D. 1830," SL.

SM135   Bright spirits have come from their loved homes [f.l.], 1864 [hymns range from 1864–73], [12]61[142]pp.[p. inserted between 42–43], 16½ cm. Flyleaf, "Andrew Fortier 1864." SL.

SM136   "A Collection of the Songs of Zion Penned by Eliza R. Avery." 1842 [hymns extend to 1848], [14]27[153]pp., 17 cm., SL.

SM137   Blessings of the Righteous [f.t.], 1864 [4]60[44]pp., 17 cm. SL; SL in 2 and 4 parts: RN.

SM138   Voice of Father [f.t.], n.d.[hymns 1839–42 period], [10]228[4]pp. [first 6 pp. repeated], 17 cm., SL.

SM139   Gospel Beauty [f.t.], n.d.[paper pasted on fly leaf: "Hyms used in the Church from 1830 to 1860 & after], [10]248[6]pp., 17 cm. Finis 1837, at end. 5-line SL.

SM140   O how I love my faithful children [f.l.], n.d.[hymns range 1838–42 period], [2]259[14]pp.[59 repeated; 2 pp. inserted between 70–71; ditto between 98–99], 16½ cm., NN; PN.

SM141   Jehovah's Promise to his People [f.t.], n.d.[1840 period?], Pt. I [10]39[5][many blank]pp; Pt. II [4]112[4]pp., 17½ cm., SL; 5-line SL.

SM142   The Call of Mother [f.t.], n.d.[hymns dated 1838–41] [13]414[4]pp., [256–265; 278–279; 345–354 omitted] 16 cm., SL.

SM143   A Funeral Hymn [f.t.], n.d.[Cover says: "Believed to commenced 1811"], [8]119[5]pp.[74 omitted; 83 omitted], 18¾ cm. No music; hymns only.

SM144   Anchors of Safety [f.t.], 1840[last hymn dated 1873], [4] 275[1]pp. [2 pp. added between 55–57; 89–90 omitted; 140 confused], 17 cm. Flyleaf, "Book of Augustus Blase For Hymns and Anthems," SL; 5-line SL; 1-line SL.

SM145   First Founders [f.t.], 1849, [11]195[4]pp.[94 repeated; 96 omitted], 15¾ cm. Flyleaf, "Harriet Storer's Book. Tyringham Feb. 12th 1849." Hymns; no music.

SM146   Fervent Devotion [f.t.], n.d.[hymns dated 1841–46]. 114 pp., 16 cm., SL.

SM147   Love to Mother, n.d., [8]61[11]pp.[31–32 missing; 37, 38, 43, 50 repeated]. 14¾ cm., Outside cover title: "MSS. Collection of Anthems: dating back to 1806." Hymns; no music.

SM148   O how pure is the way [f.l.], 1840, [2]82[5]pp.[2 pp. inserted between 5–6; ditto 7–8], 15¼ cm., 2-line SL.

SM149   The Precious Way [f.t.], 1844, 25[158]pp., 15½ cm., On cover: "Jeremiah's Book 1844," SL.

SM150   Crown of Life Eternal [f.t.], n.d.[hymns range 1835–46], [4]216pp.[23–26 torn out; 55–60 torn and cut; 75–76 missing; 205–209 missing], 14½ cm., 1-line and 5-line SL.

SM151   What comfort does flow to the true overcomer [f.l.], n.d. [1851–65 period], n.p., 13 cm. SL.

SM152   Mother Ann's Invitation [f.t.], n.d.[1841–52 period], [10]226[23]pp.[many blank pp. at end; 127 omitted], 12 cm., SL.

SM153   A Collection of Anthems Improved in our General worship. Written and Pricked for the purpose of retaining them, By Henry De Witt—A.D.—1833. [8]106[8 blank pp.]pp.[62 omitted; 105 omitted], 13½ cm. De Witt's work to p. 90, SL; 5-line SL.

SM154   A Vision Nov. 1847, n.p., 10 cm., Flyleaf, "Zilpha Blanchard's Book August, 1848." Hymns; no music.

SM155   A Collection of Verses Improved in our Worship Written for B.L., n.d., n.p., 9 cm. Hymns; no music.

SM156   Solemn Covenant [f.t.], n.d.[hymns range 1839–56], n.p., 20½ cm., SL.

SM157   The Harmony of Angels [f.t.], n.d.[1845–48 period], 145pp.[first 2 pp. missing; 138 repeated], 20½ cm. Hymns; no music.

SM158   Wisdom [f.t.], "Commenced Jan. 1st 1855. Finished July 10th 1855" (flyleaf), [8]222pp.[108–9 repeated], 19½ cm., Louise B. Blanchard, Harvard, Mass., SL.

SM159   Travelers Home [f.t.], n.d.[1868–71 period], n.p., 19½ cm., SL.

SM160   A soft sweet voice from Eden stealing [f.l.], n.d.[1879–89 period], 178[4]pp.[1 and 2 missing; 21–22 missing; 31–34 missing; 2pp. inserted 41–42; 57–64 missing; 67–70 missing], 19½ cm. SL.

SM161   Beams of Glory [f.t.], n.d.[1848–54 period], [16]44[10]pp. [many blank pp. at end], 19¾ cm., SL.

SM162   Now I am determin'd more faithful to be, [f.l.], n.d. [hymns 1842 period?], [14]144[4]pp., 19 cm., SL.

SM163   A Collection of Hymns and Spiritual Songs. Improved in our general worship . . . Began to be Writen Nov. 1825, n.p., 19 cm., Hymns; no music.

SM164   Victorious Love [f.t.], n.d.[hymns range 1827–35[last page, "Lebanon, 1834, Finished Feb y 8 1835"] [4]166 [6]pp. 18½ cm., Flyleaf, "Book 11th Thomas Hammond Harvard," CL; 5-line SL; SL.

SM165   Hymn on Truth [f.t.], [range 1834–74], [5]156[17]pp., 18 cm. Mostly hymns; 5-line SL.

SM166   Hymn 1st[f.t.] In the Lambs first revelation[f.l.], n.d., n.p. 17¾ cm. Outside cover, "MSS. Shaker Hymns." Hymns; no music.

SM167   Hour of Prayer [f.t.], n.d.[range of hymns 1847–60], [10] 240[many blank pp. at end]pp., [169 omitted; 176–183 missing; 216–217 torn out], 17¾ cm., SL.

SM168   Hour of Prayer [f.t.], n.d.[at end: Finished November 27, 1848 by Richard B. Woodrow C.H.H. Second Order], [12]345[2]pp.[108 omitted; 191 omitted; 243–4 missing; 301 omitted], 17½ cm., SL.

SM169   Hymns Improved in the Worship of Believers . . . Commenced Apl. 17th 1837.[extend to 1842], [16]264pp., Hymns; only music on Song Leaf, (p. 120) ; 17½ cm., SL.

SM170   Sweet love and union, is a flowing all around [f.l.] n.d. [1849–58 period], [12]61[158]pp.[many blank pp. at end; 2pp. inserted between 55–56], 18 cm., SL.

SM171   Grant my prayer, O mighty Father [f.l.], n.d.[funeral hymns at end collected 1859], [14]230[2]pp.[2pp. inserted 22–23]. Cover title, "Eunice Wythe's Hymns To the 168th page Thence Funeral Songs," 17½ cm., SL.

SM172   Lovely Treasures [f.t.], n.d.[hymns 1817–60], [12]226[4] pp. [141–144 cut out], 17¾ cm., SL.

SM173   O Lord of Wisdom strength and power [f.l.], n.d.[1840?– 50?] [12]106[4]pp., 17¾ cm. Flyleaf, "Justin Budine," SL.

SM174   Song of Thanksgiving [f.t.], n.d.[at end: "Finis Began February 17 1855 Finished October 17 1855"], [16]274 [2]pp.,[134 repeated; 212 omitted], 17½ cm., SL.

SM175   Glad Tidings [f.t.], n.d.[at end: "Finished October 7th 1855"] [20]279[2]pp.[241 repeated], 17¾ cm., SL.

SM176   A Collection of tunes Written Exclusively to Remember . . . Began to be written 1850, n.p. 17¾ cm., SL.

SM177   Be ye Ready [f.t.], n.d.[mostly 1845–54], [16]349[11]pp. [confusion 170–172; 182–183 omitted; 257 repeated; 303 omitted], 17¾ cm. SL.

SM178   Path of Selfdenial [f.t.], n.d.[hymns 1839–42 period], [10] 44 [175]pp., 17¾ cm., SL.

SM179   Hour of Prayer [f.t.], "Commenced 1847," Finished February 20th 1850 [By James Hollister], [17]317pp.[192 repeated; 223 repeated], 17½ cm., SL.

SM180   Happy Anticipation [f.t.], n.d.[1848–56 period], [14]215 [85]pp. [blank pp. at end; 63–64, 73–74 omitted; 180 repeated; 210–211 cut out], 17½ cm., SL.

SM181   A Collection of Anthems And Spiritual Songs, Improved in General Worship. New Lebanon April 5th 1840. [Eliza Ann's Book], Finis July 28th 1844. [10]237[2]pp. [114 omitted], 17½ cm., SL.

SM182   Song of Thanksgiving [f.t.], n.d.[1832–58 period], [20] 287pp. [Many blank pp. at end; 117 repeated; 184 repeated], 17½ cm., SL.

SM183   A Collection of Spiritual Anthems Improved in Sacred Worship . . . Transcribed by Roby Bennet, New Lebanon, N.Y. Beg' to be written March 14th 1840. [14]253 [9]pp.[147–148 torn out], 16 cm., SL.

SM184   Come come heavenly love [f.l.], n.d., n.p., 16½ cm., Cover title, "MSS. Collection of Shaker Hymns." SL.

SM185   A Collection of hymns and Spiritual songs. Improved in our general worship. Rhode Blake, n.d.[10]129[1]pp., 15¼ cm., Hymns; no music.

SM186   Let bloody wars forever cease [f.l.], n.d., n.p., 15¾ cm.,
        Cover torn off, Hymns; no music.
SM187   A Faithful Child [f.t.], n.d.[1838–41 period], 156[10]pp.,
        14 cm., SL; 1-line SL.
SM188   A Transcript of Beautiful Songs . . . Transcribed by
        Hannah Blake. Nov.^br 17th 1843. 175[1]pp.[65–78 torn
        out; 139–142 torn out], 13½ cm. Printing pasted on pp.
        and scribbling. SL.
SM189   A Collection of Songs of Various Kinds . . . Begun Nov.
        29th 1839. Finished October 11th 1840., n.p., 13 cm. SL.
SM190   O here is growing here is growing the tree of life [f.l.],
        n.d.[hymns dated 1837–38], n.p., 13½ cm. 5-line SL;
        SL; 1-line SL.
SM191   A Selection of Hymns and Anthems Used in Worship
        . . . n.d.[1847–68 period], [16]119[64]pp.[Many blank
        pp. at end], 13 cm., SL.
SM192   O things eternal and sublime [f.l.], n.d.[1837–40 period],
        [8]212[50]pp.[77 omitted; 92 repeated; 2 pp. inserted
        117–118; 119 repeated; 172 repeated; 188–189 repeated],
        11 cm., 5-line SL; SL.
SM193   Hymn from Isaiah Chapter 35th [f.t.], n.d., n.p., 24¾
        cm., Flyleaf, "Margret Denning Book 8149 It now belong
        to Hnnah Bryant 81 62," SL.
SM194   A Collection of Songs used in our General Worship . . .
        Commenced June 10, 1904 Andrew D. Barrett, [4]141
        pp.[blank pp. at end], 24½ cm., 3 loose leaves containing
        songs, SL.
SM195   Beauty Union & Love [f.t.], n.d.[hymns dated 1812–41;
        probably written 1839–41], [14]520 pp., 21½ cm., Inside
        cover, "Bound by Henry De Witt, New Lebanon," SL.
SM196   Holy Mothers Cord of Love [f.t.], n.d.[Flyleaf: "Com-
        menced writing this Book in 1851."] [5]252[13]pp., 21
        cm., Nancy Orsment's Book. Mostly hymns; a few tunes
        in SL.
SM197   Letter Music. A Collection of Hymns, Anthems & Tunes:
        Suitable for Believers worship . . . South Union, Jasper
        Valley, Logan County, Kentucky—May 1st 1834. [8]7[5]
        133pp.[2pp. inserted 36–37 and 69–70; empty pp. near
        end], 20¾ cm., 1-level SL; 5-line SL; SL; 1-line SL.
SM198   Ive quit that old relation [f.l.], n.d.[range 1811–43 or
        longer; mostly c. 1833], [16]104pp., 19¾ cm., 5-line SL;
        one-level SL; SL.
SM199   I'm truly thankful ([f.t.], n.d.[range of hymns 1843–44],

[3]109[29]pp.[p. inserted 4–5], 19¼ cm. Hymns; no music.

SM200   Sacred Songs Vol. 3rd Collected & Compiled by James P. Vail. A.D. 1857 to 1862 inclusive. [22]226[8]pp., 19 cm., SL.

SM201   A Call to Zion [f.t.], n.d., n.p.[many blank pp. at end], 19¼ cm., SL.

SM202   The Saviour's Promise [f.t.], n.d.[range of hymns 1842–46], 205[14]pp.[39 repeated], 19¼ cm., Flyleaf: "Margaret Hopkins. Zilpha Blanchard's Hymn Book." Hymns; no music.

SM203   Compete not with those who have means beyond your reach [f.l. of a writing lesson], n.d.[one hymn dated Feb. 20, 1869], 22 pp., 18½ cm., Cover title, "MSS. Shaker Song Book." SL.

SM204   A Collection of Hymns and Spiritual Songs Improved in our General Worship. By Orren N. Haskins. 1828. [10] 108pp., 18½ cm., Hymns; no music.

SM205   I'm going down to the beautiful valley [f.l.], n.d.[hymns mostly 1842–56 period], [6]298[10]pp.[188 omitted, but not missing; ditto, 288], 18 cm., SL.

SM206   Resurrected from the deed [f.l.], n.d., 96[147]pp.[55 skipped], 18 cm., Flyleaf: "Songs in this book between 1874–80 All from Mt. Lebanon & branch family at Canaan N.Y." SL.

SM207   Mother Ann's Words [f.t.], n.d.[flyleaf: 1837]. [14]67[16] pp.[many blank pp. at end], 18 cm., Inside front cover: "Bound by Henry De Witt New-Lebanon," 1-line SL.

SM208   My soul does rejoice that I have been called [f.l.], n.d. [dated tunes range 1858–73], [5]40[105]pp.[many blank pp. at end], 17¼ cm., 5-line SL.

SM209   Lift up your heads ye righteous a day of glory's a nigh [f.l.], n.d.[hymns mostly 1852–68], [4]213[30]pp., 17½ cm., 5-line SL.

SM210   Wisdom's Roll [f.t.], n.d.[hymns 1841–57 range], [6]123 [25]pp. [10–11 reversed; 78 skipped; after 79 begins with 40 again; complete new series 40–79 repeated; 51 skipped; after 57, pp. 48–57 repeated again; after 65 starts 57–58 which are 66–67; 2 pp. between 113–14 unnumbered; ditto 115–16; ditto 117–18], 17 cm., SL.

SM211   We have come says Mother Ann to prepare you for Heaven [f.l.], n.d.[hymns range mostly 1840–43], [12]119

[54]pp.[86–87 repeated, sealed and broken open], 17 cm., SL.

SM212	Va-des-ha-len-ha- [f.l.], n.d.[mostly 1838–47 period]. Begins with p. 67, used as a scrap book and pp. cut out; pp. 67–334[71–84 cut out; ditto 109–126; ditto 145–156; ditto 175–186; ditto 205–15; 224 repeated; 225–26 cut out; ditto 229–58; ditto 273–86; ditto 311–14; ditto 327–28], 16¼ cm., SL.

SM213	Mother Ann's Closing Hymn [f.t.], n.d.[range of hymns 1841–49], [8]245[many unintelligible pp. follow]pp.,[42 omitted; ditto 188], 16½ cm., SL; 5-line SL.

SM214	A Collection of Hymns By Susannah Redmon. First Order Union Village November 4, 1844. [2]206[28]pp. [21 omitted; ditto 101; 127–30 cut out], 16 cm., SL.

SM215	A Collection of Hymns and Spiritual Songs; Improved in our Worship. New Lebanon January 8th, 1832, [9] 203 [2]pp.[124–25 repeated; 155 omitted; 200–203 numbered 100–103], 16 cm., James H. Smith, Hymns; no music.

SM216	The Little Flock [f.t.], n.d., [6]5[133]pp., 15¾ cm., RN; SL.

SM217	The New Years Gift: 1817, n.d.[extends to 1838], [12] 176pp.[137–40 missing; 163 repeated], 15¾ cm., Hymns; no music.

SM218	A Collection of Anthems and Spiritual Songs Improved in the Worship of believers . . . Began to be written January 1st 1840. [10]257[33]pp., 16½ cm., Rhoda Blake, SL; 5-line SL.

SM219	Mt. Lebanon Anthem [f.t.], On cover: "4/66." [4]174 [10]pp. [36–37 repeated], 16¾ cm., SL.

SM220	The True Spirit of Christ [f.t.], n.d.[1847?], n.p., 16¾ cm., SL; 5-line SL.

SM221	The Lord has again in this temple appeared [f.l.], n.d., n.p., 15¼ cm., Cover title: "MSS. Early Collection of Shaker Hymns," Hymns; no music.

SM222	O my blessed Mother has given unto me [f.l.], n.d.[range of hymns 1840–41], [18]198pp.[73–74 repeated], 13½ cm., SL.

SM223	Wisdom's Blessing [f.t.], n.d.[hymns 1842–43 period], [6]171[3]pp.[45–46 pasted shut], 13¾ cm., SL.

SM224	Heavenly Joys [f.t.], n.d.[hymns range 1850–55], n.p., 13½ cm., SL.

SM225	A Variety of Anthems and Spiritual Songs for Believers to improve in While in their Sacred Worship. Began 1842 New Lebanon Second Order. [10]238[6]pp.[65 repeated; 68 skipped; 72 called 73; 224–33 repeated], 13¾ cm., SL.

SM226   Do cultivate and norish the tender plant [f.l.], n.d.[hymns range 1847–54], n.p., 13½ cm., SL.

SM227   A Collection of Spiritual Anthems—Given mostly by Inspiration . . . Jan 8 1842, [10]167[33]pp., 13½ cm., SL.

SM228   Solemn Trumpet [f.t.], n.d.[hymns dated 1839–40], [8]-250 [1]pp.[237 skipped], 13½ cm., Cover: "Bound by Henry De Witt, New Lebanon," SL.

SM229   A Song Book Anthems Such as are Use In our Worship Wretten by George Curtiss Begone to be Wretten Jan. 12th 1840. [18]263[4]pp.[65–66 missing; 77 omitted; 223 omitted; ditto 247], 13 cm., SL.

SM230   A few Exercises in Dynamics [f.l.], n.d.[hymns dated 1869], n.p.[16]pp., 22¾ cm., Cover, "MSS. Rules for Correct Singing. Shaker Hymns—with music." SL.

SM231   Amelia Lyman's Book Commenced Nov. 18 1855, [5]-30[101]pp. [16–17 missing], 21 cm., SL.

SM232   True Light [f.t.], n.d.[hymns mostly 1863–65 period] [2]112 [2]pp.[39–40 repeated], 21cm., SL.

SM233   Various Songs received in 1829 and 30 from different places. Some Harvard ones — n.p., 21 cm., 2-, 3-, 4-, 5-line CL.

SM234   Various Songs received in 1827 and 1828 from different places Some of them belonging to Harvard. 31[55]pp., 21 cm., 5-line CL.

SM235   Shining Silone [f.t.], n.d.[hymns mostly 1865–69; some earlier], [6]53[23]pp.[many blank pp. at end][6 repeated; 35–36 a page skipped; ditto 36–37], 20¾ cm., Loose clippings in front; 2 letters back flyleaf, 6 and 7-line SL; SL.

SM236   A Choice Collection of Divine Songs Made Use of in our General Worship. Written by Jeremiah Lowe. Commencing August 10th 1851. [8]7[105]pp.[many blank pp. at end], 20¾ cm., SL; 1-line SL.

SM237   Behold the lovely shining band of valiant volunteers [f.l.] Cover: "MSS. Oliver Woodford's Hymn and Tune Book: 1840." n.p. [32]pp., 20½ cm., SL.

SM238   *Songs to be Sung at the Boston Meeting Dec. 28–29,* n.d.

[hymns dated 1869], n.p.[24]pp., 20¼ cm., Cover: "Geo. Albert Lomas, Shaker Agent, Albany, N.Y." SL.

SM239   The Purification of Zion [f.t.], n.d.[hymns range 1838–42], 182[4]pp., 20¼ cm., Cover: "MSS. Hymns set to Music," PN; SL; 5-line SL.

SM240   Be Ye Holy [f.t.], n.d.[some dated 1842–47], 143pp.[101 skipped; many pp. cut out at end], 20 cm., Words; no music.

SM241   Solemn Praise, n.d.[range 1869–81], [1]322[8]pp.[233 omitted], 20¼ cm., SL; 4-line SL.

SM242   A Collection of Hymns & Tunes; Prudence F. Houston South Union, Jasper Valley, Logan County Ky. March 4th 1833.[extends to 1844] [6]122[5]pp.[p. skipped 1–2], 20 cm., SL; 5-line SL; SL on one level.

SM243   Wisdoms Roll [f.t.], n.d.[hymns extend 1839–69; arithmetic in back, 1902–3], n.p., 19¾ cm., PN; SL; 2–3–4–voiced SL; colored SL.

SM244   Shaker Music, n.d.[pencil inside: "George C. Bartlett. In Church Union 1889–New York."] 152[4]pp.[80 pp. scrap book], 19 cm., RN.

SM245   The funeral Hymn [f.t.], n.d.[inside cover: "Gideon Kibbee Deceased—March 1848 Alonzo G. Hollister Received Feb. 13, 1870"], [10]109[5]pp.[66 skipped; p. unnumbered between 80–81]. 19 cm. Mostly hymns; 1-line SL.

SM246   Hymn First. Celestial Fountain [f.t.], n.d.[dates range 1837–53], 266[4]pp.[179–80 skipped; 262 numbered 263], 19¾ cm. Inside cover, "Watervliet" in pencil, PN.

SM247   Holy Jubilee [f.t.], n.d.[inside cover: "at various periods from 1814 to 1859."] [10]233[21]pp., 19 cm., SL.

SM248   Pleasing Thoughts [f.t.], Inside leaf; "William C. Brackett's Hymn Book, Watervliet 7th 1829," [10]168-[3]pp.[126 repeated], 19 cm., PN.

SM249   Prepare O my children prepare you a robe [f.l], n.d.-range mostly 1840–43]. [2]270[4]pp.[13–14 missing; 2 unnumbered pp. between 125–126;pp. 215–222 torn out], 18¼ cm., SL.

SM250   A Selection of The Choicest & Most Mellodious Songs of Zion . . . Commenced March 25th 18 [Cover: "March, 1868"][range of hymns 1847–59], [18]185[103]pp, 17½ cm., Cover: "Andrew Fortier's Book," SL.

SM251   Seal of true Redemption [f.t.], n.d.[hymns range 1839–46] [2]306pp.[1–12 missing; ditto 19–24; page unnumbered between 39–40; ditto 76–77; 2pp. sealed between 183–184; skips numbering from 269–80[297–98 cut out], 12½ cm., SL.

SM252 [Incomplete] . . . love forever, Nay nay I'll be simple [f.l.], n.d.[flyleaf "Bound by Henry De Witt for Edward Fowler July—1844 New Lebanon"] n.p.[alternate pp. are upside down], 17½ cm. Book has had a lock like a diary. SL.

SM253 Matin Hymn [f.t.], n.d.[range 1860–69], [18]167pp.[2 omitted; 81–167 blank], 17¼ cm., SL.

SM254 Go away, go away every fleshly tie go away [f.l.], n.d.[Flyleaf: "received between the years 1849–59."] n.p. 17½ cm., SL.

SM255 A Hymn Book Containing A Collection of Sacred Songs, Hymns, Anthems & Poems . . . May 1846. [4]11[220]pp.-[last 40 pp. blank] 16 cm., SL; 5-line SL.

SM256 [Cover] (MSS) Musical Instructor, n.d.[tunes dated 1869 at end], [4]31[55]pp., 9½ cm., SL.

SM257 A Collection of Anthems Adapted to the Worship of Believers in the Manifestation of Christ's Second Appearing[very faint pencil], n.d.[last dated hymn 1863], [22]400[2]pp.[confused numbering 161–64], 14 cm., Inside cover: "This Book was written by Elizabeth Bates," SL.

SM258 Faithful Few [f.t.], n.d.[hymns range 1844–54], [18]149-[81]pp. 13¼ cm., SL.

SM259 Hail the sweet harmonious sound [f.l.] n.d.[1843–54 period hymns] [4]203[83]pp.[38 repeated; 164 repeated], 12¾ cm., SL.

SM260 A Collection of Anthems sent to Individuals as a Particular notice, from the Spiritual World, also many others, All given by Inspiration. Commenced Jan. 8 1840. [6]128pp. 12½ cm., SL.

SM261 [Dance tune in 6-8 measure with "Amos Bishop" written over it], n.d., n.p., 12¾ cm., Purple cover, yellowed paper, begins with section of dances in capital letteral notation, section on theory in back, 5-line CL; CL; 5-line RN.

SM262 For Eldress Ruth [f.t.], n.d.[date near end of 1849], [5]79 [23]pp. [71 repeated; 78 marked 79], 13 cm., SL.

SM263 A Collection of Anthems and Spiritual Songs Improved in our general worship. Begun to be writen in 1824 april.

Samuel Johnson. [8]126pp.[93–94 cut out; 95–126 blank], 12¼ cm., Words; no music.

SM264 Anthems Mostly given by Inspiration Used in Sacred Worship . . . Richard B. Woodrow. Begun January 27th 42, ["Finished September 27th 1844" at end], [6]330[2]-pp.[243 repeated; 261 skipped] 12¼ cm., SL.

SM265 A Selection of Choice Poems or Verses . . . Watervliet, Mar. 9th 1853.[extend to 1859], [4]14[307]pp.[6–7 omitted], 11 cm., Written by D. A. Buckingham, SL.

SM266 At Shiloh was a yearly feast [f.l.], n.d.[At end: "Finis Dec. 4th 1836"], [2]225 pp.[p. 30 numbered 31], 11½ cm., Hymns; no music.

SM267 The rolling vi and the holy Cross [f.t.], n.d.[1839–43 range] 2 sets of paginations confused. 10¼ cm., SL; 1-line SL.

SM268 Behold the time is come [f.l.], n.d.[last hymns dated 1839] [10]148[6]pp., 10 cm., PN; 5-line RN; 5-line SL; SL.

SM269 Crown of Life Eternal [f.t.], n.d.[range 1837–39] [6] 219[2]pp.[11, 77 101, 177, 213 omitted], 8¾ cm., 5-line SL; SL.

SM270 Marches, Watervliet 2.ᵈ Order [f.t.], n.d.[dates range 1828–35] [4]21[115]pp., 8¾ cm., 5-line CL; 5-line SL.

SM271 Gathering the Sheep [f.t.], n.d.[only composition dated, 1843], n.p., 29 cm., 5-line SL.

SM272 "Jan 22 1838 S.D. knows a march learned the same day." [top of p. 1], n.d.[range 1837–47], [4]115[21]pp., 21½ cm., Flyleaf, "Enfield, Connecticut," 5-line SL.

SM273 Inspirational Songs of Praise. Copied by N. Catherine Allen Mount Lebanon, n.d.[range 1889–94], [40]200pp. [starts at either end and numbers 100pp. to the middle], 18 cm. Cover: "Songs: other cover: "Hymns." RN.

SM274 The Lamb [f.t.], n.d.[hymns dated 1825–29], 162[10]pp. [1–3 missing], 16½ cm. One loose leaf hymn; one hymn on flyleaf at back., 5-line CL.

SM275 [Inside Cover: "Sally Loomis. Her Book. *1825.*"] [Extends to Dec. 14, 1828], [3]190[3]pp., 15 cm., 5-line CL.

SM276 The Beauty of Believers [f.t.], n.d., [2]59[2]pp.[5–6 cut out; p. unnumbered between 56–57.] 23 cm., Outside cover: " (MSS) Poems: The Beauty of Believers, Indiana Union, A Question, . . ." Hymns; no music.

SM277 A Collection of Hymns Improved in our sacred devotions. Written by George W. Curtiss began Mᶜʰ 29th

1835. [8]138[2]pp., 20¾ cm. SL; 1-line SL.

SM278   What a feast what a feast my soul does enjoy [f.l.], n.d.-
[one hymn dated 1863], n.p. 20¼ cm., SL.

SM279   Eternal Truth [f.t.], n.d.[flyleaf, "These hymns thought
to be given during the years 1825 to 40"], [2]90[6]pp.-
[many blank pp. at end], 20 cm. Hymns; no tunes.

SM280   Mother Anns Song of Praise [f.t.], n.d.[range 1847–54]
[4]114 [61]pp.[113 repeated], 20½ cm., SL; 5-line SL.

SM281   Beams of Glory [f.t.], January 1862, [14]117[6]pp.[many
blank pp. at end], 20 cm., Inside cover: "Lorenzo Prouty,
Shirly Village, Mass." SL.

SM282   From the heavenly shores I hear the sweet sound [f.l.]
n.d. [flyleaf: "used during the years from 1860 to 85"]
n.p. 20 cm. SL.

SM283   Glorious Pearl [f.t.], n.d.[dates range 1839–47] [16]135[1]-
pp. [many blank pp. at end], 20 cm. Mostly hymns; SL.

SM284   Source of Light [f.t.], n.d.[one hymn dated 1875], n.p.,
19¼ cm. SL.

SM285   The Children of Light [f.t.], 1821, n.p., 19½ cm., Flyleaf:
"Emeline Clark's Book Watervliet January 1st 1821."
Hymns; no music.

SM286   Hymns, and Songs of Praise, Prayer and Thanksgiving
By Eunice Wyeth. Copied by Eunice Bathrick in the
Seventy-Second Year of her age, 1865, [24]195 [3]pp.,
19½ cm., SL.

SM287   We are seen [f.t.], n.d.[flyleaf; "The last hymn copied in
this book was given in 1852. The others are mostly of
much earlier date." [6]7[133]pp.[many blank pp. at end],
19½ cm. Outside cover: "Record." 5-line SL; SL.

SM288   Gospel Adoration or Hymns of Praise . . . Watervliet,
1839 [14]349[15]pp. 19 cm. "Written by D. A. Buckingham," PN; SL; 5-line SL.

SM289   A Collection of Extra or Slow Songs, Sung by the Believers . . . Eldress Betsy Bates, Commenced January
2nd 1859., n.p., 18½ cm. SL.

SM290   A Collection of Hymns Adapted to The Sacred Worship
of Believers Commenced in the Year 1850. [12]59[1]pp.-
[many blank pp. at end], 18 cm., SL.

SM291   Love to my Home [f.t.], n.d.[hymns mostly 1848–54],
[18]280 [61]pp.[101 omitted; 139 repeated; 205 repeated],
17¾ cm. Mostly hymns; SL.

SM292   Sure Reward [f.t.], n.d.[1852–56 period], [18]295[4]pp.-
         [160–161 repeated; 295 repeated], 17½ cm. Classified
         table of contents by types., SL.

SM293   Childrens Petition [f.t.], n.d.[1849–52 period], [16]212-
         pp. [many blank pp. at end; 45 repeated; 82–83 cut out;
         86 repeated; 167 repeated], 18 cm., SL.

SM294   A Treasury of Heavenly Songs . . . Written by Elizabeth
         R. Avery, 1848, [2]42[222]pp.[many blank pp. at end],
         17¾ cm., SL.

SM295   A Collection of Hymns Improved in our Sacred Wor-
         ship. Written by Henry De Witt. Began A.D. 1835. [10]-
         182[3]pp.[65 repeated], 17¾ cm., 5-line SL; SL.

SM296   Zion's Consolation [f.t.], n.d.[1855–59 period], 297[1]pp.
         [285–90 missing], 17½ cm., SL.

SM297   The forepart of this book contains many little Songs
         Given by the Shepherdess at Canterbury: 1842. [16]167-
         [100]pp.[103 repeated], 17½ cm., SL.

SM298   Ye righteous souls be of good cheer [f.l.], n.d.[1874
         period], [12]161pp.[many blank pp. at end], 17½ cm.
         Flyleaf: "Elder Daniel Boler's Book," 2 loose leaves, SL.

SM299   Elder Wᵐ Williams Book. May 25th 1830, 26[2]pp., 18
         cm. Hymns; no music.

SM300   Sound sound the Tamborrine [f.l.], n.d.[1872–73 period],
         n.p. 20 cm., SL.

SM301   Arrangements of exercises in Singing School [f.t.], 1867,
         n.p. 19 cm., SL without lines.

SM302   I hear the Angels voices in gentle whispers say [f.l.]
         [1859–70 period] n.p.[many pp. cut out of middle], 19
         cm., SL.

SM303   Holy Savior, 1836, [6]64[9]pp[63 repeated], 18½ cm.,
         "Perline Bates' Book," SL.

SM304   Part First Marching Tunes and Verse [f.t.], n.d.[1852–61
         period] [4]130[25]pp.[pp. unnumbered 68–110], 18¼
         cm., SL.

SM305   [p.20] A Welcome for the Western Ministry[title: first
         pages are scrap book], n.d.[1853–59 period], 274pp.[pp.
         1–19 scrapbook; 21–24 missing; ditto 37–38; 59–60 torn;
         83–84 torn out; 101 skipped; 108–9 torn out; ditto 132–
         33; 140 repeated; 181–82 missing; ditto 189–90; ditto
         251–56], 17½ cm. Book badly mutilated by child, SL.

SM306   O come thou lovely Angel [f.l.], n.d.[1848–53 period],

[24]352 pp.[112 skipped; 173 repeated], 17½ cm., SL.

SM307   A collection of Songs and Anthems Improved in Worship, by Believers in Christ's Second Appearing. 1870, [24]-276[18]pp.[121 repeated; ditto 242], 17½ cm., SL.

SM308   The Saviour's Invitation [f.t.], n.d.[1844–48 range], n.p. ["294 songs"], 17¼ cm. Flyleaf: "Emma Woodworth 14 years Old." SL.

SM309   My words shall be few and well seasoned with grace [f.l., p. 19], n.d.[1847–51 period], 314pp.[1–18 missing; ditto 23–24, 37–38, 47–48, 89–90, 155–56, 205–6; 221 skipped; 248–49 half torn out; 250–51 torn out; ditto 282–85; 298 skipped; 300 skipped; 308–10 torn out], 16 cm., SL.

SM310   A Collection of Hymns and Spiritual Songs. Improved in our general worship. June 22, 1830, [11]147[29]pp.-[143 skipped], 15½ cm. Mostly hymns; SL.

SM311   Beautiful, Heavenly and Sacred Are the Gifts, etc., Began to be Written, May 4th 1846 [extends to 1849], [4]179-[113]pp., 13 cm., SL.

SM312   Call of Mother [f.t.], n.d.[1838–41 period]. [12]266[4]pp., 12¾ cm., "Horace Haskins," 1-line SL; SL.

SM313   Marching Tunes. Eleazer Stanley's 1840 [f.t.], n.d.[1838–57 period], n.p., 12 cm., SL.

SM314   Marching Tunes [f.t.], n.d.[4]261[27]pp.[27–30 missing], 11½ cm., SL.

SM315   Soldier of Christ [f.t.], n.d.[1846–50 period], [2]45[2]pp. [begins at end and numbers two ways towards middle], 11 cm., SL.

SM316   Heavenly Call to the Youth [f.t.], n.d.[1839–40 period], [16]216pp., 10½ cm., SL.

SM317   The Lord Reigneth [f.t.], n.d. [12]82pp.[many blank pp. at end], 10½ cm. Anthems; no tunes.

SM318   A Collection of Anthems and Spiritual songs Improved in Sacred Devotion. Selected and transcribed by Elizabeth Terressa Lannuier. Began to be written December 2nd 1839. [4]156[93]pp.[35 numbered 34], 10½ cm., 5-line SL; SL.

SM319   Like many others in diferent sizes and bindings [f.l.], n.d., n.p., 9½ cm. A blank book with the lines for music-writing. Inside front cover: "Like many others in diferent sizes and bindings, this little book was prepared by Russell Haskel for copying the new songs as they came.

Staff lines pale, when lettered notes were used just to guide position of same. In Library of Congress is a very large vol. copied by R. Haskel in the various notations used from time to time."

SM320   A Book of Anthems And songs; Improved by every Good Believer; Written by Rhoda Blake, n.d.[1824–5?], [4]21 [73]pp., 9½ cm., PN and RN; 5-line SL; 1-line SL.

SM321   [First page and second page, music], Third page: "7. Father James." n.d., n.p., 6¼ cm. Next to last page in book begins: "Come sisters, skip and play." 5-line CL; 5-line SL.

SM322   The Children of Light [f.t.] n.d.[1831–41 (1864) period], 187pp.[many blank pp. at end; 140–141 repeated; 143–52 missing], 18½ cm., PN; SL.

SM323   The Request [f.t.], n.d.[hymns mostly dated 1847–51], [14]225[4]pp.[145–48 cut out; 189 repeated], 17½ cm. Mostly hymns; SL.

SM324   Nathan Spier His Book, n.d.[before 1827], [6]146pp., 17 cm. Hymns; no tunes.

SM325   A Collection of Spiritual Anthems, Given Mostly by Inspiration . . . Written by Rhoda Blake. March 1840. ["Finis October 1846"] [14]364[2]pp.[267 repeated; un-numbered p. between 299–300], 16 cm., SL.

SM326   Anthems Mostly given by Inspiration. Designed for the Worship of Believers. Written by George W. Curtiss. September 1841. n.d., 13½ cm., SL.

SM327   Soliloquy [f.t.], n.d.[2]100 pp., 13 cm. Hymns; no music.

SM328   Life from the Dead [f.t.], n.d.[1839–56 period], [6]157 [7]pp.[many blank pp. at end], 12½ cm., 5-line SL; SL.

SM329   A New Years Blessing [f.t.], n.d.[1840–44 period], [10] 95[77][10pp. numbered 11–22][6]pp.[11–22 missing; bound in back of book]. 9½ cm., SL; 5-line SL.

SM330   Mansion of Peace [f.t.], [Flyleaf: "No 4, or fourth book," and "Recorded by Russel Haskell of Enfield Conn. Commenced 1852"] [4]205[15]pp., 25 cm., 5-line SL.

SM331   Hymn & Song Book Written by H. L. Eades Commencing May 9th 1858. [extends to 1867], [2]285[3]pp., 25½ cm., SL.

SM332   Book of Songs, n.d. [2]67[46]pp., 22½ cm. Hymns; no music.

SM333   [Inside flyleaf and typed on cover] Miscellaneous Collec-

tion of Very Old Shaker Hymns & Songs much used in
Enfield Conn, seventy years since., n.d., n.p., 23 cm.
Mostly hymns; SL.

SM334   This Blank is A Present from Mary Whicher . . . Nov.
1st 1856[to 1876]. [10]95pp.[many blank pp. at end],
22 cm. Hymns only; no music.

SM335   Nancy Orsments Book Commenced Writing (1845 South
Family Harvard). "Ending in 1851." [4]196[9]pp.[4 un-
numbered pp. bound in 68–69; 177 skipped], 21 cm.,
Loose leaf with poem, Mostly words; SL.

SM336   Anthems of Praise. Samantha Bowie's Book. Watervliet
Jan.ʸ 1st 1868, n.p., 20¾ cm., SL.

SM337   Hasting Storer His Book. Wrote in 1857. [14]157[15]pp.,
20½ cm. [7 loose items; some music in letteral notation.,] Hymns; no music.

SM338   Mary Ann Augur's Book Written, In the year 1859.
[Songs written much earlier recopied], [8]100,[a second
series]24[20]pp., 2 loose papers; one has music in SL.,
20¼ cm., SL.

SM339   The Righteous Are only sav'd [f.t.], n.d.[1837–49 period],
162 [3]pp., 20 cm. Hymns; no music.

SM340   A Book of Divine Songs Composed by Members of this
Society . . . By Ann Maria Love Groveland 1858. [ex-
tend to 1861], n.p., 20½ cm. Letter with 4 letteral songs
pasted on back cover, SL.

SM341   Book No. 2 A Collection of Songs of Various Kinds
Mostly Received by Inspiration. Written by Mary A.
Ayers . . . Wisdoms Lovely Vale March 14th 1853, [6]
109pp. correctly lettered,[107 repeated; 206pp. with
confused numbering], 21 cm. March, loose-leaf in letteral
notation, SL.

SM342   I know my Redeemer liveth [f.l.], n.d.[cover: "various
periods from 37—on"][1837], [52]222pp.[many blank pp.
at end; 141 omitted], 20 cm., SL.

SM343   The Shaker. Zion's Defense [f.t.], n.d., 47pp., 19½ cm.
RN.

SM344   Hymns Used in the worship of Believers Written by
Charles Stewart in the year 1823 & 56., n.p., 19 cm.,
mostly hymns; SL.

SM345   Scrap Book. These Songs were received in various Societies, mostly between the years 1862–68. 135[1]pp.[1–2
missing; 1 p. between 129–30 unnumbered], 19 cm., SL.

SM346   Angelina Anna's Book Watervliet Jan.ʸ 6th 1834. n.p., 19 cm. Mostly hymns; PN.

SM347   We are groping in darkness and woe [f.l.], June 4, 1843, 11[59]7[59]pp.[2 series of pp. started] 19 cm., loose clippings. Hymns; no music.

SM348   Lo how beautiful is the way [f.l.], n.d.[flyleaf: "somewhere in the fifties"[1850], n.p., 19 cm., SL.

SM349   A Funeral Hymn [f.t.], n.d., [4]63[13]pp., 18 cm., Outside cover: "MSS. Collection of Hymns . . . Mother Ruth's Memorial . . . The Believer . . ." [Polly Laurence]. Hymns; no music.

SM350   A Collection of Inspirational Songs Selected and Transcribed by Marrietta Strever, n.d.[range 1880–84], n.p., 17 cm., SL.

SM351   No 3, or third book. Recorded by Russell Haskell Enfield Conn. Commenced in 1848[flyleaf], [4]216[4]pp., 17 cm., 5-line SL.

SM352   Crown me Crown me With your heavenly love[f.l.], n.d., [1837–48 period], n.p., 15½ cm. Flyleaf: "Chester C. Holman Book." Hymns; no music.

SM353   Songs and Hymns book., n.d.[1843–51 range], [4]60[79] pp.[1–4 missing; ditto 78; 27 repeated; 50–51 missing], 15¼ cm. Mostly hymns; SL; 1-line SL.

SM354   A Collection of Hymns, and Spiritual Songs: Improved in our general Worship. New Lebanon June 24, 1830, confused pp., 15 cm. Hymns; no music.

SM355   Blessings for the faithful are descending freely [f.l.], n.d. [range 1841–46], [2]190pp.[77–78, 81–82, 85–86 missing; ditto 159–84], 13¼ cm., 5-line SL; RN.

SM356   Arise, and thresh, O children Of Zion [f.l.], n.d.[range 1847–50], [2]13[147]pp., 13½ cm., 5-line SL; RN.

SM357   Spiritual Warning [f.t.], January 24th 1847, n.p., 15½ cm., "Maria Lyman." Hymns; no music.

SM358   The Word of the Lord of Hosts [f.t.], n.d.[range 1841–65], [14]114[13]pp.[many blank pp. at end; 21 repeated], 13¾ cm., SL.

SM359   The Virgin Spouse bigins to rouse [f.l.], n.d.[1829–39 near end], n.p., 11 cm., 5-line SL.

SM360   Blessed Gospel Blessed Cause [f.l.], n.d. [Inside leaf: "Isabella Graves. 1875"], [2]205[2]pp.[112 omitted], 21 cm., SL.

SM361   I will be with my dear children [f.l.], n.d.[hymns near end dated 1852], [4]23[187]pp., 20 cm., SL.

SM362   Truth an Anchor [f.t.], n.d.[1854–57 period], [4]144[2] pp., 20¼ cm., SL.

SM363   A Collection of Divine And Heavenly Songs. Improved in Sacred Worship. Written by Florinda Sears. New Lebanon. September 25th 1847[extends to 1866], [12] 276[5]pp.[145, 261, 273 repeated], 19½ cm., SL.

SM364   Mary Ann Ayres's Hymn Book. Watervliet, Feb. 1849. [4]138[8]pp.[24 numbered 25; 53–56 missing; 115 repeated], 19½ cm., SL.

SM365   No. 1. Tis not in Station place or name[f.l.], n.d.[2]216 [4]pp.[105–16 missing; ditto 119–24; 127–32; 137–46; 153–56; several pp. cut out at end], 19½ cm., SL.

SM366   Musical Presents, from the Land of Souls, n.d.[range 1841–61]7[9]pp., 19½ cm., 1-line SL.

SM367   For a robe thats pure and holy[f.l.], "These songs between 1871 & 73 Mostly from Mt. Lebanon," n.p., 19¼ cm., SL.

SM368   A few of Mothers Lucy's own words [f.l.], n.d.[hymns dated 1873–80], [14]103[60]pp., [many blank pp. at end], 19½ cm. "Mary O. Elston." Hymns and writing; no music.

SM369   The Messiah has come Alleluia! will sing, [f.l.], "Begun 1861, finished 1863." n.p., 19½ cm., [M. Catherine Allen. Mt. Lebanon N.Y. "The greater part of the songs in this book originated in Mount Lebanon N. Y."], SL.

SM370   The time draweth nigh when God's powerful word [f.l.], 1871–78, [2]224[2]pp.[219–220 missing], 19 cm., "Phebe Van Houten and Elvah Collins," SL.

SM371   Where are the friends that love sincerely [f.l.], n.d.[1845 period], [2]13[181]pp., 18½ cm. Mostly hymns; SL.

SM372   Pleasant Walk [f.t.], n.d.[1857–61 period], [16]23[215]pp., 19½ cm., SL.

SM373   Our Heavenly Father's Choice [f.t.] n.d.[1846–69 range], [6]145[131]pp., 18½ cm. Hymns; no music.

SM374   The Saviour's Universal Prayer [f.t.], n.d.[1843–68 period] [6]220pp.[many blank pp. at end; 171, 189, 202 omitted], 18 cm., SL.

SM375   A Choice Collection of Sacred Holy & Divine Songs . . . Transcribed by Gabriel Thompson May 13" 1855[extends to 1860], [6]86[206]pp. 17 cm., SL.

SM376   Searching Light [f.t.], n.d.[range 1837–59], [14]33[295]
        pp., 18 cm., 5-line SL; 1-line SL.
SM377   Immortal Scenes [f.t.], n.d.[hymns dated 1842–47], [6]
        258[17]pp.[64 repeated; 108–9 missing; 122 skips to 203],
        18 cm., SL.
SM378   True Heirs of Heaven [f.t.], n.d.[hymns dated 1856–57],
        n.p., 18 cm., SL.
SM379   A Collection of Short Anthems and Marching tunes . . .
        Began to be written at the close of 1843. n.p., 17 cm., SL.
SM380   Rejoice, rejoice all ye children [f.l.], n.d.[range of hymns
        1837–44 (1867)], n.p., 16 cm. Mostly hymns; PN; 5-line
        SL; SL.
SM381   Virgin Daughter [f.t.], n.d.[hymns dated 1848–52], [6]
        225[14]pp.[78–79 repeated; 99–102 missing; 137 re-
        peated], 15½ cm., SL; PN; 5-line SL.
SM382   Presented to Elder Sister Eliza Ann Taylor [f.l.], June
        16th 1852, [2]98pp., 15 cm. Hymns; no music.
SM383   Angels Descending [f.t.], n.d. "Finished Jan 27d 1843,"
        [range of contents 1816–39], [4]254[4]pp., 17 cm. Hymns;
        no music.
SM384   Gospel truth [f.t.], n.d., n.p., 15½ cm. Hymns; no music.
SM385   A Book, Containing Songs of Praise. For the use of
        Mother's true Children. In Worshipful Devotion. New
        Lebanon Second Order, March 16th 1840[extends to
        1842] [14]145[4]pp.[121 omitted], 14½ cm., SL.
SM386   A Collection of Verses, Written and Pricked By Benja-
        min Gates New Lebanon 1836, [4]193[3]pp.[2 unnum-
        bered pp., 38–39], 12 cm., 5-line SL.
SM387   A Book of Anthems Given by Inspiration to the Be-
        lievers in Christ's Second Appearing . . . Copied by
        Rhoda R. Hollister New Lebanon. Commenced October
        1st 1848, [6]60[2]pp., 16½ cm., SL.
SM388   Whence comes this bright celestial light [f.l.], n.d.[inside
        cover in pencil: "Apr 20 1890"], 166[24]pp.[5–8 missing;
        147 omitted; 165 numbered 166], 21 cm., 2 leaves pasted
        in pp. 90–91.
SM389   Native Songs, n.d.[songs dated 1842–45], [2]21[25]pp.,
        15¼ cm., leaf pasted inside back cover: "Names of the
        fruit in our basket that Father William placed on the
        Table in our room," SL.
SM390   A Collection of Choice Songs, carefully Arranged and

Transcribed by Minerva Reynolds, New Lebanon, October 11th 1857, n.p., 20 cm., SL.

SM391   Esther Markham, A hymnbook containing 33 Hymns, Sept. 13, 1809, 96pp., 18 cm. Words; no music.

SM392   A Prayer [f.t.], n.d.[dated 1875–76], 99[6]pp. [86 omitted], 21¼ cm., SL.

SM393   A Poem [f.t.], n.d., n.p., 15¾ cm. Mostly hymns; SL.

SM394   Collection of Hymns and Spiritual Songs Improved in our General Worship: from 1817, 55 hymns [8]81pp.[3], 19¼ cm. Words only.

SM395   A Collection of Hymns and Spiritual Songs improved in our general worship: from 1817, 96pp., 20 cm. Words only.

SM396   O my children my children [f.l.], n.d.[2 periods; 1825–28 and 1848–50], n.p., 7 cm., 5-line RN; PN; 5-line SL; 1-line SL; SL.

SM397   A Collection of Hymns, 1823, [2]93[5]pp., 19 cm. Words; no music.

SM398   Early Hymns of the Shakers from 1810 on. [4]86[4]pp., 20⅔ cm. Words only.

SM399   A Collection of Hymns Improved in the Sacred Worship of Believers. Selected and Transcribed by Charles Sizer. 1846. [12]380[6]pp.,[55 omitted; 87 repeated; 2 pp. unnumbered, 163–164], 17 cm., SL.

SM400   A Collection of hymns and spiritual songs, n.d., n.p., 17½ cm. Words only.

SM401   A Collection of Anthems and Spiritual Songs Improved in our general worship: from 1811, [8]92[6]pp., 19 cm. Words only.

SM402   Stand to your Post [f.t.], n.d., 232pp.[9 pp. numbered 7–17 starting from back; 1–7 missing; 120 repeated; 135 repeated], 19 cm. Mostly hymns; 5-line SL; 1-line SL; SL.

SM403   Harmonious muse, delightful, good [f.l.], 1832, [4]184 [10]pp., 19 cm. Flyleaf: "Regular Songs by John Wood," 5-line RN.

SM404   Vany, vany, we O vene vany [f.l.], 1839, 114pp.[p. 69 repeated; 101 omitted], 16½ cm., SL; 1-line SL; 5-line SL.

SM405   Book of songs, Many from Union Village Copied by Charles Sizer, 1847 [flyleaf], [12]232[4]pp., 17¼ cm., SL.

SM406   Round Dance Songs [f.t.], n.d.[mostly 1854–61 period], n.p. 15¾ cm., SL.

SM407   I thank my God and Heavenly King [f.l.], n.d., [14]269 [1]pp., 20 cm. Some songs without music, some with SL.

SM408   A little book containing a variety of little songs by a little shepherdess who designed one for each of the Ministry Elders, Brethren and Sisters, W.V.Chh. [Watervliet, N.Y.], n.d. [1]52pp., 16 cm. Words only.

SM409   A little Treasure Book of Divine Hymns [1814–1886], written by Elizabeth R. Avery, 1835, [12]324[2]pp., 15½ cm., SL.

SM410   A Collection of Anthems and Spiritual Songs Improved in our general worship [Henry Youngs, May 1819], [12] 124[14]pp., 10½ cm. Words only.

SM411   A Collection of Hymns and Spiritual Songs Improved in our General worship for the use of good Believers. New Lebanon, 1822, [10]106pp., 19 cm. Words only.

SM412   Youngs, Isaac Newton, Book of Songs, n.d., [1836?], 40 [5]pp., on cover: "No. 3," 9½ cm., RN; 5-line SL.

SM413   Youngs, Isaac Newton, Book of Songs, n.d., confused pagination, [67pp.], 11½ cm., RN; 5-line SL.

SM414   A Collection of Marching Songs etc. Written by Sarah Bates New Lebanon 1849, [extends to 1852], [22]111[63] pp., 17¼ cm., SL.

SM415   A welcome Hymn, Gospel Truth Admired Charity, Gospel Voyage, Babylon's Fall, and Spiritual Union, n.d., n.p., 12 cm. Words only.

SM416   Hymns sung at the funerals of members of The North Union Society of Shakers, [1827–1862], [6]138pp., 9½ cm. Words only.

SM417   The Sound of Freedom [f.t.], n.d., [2]193pp.[many blank pp. at end of book; 5–6 missing], 19¾ cm., SL; 5-line SL.

SM418   Living Shepherd [f.t.], n.d.[hymns and writings 1831–84], [2]185pp.[many blank pp. at end], 19½ cm., "Lorenzo D. Prouty, Shirley," SL.

SM419   Kibbe, Gideon, Book of Songs and Poems, Jan. 11, 1811, n.p., 15 cm. Words only.

SM420   A Collection of verses and little Anthems Improved in our Worship written by Arba Noyes, 1832, [4]46 numbered pp., [69 pp. of verses and songs and 16 blank], 10⅓ cm. Words only.

SM421   Blessed Promise [f.t.], n.d.[hymns dated 1883–88], [4]152 [4]pp., [2pp. between 124–25], 17 cm., RN.

SM422   Come pretty freedom dwell with me [f.l.], n.d.[hymns cover 1866–68 period], n.p., 21 cm., SL.

SM423   A Collection of Various Songs, Composed by Ann Maria Love, 1842–55, [2]62pp., 23 cm., Groveland, N.Y., SL.

SM424   Funeral Hymn for Father David Darrow, Union Village, O 1825, 2pp., 33¾ cm., CL.

SM425   Florida [f.t.?], n.d., n.p., 8 cm., RN. No words, only titles.

SM426   Now forward Israel hasten [f.l.], n.d.[range 1855–56], n.p., 13 cm., leather flap on book like billfold, "Andrew Barrett and Rhoda Blake." SL.

SM427   Peace peace the Angels resound [f.l.], n.d.[songs dated 1862; scrap-book extends to 1905 period], [8]19[21]pp., also many pp. of scribbling and news-clippings], 17 cm., SL.

SM428   Harvest Reward [f.t.], 1867–8 [extends 1909], [5]161[9] pp., 16¾ cm., SL.

SM429   The Book of Witnesses [f.t.], n.d.[hymns dated 1859–65], [7]224[18]pp. [1–57 unnumbered; 89, 98 repeated], 19 cm. Mostly hymns and writings; SL.

SM430   Burdick, Anna, Anna Burdick's hymnbook, Oct. 2, 1811, 16 cm. Words only.

SM Miscellaneous, Container 19, Folders 2, 3, and 4, Papers relating to the practical arts, hymns, poetry, prayers, songs, music, and drawing.

SM500   A Gradual Series of Lessons in the Science of Music. Exercises selected from a variety of Authors. Arranged for the School in Enfield N. H. by James G. Russel., n.d., 72[2]pp., 18½ cm., SL.

SM501   Rules for Learning Music. Copied in 1870. n.p., 23¾ cm., SL; 4-voiced SL; 5-line SL.

SM502   A Gradual Series of Lessons In the Science of Music; Copied by Nancy Ely Moore Feby 24th 1871, [5]122[3] pp., 19¼ cm., SL.

SM503   The Patent Gamut or Scale of Music, 1823, n.p., 10¾ cm., RN and SL.

SM504   A Musical Expositor: Being an index or key to the reading and writing of music according to the letter method. Enfield, Hartford county, Conn 1831 [pencil] by Russell Haskell, n.p., [37]pp., 13½ cm., 5-line SL.

SM505   Rules of Music: musical characters and signs with their explanations, remarks and illustrations; n.d., n.p., 12 cm., 5-line SL.

SM506   Letter from Elder Henry Blinn, Chh. Canterbury, N.H.

to Bro. Jas Calver, Shaker Village, N.H., Dec. 31, 1867, n.p., 21 cm.

SM507 Musical Key; rolled chart used for instruction, by DA. Buckingham, Watervliet, New York, October, 1848.

BERKSHIRE ATHENAEUM, Pittsfield, Massachusetts

V 289.8   Mary Ann Mantle's book, lent to Eunice C. Jany 1879,
Un 3.3   [10]202[5]pp.[66–69 confused; 80–81 omitted; 162 re-
v. 1.   peated], 17½ cm., SL.

V 289.8   Move on don't be bound [f.l.], 1825–37, Mt. Lebanon,
Un 3.3   N.Y., n.p., 11½ cm., 5-line SL; some SL.
v. 2.

V 289.8   Strong Union [f.t.]. n.d.[1854–62], [4]168[4]pp., 19½
Un 3.3   cm., SL.
v. 2.

V 289.8   Mother's Trumpet [f.t.], n.d.[1840–41], n.p., 14½ cm.,
Un 3.3   1-line SL and SL.
v. 3.

V 289.8   Mother's Love [f.t., p. 1], n.d.[1825–40?], [8]208[1]pp.
Un 3.3   [54 omitted], 17 cm.
v. 3.

V 289.8   Angel of Peace [f.t.], n.d.[1839–41], [12]232[4]pp. [con-
Un 3.3   fusion in pp. 210–11]; 13½ cm., SL.
v. 4.

V 289.8   Heavenly Jerusalem [f.t.], 1839–44, [14]232 pp., 17 cm.,
Un 3.3   SL.
v. 5

V 289.8   Index. As stars and diamonds you shall be [f.t. in index],
Un 3.3   [fly leaf: "Presented to Emanuel M. Jones June 3rd
v. 6   1863 by a friend,"], 1853 [last page], [14]283[11]pp.
           [154–55 repeated], 13½ cm., SL.

V 289.8   Preface [f.t.], "Fanny C. Casey Jan. 1887, Alfred, York
Un 3.3   Co. Maine" on fly leaf; n.p., 20 cm., SL.
v. 8

V 289.8   A Collection of Hymns, Improved by the Followers of
Un 3.3   Christ in his Second Appearing. Made for Edward
v. 10   Fowler, By Isaac N. Youngs March 1833. [10]220[2]pp.
           [blank pp. at end; 101 omitted; 116–17 cut out; 124–27
           missing; 130–31 repeated; 134–35 missing; 168 re-
           peated], 17 cm., SL.

V 289.8   Shining Silone [f.t.], n.d., [18]200[18]pp.[9 repeated; 56

Un 3.3   repeated; 159–60 missing], 17½ cm., SL.
v. 11
V 289.8   A Collection of Spiritual Songs for Devotional Wor-
C 61   ship Transcribed by Betsey B. Clisbee. Canaan May
         1859. [4]151[77]pp.[2pp. inserted 26–27], 18½ cm., SL.

The Library of Congress, Manuscript Division

MT   Youngs, Isaac N. [Treatise], The Rudiments of Music.
7   Displayed and explained With a Selleted Variety of
.Y56 case Lessons and Examples. New Lebanon—1833.

Papers of "1837 Moses Eastwood Fourth Book", Watervliet, [4]
Shakers   153[5]pp., 15½ cm. Hymns; no music.
173
Ohio
Union Village[2]

183   Hymns and Prayers. O. C. Hampton, 1866 July (inside
      cover: Susanne C. Liddels Book). [4]323[4]pp.[many empty
      pp.], 20 cm., SL.
188   Hymns (fly leaf: "One of the earliest collections of anthems
      composed & sung after the opening of the Gospel in Ohio,
      Previous to that, songs were mostly even without words. This
      by Stephen Markham. See end. Mount Lebanon, N.Y., Com-
      menced 1811.") [10]78[3]pp.[71 omitted]; 12 cm. Anthems
      and spiritual songs; no music.
189   Hymns 1812–1824 (fly leaf: "Brought from Union Village
      I have understood that our first hymns were composed in
      the West—I think this a rare collection of some of the earli-
      est—perhaps written in the West & brot home by one of the
      missionaries. I esteem it of rare value. Last hym insures that
      it was composed in the West—brought here from there by
      C.A.—") [2]98pp., 16 cm., hymns; no music.
190   1818–41 Songs & Hymns (back fly leaf; "Elder Giles' Tune
      Book—Marches, quick dances, Round dances, Shuffling
      tunes, or Square Order. Slow marches & stand still songs—
      Sung to one syllable, between lo & la. Letter notes were in-
      troduced by Abram Whitney of Shirley, who informed me
      the plan originated with Mother Ann. He received it from

2. All following call numbers are identical to this one except for difference in
the case number, which appears.

her. But few among Believers could read music. The letter notes enabled many to learn both to read & to write it.") [n.p.]; 8 cm., 5-line SL.

191   Sylvia Scott's Hymn Book: containing a Selection of Hymns and Anthems; Adapted to the Worship of God. In Christ's Second Appearing. Union Village, June 1845. [6]144[10]pp. [41–42 missing; 10 repeated; 133 omitted], 19½ cm., SL. Mostly hymns.

192   1823 Covenant Hymn, (inside cover: "Anna Ervin's Book March 23, 1823.") n.p., 20 cm. Hymns; no music.

193   1823 Hymns McNemar [Richard], (Note inside: "This Richard McNemar is not the Preacher Richard McNemar but a nephew of his.") ; n.p., 22 cm. Hymns; no music.

194   A Collection of Hymns and Spiritual Songs Improved in our general worship. Written by Joseph Fearnay February 8th 1824. [4]53pp.[50–51 repeated]; 13 cm. Hymns; no music.

195   A Hymn Book 1 written by Moses Eastwood March the 22nd 1836. These Hymns, collected here has been in general use by the society of believers at Watervliet Ohio Montgomery County. [4]116[4]pp., 15½ cm. Hymns; no music.

196   Moses Eastwood November the 7. 1839 His Hymn book. The hymns collected in this book are those used by believers in the beginning at Watervliet Montgomery County Ohio. [4]175[3]pp., 16 cm., [in letter folder]. Eastwood's second book. Hymns; no music.

197   1839 Hymns [f.l.] Come lovely vigins now arise. [4]113[11] pp., 15 cm. Hymns; no music.

198   Edwin H. Burnham's Hymn Book Bot at Cincinnati November 27th 1841 Price 56¼ ct. (inside page: "A Selection of Hymns and Pomes. For the use of Believers. White Water Village Ohio") [4]153[47]pp., [13–14 cut; 25–26 cut], 18 cm. Leather folder; SL.

199   The Gospel Child [f.t.], (Cover: "1842–45 Songs and verse.") . n.p., 15½ cm. Hymns; no music.

200   1842–56 Hymns Vincy McNemar (inside: "A Selection of hymns Composed After the year ending 42 written mostly By Vincy McNemar Sketches From 1842 till 1856.") [4]101 [33]pp., 17 cm. Binding damaged; SL.

201   A Collection of Gospel Anthems Given to the followers of Christ In his second Appearing Selected and Transcribed By Hannah Wilson Canaan, N. Y. March 19th 1843. [2]52

[14]pp. [30–31 sealed]; 15 cm. Anthems; no music.

202   A Funeral Hymn Sacred to the memory of Brother Andrew C. Houston Oct. 8th 1844. [f.t.], n.p., 16 cm., SL.

203   Omar Pease's Book. Enfield Conn., n.d. [up to 1845], [6]112-[10]pp., 15 cm., SL. Mostly hymns; words.

204   How lovely the place where thy children do meet [f.l.], 1846; n.p., 21½ cm. Hymns; no music.

205   The Angel's Call [f.t.]. 1846, 79[4]pp., [Confused pagination;]20 cm., SL.

206   James McNemar's Book of Anthems, December 27, 1846. [4]279[15]pp., [103 repeated; 245–49 skipped in series], 19 cm., SL.

207   Containing A Choice Selection of Hymns Anthems & spiritual songs used by the children of Zion . . . January *th* 11, 1846. [4]9[189]pp., 20 cm., SL.

208   Edwin Burnham's Hymn Book. January 15th 1855, [4]128-[67]pp., 18½ cm., SL.

209   Hymns selected & transcribed by J.W.B. 1848 to 1854. [4]35 intermittently numbered[145]pp., 15½ cm., SL.

210   Hymns and Songs, 1847. [2]180[4]pp.[at 65 pages cut out], 16 cm., SL.

211   1849–50—Hymns Prayers. [6]160pp., [13–14 cut out; ditto 79–80; ditto 151–2], 16 cm. Hymns; no music.

212   1849–50 Records of Hymns for Use of J. Morris, n.p., 19 cm. Hymns; no music.

213   Shakers Hymn Book 1850 Index. 384[4]pp. [57–58 cut out; 323–46 missing], 16½ cm., SL.

214   Lines Addressed to Sister Anna [f.t.]. 1851; n.p.; 21 cm., In a printed book: "The Scholar's Record Book." Hymns; no music.

215   Mary Ann Holland's Book of Spiritual Songs; Commenced October 5th 1852. n.p., 21 cm., SL.

216   Hymns by S. M. Brady 1856–1858, n.p., 20 cm., SL.

217   No. 3 Hymn Book 1858. (Inside cover: "Hymn Book The Property of Isaac N. Houston; Second Family, Union Village, Ohio, December 25th 1858.") [6]170[12]pp. [133–40 cut out], 16 cm., SL.

218   [Index] Come my beloved companions come [f.l.], [Carolyn Jaynes on fly leaf], 1863. [10]172pp.[52 repeated; 77 omitted; 173–76 torn out], 20½ cm., SL.

219   The Angelic Train [f.t.], 1868, n.p., 20 cm., SL.

220   Millennial Praises Collected by Susannie M. Brady. 1868.

[3]242[1]pp. [199–200 cut out; 223–24 cut; 229–32 missing], 22 cm., SL.

221   Wm. Redmon's book. 1872. [4]284[15]pp.[100–101 repeated; 144 repeated; 158 omitted; 233 repeated; 276–79 cut out], 20 cm. One page of modern round notes near end. SL.

222   Christmas Hymn [f.t.], 1873, [7]163pp. [161 repeated; printed pp. from *Shaker and Shakeress* inserted], 13½ cm., SL.

223   Elizabeth Farr's Book. March 9th 1878. 122pp., 22 cm., SL.

224   Love floats on the breeze of the changes [f.l.], 1891, n.p., 20 cm., SL.

225   The Harmony of Angels [f.t.], n.d., [songs range 1843–8], 247[11]pp., 11½ cm., SL; one, 5-line SL.

226   The Gospel Trumpet [f.t.] (On inside cover: "Recorded by Anna Granger, Enfield Conn"), n.d., 42pp.[13–14 omitted], 16 cm. Hymns; no music.

227   Who will bow and bend like a willow [f.l.], n.d., [4]305-[13]pp., [skips 90–100], 17½ cm., SL.

228   [Fly leaf] "Mary Ransom" [p. preceding p. 1 has a table of Improved Modes], n.d., [4]106[4]pp., 15 cm., buckwheat notes (black) on 5 lines.

229   The Angels are sounding on their golden trumpet [f.l.], n.d., n.p., 19 cm. Hymns; no music.

230   *B*. A Brief Collection of Hymns Improved in Sacred Worship, Written by Isaac Newton Youngs, Beginning January 1st 1826 (finished September 16th 1832). [10]145[3]pp., 16½ cm. Hymns; no music.

345   Contains some loose leaf hymns. Also an index for *Millennial Praises,* identifying composers of hymns.

346   Contains recent copies, made by Susanna C. Liddell of the hymns (words only) printed in *Millennial Praises* and some of the 1833 hymnal.

349   (sec. 1) Loose leaf hymns and a few with music included (Manila folder).

349   (sec. 2) McNemars Hymns (Manila folder). Loose leaf copies of many of his hymns.

349   (sec. 3) Will you be good both night and day [f.l.], (loose leaf inside states: "Vincy MacNemar's Hymn Book written by herself in time of the spiritual work of Mother's Wisdom in all the Shaker societies In the early forties") [1840], n.p., 17½ cm. (Manila folder). Hymns; no music.

360   Anthems Given on Gold Plates; August 30th 1846, Union

Village, Ohio, [Charles D. Hampton] 252[10]pp.[pages cut out near end], 21 cm., SL.

361 A Hymn Book; Containing a collection of Ancient Hymns; . . . by Paulina Bryant. 1854. [4]405[11]pp., 32½ cm., SL and 5-line SL.

CONNECTICUT STATE LIBRARY, Hartford, Connecticut

289.84   A Collection of Hymns & Spiritual Songs Improved in
Sh ll   our General Worship.
         Written in the year of our Lord 1828! n.p., 18½ cm.
1828   Words only, except for two examples of SL added later
         in pencil.
289.84   The Harmony of Angels [f.t.], n.d. [1840–50?], [2]345pp.-
Sh ll   [many blank pages and index at end; 2 pp. inserted 261–
         62], 10½ cm. Harmony of Angels in 5-line SL with
         colored ink; remainder SL.
289.94   Hymn Book Written in the Summer of 1852. [12]211[8]-
Sh ll   pp.[85 repeated; 2 pp. inserted 91–92; ditto 95–96; ditto
1852   98–99; 128–33 confused; 193 repeated], 17½ cm., SL.
289.84   Beauty Union and Love [f.t.] n.d., [1863–74 date range,
Sh ll   but contains hymns written earlier], [10]309[31]pp.[20–
         23 omitted; 66 omitted; 85 omitted; 101 omitted; 235
         omitted; p. between 273–74; ditto 296–97], 11 cm., SL.

COLLECTION OF AUTHOR

A Selection of Spiritual Songs Used in the Sacred Worship of Believers. Transcribed By Eliza Rayson Commenced March 4th 1867, [6]346[4]pp. [144–45 repeated; 310–20 repeated], 18 cm., SL.

Spiritual Songs Adapted to Believers Worship. Transcribed by Martha Ann Burger. January 1875. [4]289[3]-pp., 20 cm., SL.

A Collection of Spiritual Songs, Transcribed by Sarah J. Burger, January 1886. n.p., 20 cm., SL.

GROSVENOR LIBRARY, Buffalo, New York

BV 442   A Valient Worrior [f.t.], n.d., [date range of songs
M2   1840–1845], [4]109[259]pp., [blank pages near end;
Acc. No. songs numbered 1-567, and 5 unnumbered songs; 81

282264   numbered, and 10 unnumbered, noted songs], 20
              cm., SL.

SHAKER COMMUNITY, *Hancock, Massachusetts*

Jacob's Ladder [f.t.], n.p., n.d., 20 cm., SL.
I feel a sweet influence Upon us, [f.l.], n.d., [1849–1902],-
[2] 203[15]pp., 20½ cm., SL.

UNIVERSITY OF MICHIGAN, *Ann Arbor, Michigan*

Rare book room 51508	A Selected Variety of Spiritual Songs. Used by Believers in their general Worship. Compiled by Levi Shaw. Canaan, N.Y., 1840. [4]309[15]pp., 19½ cm., SL. 5-line SL; 1-line SL. (Flyleaf: "Bound by Henry De Witt, New Lebanon.")
Rare book room 50865	The Song's of Zion Copied by Anna White 1858, [date range of hymns 1858 to 1863]; [6]256[6]pp., 19½ cm., SL.
Rare book room 50865	Sacred Songs [n.d.], [range of dated hymns 1876–1880], [4]290 [2]pp., 20 cm., SL. (Flyleaf: "Martha J. Anderson.")

SHAKER COMMUNITY, *New Lebanon, New York*

The path of the just shineth brighter each day [f.l.],
n.d., [1880]; [4]288[4]pp., 20 cm., round note notation. Copied in the hand of Sister Rosetta Stephens.

NEW YORK STATE LIBRARY, *Albany, New York*

CM 354	"This Collection of Sacred Songs was Compiled and Transcribed by Rollin Cramer of Watervliet N. Y. Songs received mostly during the years from 184 [sic.] to 1847. M. C. Allen." [8]115 pp. [Many blank pp. at end], 17 cm., SL. Harmony of Angels. Colored inks and 7-line letteral.
CM 355	A Collection of Hymns Improved in our Sacred Worship. Written by Henry De Witt Beginning August 2nd 1852 New Lebanon Columbia Co State N. Y. Peter H. Long's Hym Book Feb. 1854. [14]178-pp.[many unnumbered pp. of music & many blank

pp.; 13 repeated; 45–46 repeated; 55 omitted; 103 repeated], 17½ cm., SL.

CM 10243 (5)   "Louise Russell" (inside cover); "Polly C. Lewis, New Lebanon, 1851. Alice Spooner Groveland 1870," following page; [16]400[24]pp. [45–62 cut out; all blank pages after 43], 20 cm., SL.

CM 10243 (6)   A Choice Collection of Sacred Holy & Divine Songs. And Hymns Improved by the Believers in The Solmn & Devotional Worship of God . . . Written by Gabriel Thompson June 1st 1854. [12]119pp. [many unnumbered and blank pp. follow], 17½ cm., SL.

CM 10243 (7)   Path of Sorrow [f.t.], n.d., [1845–1876], [12]68pp.- [many pp. cut out after 69 and followed by blank pp.], "Fletcher" pasted on inside cover. 18 cm. Hymns; no music.

CM 10243 (8)   Illumed is our pathway, with scenes which brighter grow, [f.l.], [dated range 1865–71], ["Lydia Dole, Groveland" on inside cover], n.p., 18 cm., SL.

CM 10243 (9)   A Choice Selection of Divine Hymns Sung in our Sacred Worship. Written by Louie Russell, Groveland May 14th 1887. [6]288[6]pp. 19½ cm. One hymn in SL. ["Elizah Boardman" on leather cover; "Hymns" on binding; 1 page from *The Shaker* pasted on inside cover], mostly words only.

CM 10243 (10)   A Collection of Millennial Hymns Adapted To the present Order, of the Church . . . Laura Dole Groveland, Apr. 10th 1864. [4]37pp. [many blank pp. at end], 19½ cm., SL.

CM 358   A Treatise on Music; agreeably to the Plan established and adapted at New Lebanon & Watervliet, N. Y. 1840 [pencil] Isaak N. Youngs & David Austin Buckingham. 36 pp., 12 cm., SL.

WILLIAMS COLLEGE LIBRARY, Williamstown, Massachusetts

A Little Book Containing the Songs Given by the Shepherdess in the Church at Shirley Commencing Nov. 3rd 1844. Each Numbered as They were Given. [n.p.], 15 cm., SL.

Katie Dillon West Pittsfield Mass. Dec. 28th, 1884. List of songs I know. [f.l.], n.p., 16½ cm. Words; no music.

A Collection of Noted Songs. Written by Abm. Perkins, Enfield

1839. n.p., 12 cm., CL on 5 lines; SL on 5 lines. Signature in Shaker shorthand. All dancing tunes; no words.

A Poem [f.t.]; n.d., [songs dated 1844], [4]30 (confused) [110] pp. [many blank pp. near end], 15½ cm., SL.

Songs . . . Martha J. Anderson July 1867. [extend to 1871], [2] 210[8]pp., 19½ cm., SL.

There is a calm for those who weep [f.l.], n.d.,[dates range 1836–55]; n.p., 14½ cm., SL. A few dance tunes.

Ye are Gods Building [f.t.] n.d., [2]367[11]pp.[181 omitted; 190–93 cut out; 2 pp. between 299–300; 357 omitted], 17½ cm. Hymns; no music.

Fellow Travellers [f.t.], n.d., [1849 on dated hymns]; [1]55 [16]pp.[3–9 confused; 11–20 omitted; last half of book cut out and rebound], 17½ cm., SL. on 5 lines; SL.

Angels' Declaration [f.t.] n.d., [1851–59 range] n.p., 17½ cm., SL.

Farewell Blessing of our Heavenly Parents as they left our Meetingroom with Holy Mother Wisdom, 20 minutes before 9 Tuesday Evening December 6th 1842. [f.t.], [flyleaf: "Book commenced December 8th, 1842."] n.p., [311 numbered songs], 20 cm., SL.

Appendix: Printed Shaker Hymnals

1813   *Millennial Praises;* Hancock [Massachusetts], Printed by Joshiah Tallcott, Junior [Four parts printed separately in 1812] [No music], 17 cm.

1833   *A Selection of Hymns and Poems; For the Use of Believers,* collected from sundry authors, by Philos Harmoniae; Watetvliet [*sic*] (Ohio), [No music], 17 cm.

1847   *A Collection of Millennial Hymns; Adapted to the Present Order of the Church,* Printed in the United Society, Canterbury, N. H. [No music], 13½ cm.

1852   *A Sacred Repository of Anthems and Hymns for Devotional Worship and Praise;* Canterbury, N. H., [Printed letteral notation; no harmony], 20½ cm.

1875   *Shaker Music—Inspirational Hymns and Melodies Illustrative of the Resurrection Life and Testimony of the Shakers.* Albany, N. Y., Weed, Parsons and Co., [4-part harmony, round notes, some 1-line melodies], 19 cm.

1875–92 *Shaker Music* [printed at different periods; bound together], Canterbury, N. H. [Round notes, 4-part harmony; some single-line melodies, round notes], 24½ cm.

1876   *A Selection of Devotional Melodies; Simple in Arrangement, Yet,—Inspirational,* Canterbury, N. H. Pub. & Printed at Shaker Village, [Round notes; mostly single-line melodies; some 4-part harmony], 14½ cm.

1878   *A Collection of Harmonies and Melodies, Adapted to Sacred Worship,* Pub. and printed at Shaker Village, [Round note; 4-part harmony; single-line melodies], 23 cm.

1878–80 A volume of loose-leaves printed; mostly marked Canterbury, N. H., [4-part harmony, round notes], 26 cm.

1883   *Shaker Anthems and Hymns, arranged for Divine Worship,* Shaker Village, N. H., [4-part harmony; round notes; nearly all marked Canterbury, N. H.] 23 cm.

1884   *Shaker Music. Original Inspirational Hymns and Songs Illustrative of the Resurrection Life and Testimony of the Shakers,* New York; Pub. for the North Family, Mt. Lebanon, N. Y., by Wm. A. Pond & Co., 25 Union Sq. Copyright 1884 by Daniel Offord, [Round notes; mostly 4-part harmony; a few single-line melodies], 21 cm.

1887   *Shaker Anthems and Hymns, Arranged for Divine Worship,* Printed at Canterbury, Shaker Village, N. H., [Round note; 4-part harmony; almost no 1-line melody], 24 cm.

1892   *A Collection of Hymns and Anthems Adapted to Public Worship.* Published by the Shakers. East Canterbury, N. H., [Collected from *Manifesto* over 14-year period; round note; mostly 4-part harmony], 23½ cm.

1893   *Original Shaker Music,* Published by the North Family of Mt. Lebanon, Col. Co., N. Y., New York: Wm. A. Pond & Co., 25 Union Sq., [4-part harmony in round-notes], 21 cm.

1896   *Shaker Hymnal,* Canterbury, N. H., [Melodies and 4-part harmony in round notes; loose leaf, bound], 22 cm.

1908   *Shaker Hymnal by the Canterbury Shakers,* The Canterbury Shakers, East Canterbury, N. H., [Round note; 4-part harmony; a few melodies], 23½ cm.

n.d.   *The Musical Messenger; A compilation of Hymns, Slow and Quick Marches, Etc., Used in Worship by Believers.* Published by The United Society of Believers, Union Village, Ohio, F. Estes, Lebanon, Ohio, [Letteral printed in written script style all on one level], 20½ cm.

Bibliography

Printed Material

The American Vocalist. Boston, n.d. (title page partly torn off) .

Andrews, Edward D. *The Community Industries of the Shakers.* New York State Museum Handbook 15, Albany: The University of the State of New York, 1933.

———. *The Gift to Be Simple,* New York: J. J. Augustin, 1940.

Apel, Willi, *The Notation of Polyphonic Music 900–1600,* Cambridge, Mass.: The Mediaeval Academy of America, 1945.

———. *Gregorian Chant.* London, 1958.

Barry, Phillips. "Communal Recreation." *Bulletin of the Folk-Song Society of the Northeast* 5 (1933) : 4–6.

———. "Heavenly Display." *Bulletin of the Folk-Song Society of the Northeast* 1 (1930) : 6–7.

———. "Polish Ballad. Trzy Siostry (The Three Sisters) ." *Bulletin of the Folk-Song Society of the Northeast* 11 (1936) : 2–4.

Blinn, Henry Clay. *The Manifestations of Spiritualism Among the Shakers, 1837–47.* East Canterbury, N. H., 1899.

Brown, Thomas. *An Account of the People Called Shakers: Their faith, doctrines, and practice, etc.* Troy: Printed by Parker and Bliss, 1812.

Burney, Charles. *A General History of Music.* 2 vols. New York: Harcourt, Brace Iovanovich, Inc., 1935.

Carden, Allen D. *The Missouri Harmony.* Cincinnati: Morgan and Sanxay, 1835.

Christian Songster (title page missing; no data.)

Cole, Arthur C. "The Puritan and Fair Terpsichore." *Mississippi Valley Historical Association Bulletin,* XXIX (June, 1942) .

A Collection of Hymns and Anthems Adapted to Public Worship. East Canterbury, N. H.: Published by the Shakers, 1892.

Cutten, George Barton. *Speaking with Tongues. Historically and Psychologically Considered.* New Haven: Yale University Press, 1927.

[Darrow, David, Meacham, John, Youngs, Benjamin S.]. *Testimony of Christ's Second Appearing, Exemplified by the Principles and Practice of the True Church of Christ*. Albany: Published by the Shakers, printed by Van Benthuysen, 1856.

The Day-Star. Cincinnati. v. 1–13, No. 3; 1841–July 1, 1847 (?) v. 1–4, No. 13; 1841–Feb. 7, 1845, as the *Western Midnight Cry! The Day Star* was published in New York, August 8 and 25, 1846; in Shaker Village, Merrimack Co., New Hampshire, Sept. 19, 1846; in Union Village, Ohio, Nov. 7, 1846–

Dictionary of American Biography. Edited by Dumas Malone. 20 vols., New York: Charles Scribner's Sons, 1933.

Dixon, Harold F. "Three Men on a Raft," *Life Magazine* 12 (April 6, 1942) : 76.

Dyer, Mary. *A Portraiture of Shakerism* [New Hampshire?], 1822.

Ely, Richard T. *The Labor Movement in America*. New York and Boston: Thomas Y. Crowell Company, 1890.

Evans, F. W. *Shakers Compendium, etc*. New York: D. Appleton & Co., 1859.

Ferguson, Donald N. *A History of Musical Thought*. New York: F. S. Crofts & Co., 1940.

Fillmore, A. D. *The Temperance Musician*. Cincinnati: Applegate & Co. (?) , 1853.

————. *The Violet*. Cincinnati: R. W. Carroll & Co., 1867.

Fillmore's New Nightingale and Sunday School Singer. Cincinnati: Applegate & Co., 1862.

Fletcher, Alice C., *Indian Story and Song*. Boston: Small, Maynard & Co., 1900.

Gabriel, Ralph Henry, ed. *The Pageant of America*. 15 vols. New Haven: Yale University Press, 1925.

[Green, Calvin, and Wells, Seth Y.] *A Summary View of the Millennial Church, or United Society of Believers. (Commonly Called Shakers)*. Albany: Packard & Van Benthuysen, 1823.

Grove's Dictionary of Music and Musicians. "Tune-Books," 6: 385–92, New York: The Macmillan Company, 1928.

Harrison, Thomas. *Juvenile Numeral Singer*. 1852.

Haskell, Russel. *A Musical Expositor, or a Treatise on the Rules and Elements of Music*. New York: George W. Wood, 1847.

Haskett, William J. *Shakerism Unmasked; or the History of the Shakers*, Pittsfield: E. H. Walkley, Printer, 1828.

Hicks, John D. *The Federal Union*. Boston: Houghton Mifflin Company, 1937.

Holyoke, Samuel, ed. *The Instrumental Assistant*. Vol. 1. Exeter, Newhampshire [*sic*]: H. Ranlet, n.d.

Idelsohn, A. Z. *Jewish Music in Its Historical Development*. New York: Holt, Rinehart and Winston, Inc., 1929.

Jackson, George P. *Down-East Spirituals and Others*. New York: J. J. Augustin, 1939.

———. *Spiritual Folk-Songs of Early America*. New York: J. J. Augustin, 1937.

———. *White and Negro Spirituals*. New York: J. J. Augustin, 1943.

Laloy, Louis, *La Musique Chinoise*. Paris: Librairie Renouard, n.d.

Lamson, David R. *Two Years' Experience Among the Shakers*. West Boylston: Published by the Author, 1848.

Lane, Charles. "A Day with the Shakers." *The Dial* 4 (1844) : 165–73.

MacLean, John P. *A Bibliography of Shaker Literature*. Columbus, Ohio: Published for the Author by Fred. J. Heer, 1905.

M'Nemar, Richard. *The Kentucky Revival*. New York: Printed by Edward O. Jenkins, 1846.

Manifesto (The). Monthly Vols. 1–29. 1871–1899 Shakers, New York: East Canterbury, New Hampshire; title varies: *Shaker*. 1871–72, 1876–77; *Shaker and Shakeress*, 1873–75; *Shaker Manifesto*, 1878–83; *Manifesto*, 1884–99.

Millennial Praises. Containing a collection of Gospel Hymns in Four Parts: adapted to the Day of Christ's Second Appearing. Composed for the use of His People. Hancock: Printed by Josiah Tallcott, Jr., 1813.

Mursell, James L. *The Psychology of Music*. New York: W. W. Norton & Company, Inc., 1937.

The Musical Messenger. Union Village, Ohio: United Society of Believers; Lebanon, Ohio: F. Estes, n.d.

Phillippi, J. M. *Shakerism or the Romance of a Religion*. Dayton, Ohio: The Otterbein Press, 1912.

Philos Harmoniae [Richard McNemar]. *A Selection of Hymns and Poems; For the Use of Believers*. Watetvliet [sic], (Ohio), 1833.

A Prayer Meeting and Revival Hymn Book. Harrisburg, 1825.

Reese, Gustave. *Music in the Middle Ages*. New York: W. W. Norton & Company, Inc., 1940.

Richardson, A. Madeley. *The Mediaeval Modes*. New York: H. W. Gray Company, 1933.

Ritter, Frédéric Louis. *Music in America*. New York: Charles Scribner's Sons, 1890.

Sachs, Curt. *The Rise of Music in the Ancient World East and West*. New York: W. W. Norton & Company, Inc., 1943.

A Sacred Repository of Anthems and Hymns. Canterbury, N. H., 1852.

Schweitzer, Albert. *J. S. Bach*. 2 vols., Leipzig: Breitkopf & Härtel, 1911.

Sears, Clara Endicott. *Gleanings from Old Shaker Journals*. Boston and New York: Houghton Mifflin Company, 1916.

Shaker Broadsides (in The Western Reserve Historical Society).
Instruction in Vocal Culture (mounted on board)
Song Leaflet, "Christ's Sufferings," Vols. 2, 5.
Song Leaflet, "Happy Land," Vols. 5, 6.

Shaker Music, Inspirational Hymns and Melodies Illustrative of the Resurrection Life and Testimony of the Shakers. Albany: Weed, Parsons and Company, 1875.

Sharp, Cecil J. *English Folk-Song Some Conclusions*. London: Simpkins & Co., 1907.

Sharp, Cecil J., and MacIlwaine, Herbert C., eds. *Morris Dance Tunes*. Set II (new ed). London: Novello & Co., Ltd., 1912.

The Sweet Singer of Israel. Pittsburgh: John I. Kay & Co., 1837.

Taylor, Leila S. *A Memorial to Eldress Anna White and Elder Daniel Offord*. Mt. Lebanon, N. Y.: North Family of Shakers, 1912.

Tovey, Donald Francis. *Musical Articles from the Encyclopaedia Britannica*. London: Oxford University Press, 1944.

Voltaire. *Oeuvres Complètes*. 52 vols. Paris: Garnier Frères, 1879. Vol. 22.

Wakefield, Esq., Samuel. *The Christian Harp*. Pittsburgh: D. N. White, 1836.

Walker, William, ed. *The Southern Harmony and Musical Companion*. New York: Hastings House Publishers, Inc., 1939.

White, Anna, and Taylor, Leila S. *Shakerism Its Meaning and Message*. Columbus: Fred. J. Heer, 1904.

Youngs, Isaac N. *A Short Abridgement of the Rules of Music*. New Lebanon [New York], 1843.

Manuscript Material

(in The Western Reserve Historical Society, Cleveland, Ohio, unless otherwise specified)

Avery, Giles B. Daily Journal 1836–1838.
———. Diary (1869).
———. Diary (1876).
———. Diary (1880).
———. Journal (1834–36).
———. Notebook (pencil) 184–.

Barrett, Andrew D. A Collection of interesting matter written for the Edification & perusal of writer Commenced Oct. 12, 1867.

Buckingham, David A. Journal B. Church or 1st Order, Watervliet, N. Y., 1848–1854.

Bullard, Eldress Harriet. Journal of a trip to the southern and western societies. Mar. 22–May 29, 1889.

Cramer, P. C. Common-place Book. 1836.

DeWitt, John. Journal. 1825

Green, Calvin. Remarks on Music, Instrumental and vocal.

Grove, Betty, John O., & Sally L. Journal. Harvard, Mass., Aug. 31, 1840.

Hammond, Lucy Ann. Journal. 1830.

Hammond, Thomas. Church Journal. Harvard 1816–1872.

Haskell, Russel. A Musical Expositor: Being an index or key to the reading & writing of music according to the letter method. Enfield, Hartford County, Conn., 1831. (Inscription on fly-leaf to Br. Austin.)

Hollister, Alonzo Giles (1830–1911). The Book of Moses and of Miscellaneous writings deemed worth preserving. Copied by A. G. Hollister, chiefly from original manuscripts.

Letter from Samuel [Hooser], Union Village, Ohio, Feb. 28, 1808 to Calvin [Green], New Lebanon, N. Y.

Letter from Caleb, Daniel, Ruth, Betty, to the Elders of the first Family [?], Harvard, July 10, 1808.

Letter from Daniel [Moseley], Union Village, Warren County, Ohio, Feb. 19, 1812, to Richard Spier.

Letter from Isaac N. Youngs, New Lebanon, N. Y., June 18, 1818, to Eldress Molly (?), Union Village, Ohio.

Letter from the New Lebanon Ministry, Feb. 18, 1821, to the Ministry, Buaro, Ind.

Letter from the Canterbury Ministry to the Harvard Ministry, Apr. 10, 1821.

Letter from David [Darrow], Union Village, Ohio, July 31, 1824, to the Ministry.

Letter from Harvard Ministry, Jan. 21, 1830, to "Beloved and much esteemed Ministry," (?)

Letter from the Enfield, N. H., Ministry, Feb. 11, 1830, to the Harvard Ministry.

Letter from Thomas Hammond, Harvard, [Mass.] June 7, 1830, to Isaac Youngs, New Lebanon.

Letter from Isaac N. Youngs to Beloved brother Andrew [Houston?], New Lebanon, Aug. 6, 1830.

Letter from Hervey L. Eads, South Union, Ky., Apr. 22, 1833, to Isaac N. Youngs.

Letter from Russel Haskell, Enfield, Conn., Feb. 10, 1834, to Isaac N. Youngs.

Letter from Russel Haskell, Enfield, Hartford County, Conn., to D. A. Buckingham, Watervliet, N. Y., Sept. 25, 1834.

Letter from D. A. Buckingham, Watervliet, N. Y., Nov. 12, 1834, to Russell Haskell, Enfield, Conn.

Letter from Abraham Whitney, Shirley, Mass., May 25, 1835, to Isaac N. Youngs.

Letter from Isaac Youngs, New Lebanon, N. Y., to Beloved Brethren (?), Aug. 11, 1837.

Letter from the Ministry at Shaker Village, Merrimack Co., N. H., Jan. 29, 1838, to the Ministry at Watervliet.

Letters from different societies written 1817–1841, letter No. 15; Hancock, June 29, 1838, to the Ministry, by Olive Spencer, 111–2.

Letter from (?) New Lebanon, N. Y., Jan. 10, 1840, to Beloved Ministry.

Letter from Isaac N. Youngs, New Lebanon, N. Y., Sept. 1, 1840, to Brother (?) in SM 162, 131–138.

Letter from Giles B. Avery, New Lebanon, N. Y., Sept. 6, 1841, to Abraham Perkins, Enfield, N. H.

Letter from Andrew Houston, Union Village, Ohio, Oct. 16, 1841, to Isaac N. Youngs.

Letter from Isaac N. Youngs, New Lebanon, Nov. 16, 1842, to D. A. Buckingham.

Letter from Lovely Vineyard to the Ministry, Feb. 9, 1843.

Letter from D. A. Buckingham, Watervliet, Jan. 24, 1844, to the Societies.

Letter from (?) New Lebanon, N. Y., Feb. 2, 1845.

Letter from (?) Watervliet, N. Y., Jan. 1847, to "Beloved Brother."

Letter from Benjamin B. Dunlavy, Pleasant Hill, Ky., Sept. 1, 1847, to Isaac N. Youngs.

Letter from B. B. Dunlavy, Pleasant Hill, Ky., Apr. 9, 1852, to Beloved Brother Isaac [Youngs].

Letter from North Union, June 16, 1852. Copied by i.y. [Isaac Youngs].

Letter from David Parker, Shaker Village, N. H., Sept. 20, 1854, to Giles B. Avery, New Lebanon, N. Y.

Letter from Lorenzo D. Grosvenor, South Groton, Mass., Dec. 13, 1855, to Giles [B. Avery].

Letter from Elder Henry C. Blinn, East Canterbury, N. H., Sept. 3, 1897, to Elder Joseph Holden.

Letter from Anna Case, Sabbothday Lake, Maine, Nov. 1, 1933, to Walter [sic] M. Cathcart, Cleveland, Ohio.

Little, William, and Smith, William. The Patent Gamut or Scale of Music. 1823.

Meacham, Father Joseph, and Wright, Mother Lucy. Millennial Laws, or Gospel Statutes & Ordinances adapted to the day of Christ's Second Appearing by Father Joseph Meacham & Mother Lucy Wright. Aug. 7, 1821.

[Meacham]. Father Joseph's Writings, begun Nov. 27, 1873 [collected].

Melinda's Record. Copies of Instructions, Letters, Hymns & Anthems, Remarkable Events, &c., South Union, 1821.

Papers of Shakers. Nos. 149 and 150 (two copies) (in the Library of Congress).

Papers of Shakers. No. 189, Ohio, Union [Village], Ohio (in the Library of Congress).

Papers of Shakers. No. 190 (in Library of Congress), Box 33. Elder Giles Tune-book.

Papers of Shakers. No. 208. Union Village (in Library of Congress), 70.

SM numbers. SM numbers will be found listed in numerical order in the collation of manuscripts.

Songs & Anthems given in Mother's Manifestation. Jan. 30, 1848.

A variety of little Songs Designed for each of the Ministry, Elders, Brethren and Sisters. Watervliet, N. Y., 1844.

Youngs, Isaac N. Diary. Papers of Shakers, No. 32 (in Library of Congress).

Journal by Isaac Newton Youngs. Papers of Shakers, No. 42, Shakers, N. Y. Canaan, 1815–1823.

Youngs, Isaac N. Sketches of Visions and various spiritual gifts of which I obtain Information in various ways. 1838.

Index

MacLean, John, 38

McNemar, James: uses gapped scales, 135

McNemar, Richard, 15, 16, 19, 38, 165, 201, 205, 206

Manchester, England: Shakers in, 14; state of music in 1747, 32

Manifestations of Spiritualism among the Shakers 1837-1847, The. See Blinn, Henry C.

Marches, 190-91, 215-16

Mariah, The (ship), 13

Mather, Cotton, 29

Matthewson, Anna, 21; her funeral song, 241

Meacham, Father Joseph, 22, 23, 24, 183

Meacham, John, 15

Mediaeval Modes, The. See Richardson, A. Madeley

Membership, 19; decline after Civil War, 131; transients, 162

Memorial to Eldress Anna White, A. See Taylor, Leila S.

"Merry Dancers," 29, 38, 165

Meter, 143-45; measure, 145, 228, 238

Methodists, 29, 38, 165

Metronome markings, 119-20, 127-28

Millennial Church, established in America, 13

Millennial Laws. *See* Meacham, Father Joseph; Wright, Mother Lucy

Millenial Praises Hymnal (1813), 27, 29; alternate tunes for, 44-45; furnishes words for other sects, 45-46; includes work from other sects, 40, 43, 45; printed, 40; quoted, 50, 166, 182, 185, 187, 195, 196, 198, 200, 208; "The Seasons," 34-35; tunes for, 40, 43

Missionaries, Shaker, 38, 76

Mississippi Valley Historical Review. See Cole, Arthur C.

Missouri Harmony, The. See Carden, Allen D.

Modal scales, 114-17; shift in tonality in different versions of tune, 177-78; transposed, 135

Modes of time, 120; application in Shaker song types, 122; "Improved," 122; no longer mentioned, 130, 143-44

Modulation, rare in Shaker harmony, 162

Mormons, 60

Morris dance ("The Black Joke") adapted to Shaker worship, 34

Morris Dance Tunes. See Sharp, Cecil

Moseley, Daniel, 198

Mother Ann Lee, 13-17, 22, 28; birthday of, 209; celibacy and, 30, 35; inspires notation system, 77, 83; mentioned, 214, 222-23, 232, 236, 237; reputed to have spoken foreign tongues, 64; song from, 53; voice of, 164, 190, 193; welcomed home to New Lebanon, 43

Motioning, 194, 210-12, 215-16, 235-36

Motives: common to two periods in form, 155; common to two tunes, 156

Mountain meeting songs, 233-34

Mount Lebanon. *See* New Lebanon

Mursell, James F., 141

Musica ficta, 179-81

Musical characters, 110-14

Musical Expositor, A. (Haskell): on accent, 129-30, 133, 148, 178-79, 182; published and reprinted, 110, 124

Musical illustration, 157-59

Musical instruments, 130, 182, 184; harmonium, 136, 163

Musical Messenger, The, 43, 103

Music articles from *The Encyclopedia Britannica. See* Tovey, Donald Francis

Music in America. See Ritter, Fred L.

Music in the Middle Ages. See Reese, Gustave

Music readers, adopted 1870, 130, 184

Music teaching among Believers, 28, 162, 166-67, 183-84

Musique Chinoise, La. See Laloy, Louis

Mutation, 135, 140-41; table, 136

Names of musicians, 67-74

New Lebanon, meeting house (1795), 28: abandoning five-line staff, 91-92, 108; education at, 182-83; mentioned, 43, 196, 213, 221, 231, 237, 241; small letteral approved, 84-85; songs exchanged, 76-77, 83; Youngs' Abridgement published, 110, 118, 133, 135, 171

"New Lights," 38, 165

Niskayuna, N.Y. (Watervliet), 14, 33, 38

North Union, Cleveland, O., 49, 211

Notation of music, 28; beginning of, 39; difficulties of dating, 75-79; uniformity approached, 94

Index of Songs

The numbers in parentheses are the numbers assigned the songs.

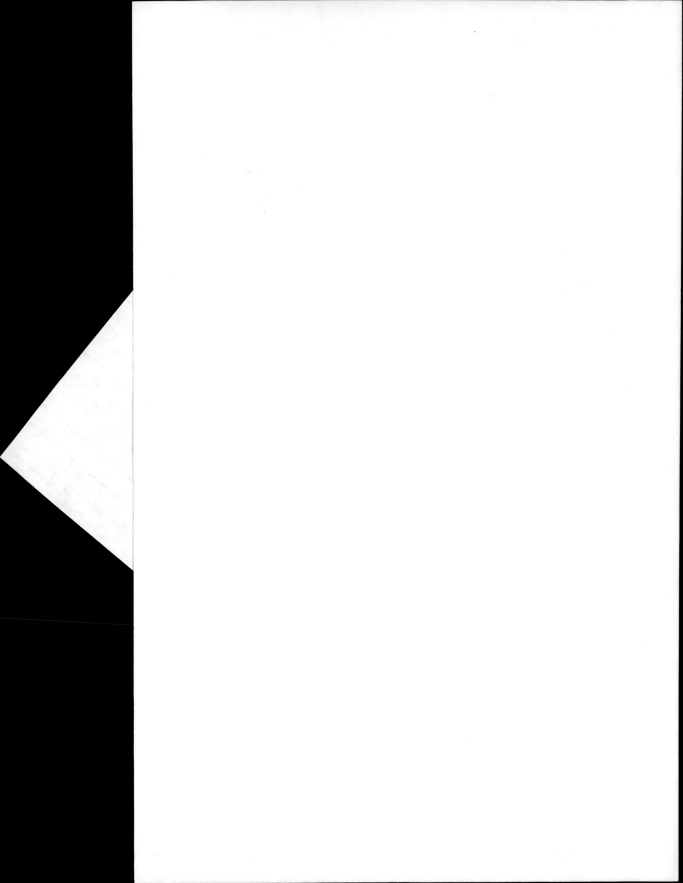

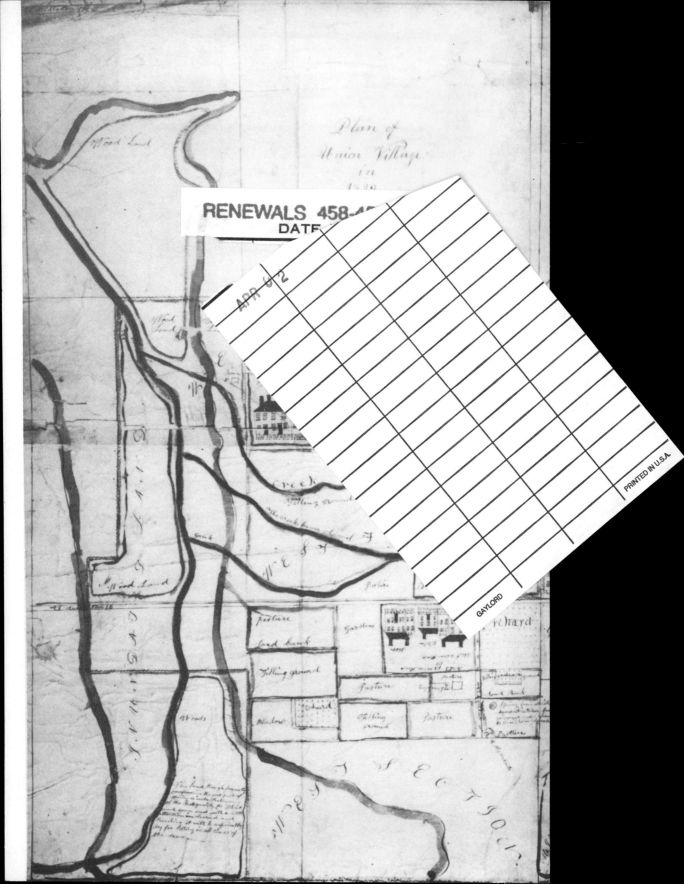